About the Author

Alexandre Yambanis is a gifted linguist, fluent in six languages and holds a bachelor's degree in Business Administration. His long career as an international executive has not precluded him from remaining a dreamer and an acute observer of the human psyche. His diverse cultural background coupled with multiple life settings and travels spanning the globe, awarded him a strong sense of understanding, compassion and sympathy towards the paradoxes of our existence where our weaknesses constantly meld with our greatness to create a constant struggle for survival. Nature seems to hold the key in solving our dilemmas. Women have been extremely influential in Alexandre's spiritual growth hence he nurtures a great deal of gratitude and respect towards them. Alexandre is a father of two and lives in Estoril, Portugal where he gets his inspiration from nature and people from all walks of life whom he crosses on a daily basis when walking and day-dreaming on the beach…

Woman

Alexandre Yambanis

Woman

Olympia Publishers
London

www.olympiapublishers.com
OLYMPIA PAPERBACK EDITION

A CIP catalogue record for this title is
available from the British Library.

ISBN: 978-1-80074-219-2

This is a work of fiction.
Names, characters, places and incidents originate from the writer's
imagination. Any resemblance to actual persons, living or dead, is
purely coincidental.

First Published in 2021

Olympia Publishers
Tallis House
2 Tallis Street
London
EC4Y 0AB

Printed in Great Britain

WOMAN

The threatening wave

Silent like a defector

Explodes in fury, passion, spluttering foam

Indomitable

Intractable

Suddenly submissive

Like a whisper

Wets my feet

Softly

Warmly

Woman

GENESIS

The raindrops were the size of big mushrooms and would relentlessly hit the roof of the shack like a frantic drummer stubbornly attempting to match a rhythm to a preset wild and unknown song... She was there, on her knees, very close to me, naked, staring at me with her big, almond-shaped eyes with a glow reflecting from her silky, golden skin and her unbelievably firm pear-like breast tips pointing towards the ceiling, defying gravity, shining and hardened by her extreme excitation! I was myself so aroused that I would simply fall into a state of wonder, sensuality and expectation that I had never experienced before. At this point I was completely immersed in some kind of trance, certainly as a result of the herb we had chewed together some hours ago; one that was commonly offered to young, first time couples with a view to breaking the ice, encouraging the bride, and enhancing the experience. I did not have a clue as to what her next gestures would be although my excitement would definitely grow with the anticipation... she bent towards me, softly and posed, her tender and meaty red lips against mine making me shiver and shake out of desire. She exhaled a mysterious perfume, and I couldn't tell whether it was her natural scent or a fragrance of some of the exotic plants from the jungle surrounding the primitive yet well-organized hamlet. Her breathing was short and loud, exhaling an odor of passion and craving, charged with lust... she then slowly laid down by my side better disclosing the full extent of her magnificent forms!

She was athletic, yet extremely feminine, possessing a corporal expression that would transmit vigorous youth, extreme beauty, deep voluptuousness and a feline demeanor. Then, very slowly, she touched my intimate parts and caressed them in movements that would denote discovery, performing it in such a manner that I felt as if the whole world was unravelling in my solar plexus… then, again very slowly, she started licking my body whilst swallowing the droplets of rain that would hit my skin after having persistently permeated the fragile roof made of palm leaves. The same warm lips that kissed mine just moments ago were now avidly kissing my entire body and gently sliding through my skin while her firm breasts would caress my chest and belly in a rhythmic movement that would take me straight into a climax of pure frenzy if it weren't for the effects of the plant that quite surprisingly would give me the ability to exercise full control over my instincts and its most profound senses… She would then rub her wet sex all over me as if exploring sensitive parts of my upper chest and neck until that superb vulva reached a point where my mouth would be just some inches away. I could feel the strong and highly stimulating perfume of her most intimate parts. It was an extremely seductive odor that somehow magnified all the impulses of my unbending hotness. I then languidly kissed and licked that marvelous virginal flower for what seemed to be an eternity, then pushed her back very gently in order to penetrate her wet vagina sweetly, slowly and carefully since this was her first time, thus ardently controlling my wildest impulses in order not to hurt her. Her exhalations were totally uncontrollable, and her breath became heavy and loaded with voluptuous gradations that would make her avid kisses feel like a full sexual intercourse. We made love in a slow motion that would carry us both to a yet unknown feeling of extreme delight, making us reach a joint outburst of intense multicolored pleasure We were united in a one and whole universe which seemed as an extension of our bodies and souls. The multitude of noises emanating from the forest were reaching our ears like a perfect symphony. She had grasped all of my feminine sensitivity and I had grasped her sensuous masculinity in such a profound carnal and soul exchange that it was as if Yung's collective unconscious anima and animus theory had been evidenced in praxis by both of us in the middle of the Amazon. This sense of perfection and unity and the sublime ability to meld perfectly into infinity even for some few furtive moments, was indeed a gift from heaven, perhaps an unquestionable evidence that we are all an intrinsic part of the whole… and that love is the whole itself… it is all there is! We felt as if a mysterious entity had given us permission to surpass all censorship, preconceived barriers and cultural limitations in order to allow us to become united under the bright light emanating from the stars and the moon now shining in a clear, diaphanous sky, following the storm. Obviously, all this could easily be construed as a mere hallucinogenic experience devoid of any spiritual sense. But this would simply be an impossibility on its own. Why would the universal powers conspire in such a pervasive way as to make two human beings with absolutely nothing in common be it ethnic, cultural, racial or otherwise share a mere superficial and meaningless common experience enhanced by the effects of a hallucinogenic drug? This would be especially intriguing considering that most initiatives even before our permission to stay together as a couple came from Yana herself obviously with the blessings of the whole tribe, besides the council of ten sages and last but not least, the Big Chief himself in a totally unique and unprecedented concession to this young woman and to me. She had somehow

13

decided to postpone her initiation several times in the past, rejecting young and beautiful aspirants as if feeling that I would be there sooner or later, defying all odds, all logical paths and possibilities, not to speak of the cultural precepts of that matriarchal society, a society that had naturally evolved to reach a level of collective wisdom only envisioned by a handful of modern world scientists, scholars, philosophers and thinkers who would write treaties on psychosocial behavior, ethnicity, anthropology, you name it, just to find themselves invariably wrong or at least imprecise in their studies and analytical research. When I finally stood up, I could see a stain of blood on the rattan on which we were lying. She stared at it and smiled at me with an expression of complicity and achievement. We were deeply in love!

I was then a young adult, and suddenly I had fathomed that all my perceived understanding and conceptualization of love that had been acquired and accumulated through all the wonderful women I had the privilege to meet and love (and be loved by), faded in the face of what Yana had just shared with me with all the overwhelming intensity. Not that it would, in any shape or form, mitigate or diminish the crucial importance of all my past relationships, but I knew, right there and then, that Yana was the twin soul I had been looking for during my entire life! My love life had in fact started somehow precociously, well before our meeting, in a variety of different environments and circumstances that had definitely shaped my inner curiosity, passionate admiration and deep empathy vis a vis the feminine soul… and, I must admit that all those wonderful life experiences were tantamount for that culmination so purely shared with Yana! My life had been indeed an extraordinary journey of survival, learning and better understanding of life, through and thanks to all the wonderful women I had the privilege of sharing my existential fervor with. It goes without saying that I can only be grateful towards all those amazing women who crossed my path and who, so painstakingly yet patiently, taught me so many secrets leading to the path of love!

Indeed, no words can ever make justice to those fantastic human beings! I offer my entire recognition and incline myself very humbly and respectfully before all our female counterparts who are definitely in the forefront of our evolution, and who are also at the origin of our existence, of our genesis, of life itself… women! They certainly are the only ones capable of steering our species away from the apparent catastrophe we're inexorably heading towards…

Most human societies place terrible taboos and preconceived ideas on the sexual relationship between a woman and a man, not to speak of those occurring between two individuals of the same gender. Sex itself is tremendously overvalued and its pure, sacred, wonderful and spontaneous nature has been distorted since immemorial time because of the so-called cultural traditions, beliefs, religions, racial and social values, and especially laws! I am obviously not referring to the natural ones, but to those created by men and that bear no connection with instinctive, true and spiritual laws and reality… and I could go on indefinitely on this highly sensitive issue. My incredible and sometimes terrible upbringing quite paradoxically inoculated me from most of those invisible chains, maybe because of my sheer instinctive determination or simply because of my consequential behavior expressed in the form of my insatiable thirst for love and understanding. This is probably how I managed to shelter myself from a pre-formatted education that we all fall victims to and that blinds us from the true and genuine values of our existence. This acquired predisposition defined most of my search for meaning throughout my entire life, and was paramount to the radical turns and twists that yielded the quite fantastic epilogue of my life story.

I'm part of a torn generation caught between WWII and Viagra. Some of our most important societal 'values' have been turned upside down more than once during the 20th century and the phenomena still goes on now that we are practically reaching one fourth of the 21st!We are indeed destroying all remaining objective references without bothering to replace them, leaving instead an existential void resulting inexorably in the acute state of despair we find ourselves immersed in… all the way from the infamous 'sixties' through the 21st century that started with an explosion of high, very high expectations and settled, at least so far, as the most flabbergasting, extravagantly disturbing, chaotic and directionless period in recent memory. It looks as if the majority of people around the world have lost their way and sense of purpose in life. We all, or should I say the vast majority of the human race, navigate in the midst of a foggy universe composed of fear, anguish, despair, and depression. There are probably more wars currently being fought simultaneously in the world, yielding record levels of 'collateral damage' than any other period in history. Hatred-borne horrifying acts being perpetrated in the name of religious supremacy or simply out of sheer despair, total lack of true leadership, senseless violence, such as rapes, pedophilia, horrific murders, not to mention mass exterminations of human beings including and especially children, the disappearance of entire species and the consequent depletion of entire ecosystems ,are now part of our daily news and have been incorporated by the media in the status quo of our lives to such an extent that our minds and souls have become literally numb.

The western and now even most of the eastern ways of life have become so individualistic and competitive that we simply have no time to stop our relentless minds in order to assess our pervasive environment and try to bring some positive spin into it. We simply and systematically reject reality itself without pondering or at least halting our frantic pace in order to evaluate its validity or veracity any more. Instead, we fight fiercely in order to create the ultimate illusion of adapting it to our wildly egotistic wishes! Most of us are seemingly guided by an irrational alternation of fear and hatred... we basically use hatred to face what we do not understand or accept, ultimately in an attempt to neutralize our fear! We prefer to trust the scientific breakthroughs that promise an extended life to the ones that will be able to afford it, thus enabling us all to ignore critical issues in order to postpone solutions that could stop all the craziness that is at the origin of the huge depletion of our vital resources... by doing so however, we relinquish and ultimately end up forgetting its potentially catastrophic consequences which are happening right now before our eyes!

Quite dramatically, there is nothing and especially no one out there that warrants those better days are to come anytime soon, and this is in itself very frightening and obviously adds to the collective madness by enhancing the sense of separateness among humans. And still, the irony is that in reality we live in a totally interdependent and interconnected systemic universe where literally everything influences everything else. It is quite unbelievable that we reached this state of affairs despite all the science and the huge technological development that has been made available to us lately and this, exponentially! Perhaps the blind-for-profit exploitation of all this technology is at the origin of the conundrum we face, whereas possible solutions still exist right here, around us, but are dependent of course on our willingness to face our problems with clarity and consciousness and start healing our species through the healing of our planet and of all the other species who are intrinsically with us for the ride and that contribute likewise to support our fragile ecosystem! We must start immediately healing the sufferance that we, humans, have inflicted upon our planet and its wonderful animal and vegetal species, that wonderful and complex ecosystem that supports life itself! As so well put by a notorious conservationist organization, 'Nature doesn't need us, we need nature!'

I simply couldn't put things in a more straightforward way in the face of all the evidence made available to us by our own planet which has issued dire warnings through catastrophic events that are becoming more and more frequent as time goes by... yet we insist on going on without contemplating any changes immersed as we are in our indifference and oblivion! One simple paradigm lies in the fact that scientists are now starting to literally unearth evidence according to which we are getting inexorably closer to a tipping point whereby the cooling systems of the planet such as the poles will reverse themselves and start emitting heat due to the vastly proven global warming effects on the latter!

Where lies the potential solutions for this dramatic reality? Birth control seems to be an obvious reply to this at least in terms of mitigating the destruction we cause to our environment. However, I do not believe that mankind is anywhere close to being capable of adopting global solutions that would go against political, religious or even social and too well established not to say frozen beliefs. We are certainly among the most adaptive creatures presently roaming the earth, yet we seem to be paralyzed and unable to unite our individual resources in order to correct what seems to be a fatalistic race towards self-destruction. We seemingly will not change for the better unless strong and radical external events force us to unite in order to protect our own survival as a species. What if, as an example, we were all confronted by a global external threat of such magnitude that it would leave us with no other choice but to pull together our collective resources in order to fight that common and fantastic hazard, but then, it might be too late depending on the 'enemy's' might. Maybe there's simply no collective solution and the only way out is through individual spiritual growth which could lead to different stages of personal spiritual wisdom and ultimately to illumination. This hypothesis, however, is restrictive by its own merits and would only benefit privileged groups of seekers and their masters and would probably not gather enough momentum to save us all in due course from the potential cataclysmic events that are taking shape as we continue to obliviously destroy our environment. Another restrictive contradiction to this theory is that if this was a meaningful probability, one could presume that those groups of privileged individuals have been around for millennia since spiritual knowledge has always existed at least for as long as spirit itself. How come therefore that evidence seems to show that man-made destruction takes over by far the pace of human spiritual development? Unfortunately, the conclusion is that we cannot simply lay back in a laissez faire stance and wait for miraculous solutions emanating from small groups of enlightened ones to save us all from our own, disgraceful destinies. We most likely have to act and act fast pulling together consciousness, intelligence, instinct, savoir faire, not to speak of leadership, global governance and, last but not least, a deep sense of respect for our own race as well as all the other forms of life that share the finite space of our planet. This however has to be achieved with some kind of universal form of communication that would have the power of uniting us instead of separating us from one another. No matter which way we turn the problem, there is only one word that could encompass that highly complex solution and that word is LOVE! We men have been the dominant genre on our planet for millennia and our apparent supremacy has been granted by the fact that in most of our relatively short history of existence, physical strength was vital for the survival and consequent procreation of our species. This reality has definitely changed radically ever since mankind has created and developed an infinity of tools that by far surpass and multiply our physical capabilities and cater not only to our present but also to our future needs. The fact of the matter is that women are as able as men, if not more, in terms of manipulating and making good — or bad — use of those tools. Hence the physical supremacy of men consists nowadays in more of a surviving myth than anything else, so much so that we see more and more women taking over the helm at a series of institutions that used to be exclusively men's territory ranging from global companies to governments, to international agencies, to international tribunals, to name just a few. Isn't it absurd, on another wavelength and just to cite a single example, that wealthy companies do not invest in nurseries which would enable women to work whilst nourishing and bringing up their babies? And why couldn't we imagine a western society where all women would be mothers of all babies regardless of their affiliation? Needless to say, those institutions have for the most part been shaped by masculine individuals with a masculine hegemonic perception of the world. The next leap forward will probably be a world shaped by different values and priorities brought about by women with a totally feminine philosophy that will better respond to the urgent needs of our time. A new era is hopefully emerging, one that will ultimately replace the current macho cultural paradox in favor of a female profound and intuitive supremacy which will finally impose new, creative societal changes and jump start what has to be urgently done in order to save our civilization... if there's still time for this badly needed rescue of course!

Notwithstanding the fascination that is inherent to those considerations, this is not intended to be a sociological essay! It is the story about the recognition of my feminine identity which is intrinsically part of my own being and as such my extraordinary relationship with women and all the precious teachings that the latter brought about into my existence, thus helping me to cope with it in a better, more fulfilling, way. All women who crossed my life have, in their vast majority proven to be wiser, and especially more loving and courageous than men. I nurture a great respect for their unique nature and acknowledge that they have helped me to better deal with myself by helping me to gradually unveil a wisdom that is usually hidden in one of the most intimate parts of our masculinity... our feminine antipode that paradoxically coexists with our masculine nature and if anything enhances the latter in a judicious way. I certainly became a better man thanks to my often-fantastic relationships with women and the cohabitation, albeit far from being comprehensive I must admit, with the most amazing aspects of their minds and souls.

SÃO PAULO

I will therefore start from the very beginning, from a hazy place where my memories are clouded like one of those old military trucks lost in a sandstorm in the middle of the desert. I am one and a half years old or so and I still recall the taste of that stirred raw egg yolk. As a matter of fact, this is probably my first memory as an existing human being… my old aunt would make me gulp one of those daily and I remember the big shadow of my moribund grandma lying on the other bed by my side… her sister would serve me the egg concoction while my grandmother would moan and at times cry out with pain and impatience… as if death was dancing around her, trying to find the right circumstances to get closer to her, hesitating, before finally deciding to carry her away. My father would then come in and ask his mother the same stupid question with his guttural voice: are you feeling better? My mother would then enter the room and ask the old aunt quite aggressively whether I had swallowed the whole stuff. They literally hated each other. My mother also disliked me, simply because I was a male and as such would bring back old wounds that were deeply inflicted in her being by men throughout her miserable existence. This would strangely enough push me towards women in lieu of rejecting them, feeding my passion and thirst for conquest of the latter, instead of nurturing any negative feelings. Obviously, she also hated my father; firstly, because he was a male himself and then because he had developed alcoholism in part as a result of my mother's unfaithful escapades, and then there was my rebellious sister trying hard to develop her own survival skills to counteract that heavy environment. Those six antagonistic souls lived on the ground floor of a small house that my father had built in the poor outskirts of São Paulo, Brazil, currently one of the less attractive, most violent cities in the world. Besides the ground floor, there was also a kind of basement where my grandma's brother and his very old, French wife would share a tiny bedroom with no bathroom. The only bathroom in the house was located on the ground floor and all eight individuals would fiercely compete for its usage in the early morning hours. My father, as the main breadwinner would of course have the right to go first, and we would all be reminded about it by his loud and endless farts that could probably even be heard by the neighbors.

Finally, on a cold morning my grandmother passed away peacefully. Her death brought some temporary peace in the house, until my mother decided that my grandma's sister was as monstrous as the latter, hence her evil heiress. And hell would occasionally break loose again and again... life was definitely not boring at home let me tell you! But it was not a walk in the park either. Years passed by, slowly at that time, at least for me who was not yet taking part in what was defined as the 'real world' by adults. Instead, I was more often immersed in my dreams, exercising my fertile imagination as a way out from that difficult environment. Eventually I grew up to be a very shy and scared boy who was sick most of the time which would create havoc in the family since nobody was patient enough to give me what I needed most — love and tenderness. My mother would become very impatient and sometimes desperate with my poor health which would in turn create a chain reaction with my father having a burst of rage in the face of the risk that his alcohol rich weekend outings would be spoiled or even compromised…

The now three remaining old individuals would hate each other's guts and together they would hate my mother, who would in turn encourage my father's rage and violent behavior towards them in a fruitless attempt by him to display his bravado and convince her that, after all, he was on her side. Yes, life was a self-inflicted hell indeed if it weren't for the marvelous and friendly animals that we had around the house: a baby duckling that would systematically run ahead of my grandma's doctor at each visit and poo in front of him. Apparently, the good old doctor possessed hidden laxative powers towards the duckling. Then there was 'little tail' ('Uritssa' in Greek), the female dog that had been found on the streets by my father in the middle of the night. He was totally drunk as usual, so the following day he could not remember how the dog ended up in the kitchen, but his sense of guilt forced him to cave in and our tenacious opposition won the permission for Uritssa to stay in our home. Kitchiko was the goat with her enormous tits that inspired comfort and made me feel as if some form of a second, loving and understanding mother was there available to me without any of those horrifying, negative sentiments. She was simply wonderful when she was offered to us as a baby goat and grew up to become a naughty youngster eating everything that became available within her sight including plants, shoes, clothes etc.

My second direct contact with death happened when the rabbit we kept in the backyard was violently killed by street dogs in the middle of the night. I still remember very vividly my mother rushing out the door in a fruitless attempt to save the poor animal to no avail. By the time she reached his fragile and delicate tiny body, he was covered in blood and, as I reached the scene, I could see his last reflexive quiver before the rendering of his small and wonderful soul... I remember that I couldn't stop crying for the following three days...

I guess that by now I have introduced all the inhabitants of the house. Aside from them however there were quite a few itinerant habitués such as Theodore, the big and flamboyant uncle recently arrived from Alexandria, Egypt, like all the others. Theodore was a tremendously captivating character with an impressive array of stories and memories — some certainly real, others imaginary — but all told with such an emotional zest and incredible details that one could spend hours listening to them even when Theodore would repeat the feats over and over again especially during occasions when one or more attractive females would be among the listeners. Theodore's stories definitely marked my life and nurtured my imagination despite the fact that he ostensibly rejected me... maybe because I would remind him of an important facet of his being, that he would dismiss as weakness. He was never alone, probably because he would panic in loneliness, one of his most frightening inner ghosts reminiscent of a dramatic and adventurous life in Egypt right before the Nasser era and all the way through a bloody war in reality fought without a real cause as it is often the case. My grandparents had immigrated from Greece to escape famine and their children were born in Alexandria at a time when foreigners and their families were welcomed and helped build the Egyptian economy of that time. Theodore was drafted at the age of eighteen and sent to the front, like my father, with the only difference that he had luckily enrolled in the air force hence becoming a 'spitfire' pilot along with the RAF (The highly renowned British Royal Air Force). His entire training took place in South Africa and his major achievement as a warplane pilot was to bring down two aircrafts... more precisely, the ones he was piloting himself! He was a very handsome man, tall and dark-haired with exquisite communication skills, lots of charm and a spicy humor, a classical music lover and connoisseur and last but not least, an enormous generosity towards women, a quality highly praised by the latter and something that I would learn to emulate and put into practice throughout my own life… all those qualities made Theodore the perfect Don Juan. He commanded such a strong presence that no matter what the environment, Theodore's arrival would act like a magnet thus attracting all the attention no matter what the style or the caliber of the other participants or even the subjects being discussed. Theodore, besides his vast general knowledge, would invariably present his own version of a given story by charmingly coloring it with his own sprightly statements, not always as accurate as they appeared though, but his brilliant ability to twist some of the facts would make them much more palatable than reality itself. Among his countless lovers, the most vivid ones in memory were 'in order of appearance' Jeanne the smelly, French, passionate and voluptuous woman, Paulette the Belgian also called the 'French madness' by one of his Greek friends who couldn't distinguish a Belgian from a French person given the similitude of both accents when speaking Portuguese, the chin dropping Greek guerilla female captain, who he met in a remote mountain camp in Northern Greece by virtue of one of his plane crashes during the Greek civil war, and I could go on for hours. What I most retained from the female captain's description, were her enormous and perfumed tits that she would so sensuously display through nonchalantly unbuttoned fatigues as a defiance to her own battalion but this in its turn would seemingly serve as a hell of a stimulant and a great motivator for the troops!

Paulette, yet another of Theodore's multiple conquests, was

probably one of the most beautiful women I ever met in my entire life. Her eyes were topaz blue, and she used to paint her eye lashes in a contrasting blue that would enhance her malicious glances and extraordinarily beautiful face. I was simply fascinated by her looks already at the age of six especially by her extraordinary eyes but also by her smell and her sensuous smile and demeanor. At that time, and well beyond, I was completely in love with Paulette, period! A love that would endure time, before emerging from the Platonic caves to a dreamy, fantastic, passionate albeit short lived love relationship. I must confess that at that age, falling in love at first sight was the norm…

Besides Theodore, the weekends would also bring in a parade of a series of intriguing personages, some quite bizarre, like Yiannis, Theodore's younger brother and a 'copie ratée' of the latter. A father of three, he was usually depressed and quite theatrical when it came to a well-rehearsed money extortion play, vis a vis my mother who would invariably cave in and gave him the money despite being a woman who used to work six days a week, ten hours a day, fighting off sexual abuses during a four hour back and forth bus commute to her workplace. Theodore would see his alter ego in his younger brother like a bull sees a red flag and would consistently batter him psychologically which would secretly give me a sense of accomplished revenge for the money that Yiannis would constantly extort from my mother… another assiduous visitor was Uncle Nicholau, my father's brother. An extremely sensitive, brilliant and cynical man as it is often the case, with a trenchant sense of humor, who would compensate for his frustrations in life by indulging in enormous quantities of food! His average weight was never less than 130 kgs which was huge indeed for a rather short man. He was in turn my own father's alter ego which would trigger awful confrontations between the two, enhanced by an enormous consumption of alcohol. This would often have a catastrophic effect for the already tenuous balance and serenity of the day... To my delight, aside from those strong and tortuous personalities there was Sophia, my aunt, recently married to Theodore and twenty years his younger. She was therefore in her early 20s at the time when I had just turned seven. I fell instantly in love with her too, admittedly without any guilt feelings! Sophia was, and will always be, among my most significant love stories. My falling in love with her happened soon after she proposed kind of jokingly to adopt me, probably inspired by my blatant melancholy which was reflective of hers. Sophia's presence in my life would grow to become much more than a furtive encounter with a replacement mother, which I will describe later. For now, however, suffice to say that her presence, contrary to the endless harassment, conflicts and the entire drama that were a constant factor in my early existence, marked and acutely increased my perception and understanding of the female soul in a very poignant and profound way... during my childhood years, Sophia would unconditionally side with me and vigorously defend me from my father's maddening verbal and physical aggressions. She would also treat me with love and respect, listen to my stories and take me seriously, all of which was like a balm to my soul amidst all the bullying and sheer disrespect in the wild and crazy environment of my miserable early existence. Finally, as I grew up, she would slowly and sweetly introduce me to the subtle side of her feminine essence and her sweet, impressive and attractive spiritual and physical attributes. Yes, Sophia was of vital importance in the building blocks of my romantic life and in my irresistible attraction to women that ensued.

A typical Sunday would start with Theodore announcing

himself loudly by suddenly appearing at the turn of our unpaved street with his strident 'Lambretta', the famous Italian two-wheeler which was all he could afford in those early years as a poor immigrant with Sophia sitting on the back seat struggling to keep her body on the tiny and uncomfortable seat! His favorite person was by far my sister, firstly because she was a female, and then mostly because of the notable contrast in personality between both of us. I must say that my sister was also coping with a highly complex and difficult childhood of her own. Her reaction to our parent's unbalanced and aggressive relationship was different though. She would react by becoming very extroverted and aggressive herself which would stand in sheer contrast to my introverted and melancholic looks. The real shame besides all the surrounding psychological chaos, was my mother's subtle attitude which was a reflection of her own deep psychic distortions, which would instill competition between the two siblings. My relationship with my sister had therefore been damaged from the start by circumstances that in fact had nothing to do with either of our characters and had also nothing to do with the love that we felt for each other notwithstanding.

On top of all that, I would stutter which would spook Theodore and reinforce even more his unfriendly attitude towards me since I would somehow incorporate all his fears towards his own weaknesses against which he would react by being aggressive, flamboyant and very naughty towards me, a defenseless toddler. When I was still a little baby, he would pull my penis in order to make me cry and provoke the ire of the old owls who would run and rescue me from him. Nonetheless as an adolescent I would simply adore the bastard maybe because he would represent everything I wanted to be in terms of strength, charm, charisma, apparent invulnerability and domination but couldn't in view of my underdog demeanor and very shy personality at that time. He would have some sort of a liberating effect upon me probably as an act of deliverance from himself towards all the weakness and psychological blockage I would represent in sheer contrast to his at all times overassertive attitude!

One of Theodore's typical hallmarks was characterized by the fact that he would carry lots of food around like, for example, the odd 15lbs of raw squids to be cooked by one of his chosen victims whom he would very ably yet insistently call to the task. That 'volunteer' was usually my mother simply because she was a great sister besides being a great cook as well and Theodore was very well aware of it. If by any reason my mother was unavailable, he would resort to any other member of the old clan or even the eventual forced volunteer who would feel unable or afraid to confront him. In the end, I must say, Theodore would get his way by having his squids cooked according to his own, favorite recipe!

Then, by order of appearance, Nicholau, my uncle from my father's side, Stephane, my mother's younger brother, Jeanne and Paulette, my mother's friends followed by Bertrand, Paulette's husband, Amely another friend who had started to look like a compulsive spinster together with her parrot who would curse everybody that stood in his or her way for the matter, as well as some other secondary souls who would arrive later. Voilà, the whole circus and its outstanding performance director... who else than Theodore, of course? At the start of a meal, our so-called home would literally look like a mad house inhabited by a host of awkward characters with incredible life stories that would nurture and indelibly mark my imagination for the rest of my life. As such, I would for instance be carried away through space, at times even faster than the speed of my own very fertile imagination to Alexandria, Egypt where right before the war, a quaint and peaceful life still existed not without the highly attaching accounts of Theodore's first street fights and love stories, or to Johannesburg, South Africa, where some of the RAF training would take place before the real and terrifying deployment in Northern Africa, where Theodore would spend his time courting and having incredible love adventures with many Red Cross nurses also undergoing training. I would literally transform those already incredibly rich narratives into even more unbelievably extraordinary experiences by adding my own fantasies to the memorable passages dating from the eve of WWII as well as from the Great War itself when all of those personages' lives had started to be shaken and were at times hopelessly dismantled by the dire circumstances of those very trying times. Many close family members or close friends' lives ended totally messed up by the tragic and catastrophic events that ensued.

What intrigued me the most though, was the radically different ways that each one of them had coped with that highly intense period, forging their own interpretation of reality and reacting to it in ways that would defy the most fertile of imaginations. My father, for example, took everything in a most dramatic way by allowing himself to become a hostage to the situation not only in the years he had spent battling in the front, but for the rest of his life, so much so that his memory would practically erase the most enriching passages of his participation in the great war in favor of the most terrifying ones which he carefully memorized together with their most despicable and sordid details. As an example of the positives that he elected to erase from his endless narratives but were described in details by a certain number of witnesses outside the family circle, was my favorite story whereby that same man who became an alcohol addict for the rest of his life, had been capable of a heroic defection in the final stages of the war when he acquired a 1,200cc3 Harley Davidson motorcycle and guided several groups of women and children through the desert towards battle free safe grounds, being subsequently hidden by a Bedouin tribe who would taint his skin and disguise him as a goat shepherd to the point that the British secret service wouldn't be able to detect his presence despite several face to face rather dramatic encounters. Every time I would hear this narrative, I would shed abundant tears of pride towards a precociously buried, yet badly needed image, of a father I had always wanted to have, but was so elusive that I had to often reinvent by stretching my imagination and my benevolence beyond any reasonable or possible boundaries! Paul would shrug this story in favor of tales of sheer misery and drama as if to justify his own, inner defeat. Those stories would be told under the influence of lots of alcohol and quite often with the sound effects of Beethoven's sixth symphony, one of his favorites. This is how I became familiarized with Rommel (a Nazi general aka 'the fox of the desert' due to his ruses in the battlefield) and the battle of 'El Alamein' (one of the most-bloody battles during WWII where he participated). Unfortunately, and to my utter disarray, I was quite often the incarnation of the enemy, suffering, as a consequence all the might of his tremendous hatred, resentment and sorrow. This would translate into violent beatings, often accompanied by shouts of indescribable destructive power that would mark my soul for the rest of my life and oblige me to spend years searching for answers and potential solutions to the dead ends that had been encroached in my being. My enormous attraction to women originated largely from the fact that I needed to be surrounded by sensitive and understanding beings in order to compensate all the ravages created by that situation.

Conversely, Theodore's narratives made one feel as if war had been an amusement park of the absurd, full of daring adventures and discoveries that would strangely enough make you want to be there in order to participate in that ludicrous party as my uncle would so ably describe or perhaps even invent some of its passages in order to make it more appealing. It took a great share of discernment for any of the accidental listeners to realize that, paradoxically, both experiences were born from the same dramatic set of events. Practically all of Theodore's adventures would involve women of different nationalities and social categories that I would invariably identify with! Those would of course include Theodore's several wives and mistresses of that time such as Sophia, Paulette, Jeanne, Aldersley, Brita, Brigitte, just to name a few. The fact that they were around during different stages of my growing up years and at times sharing Theodore's company concomitantly, added to the sensual feelings of sound, touch, smell not to speak of the furtive wicked looks that I earned from time to time... not only because women are naughty and terrific at the same time given the fact that this is their nature, but also because they would challenge my insistent and at times lavish staring at them as if they tried to find out whether I was really in a state of sexual attraction towards them despite my young age! As such, and in order to test their intriguing feelings or maybe just second thoughts, they would take me in their arms and caress me, holding me tight against their breasts. What man on this earth, no matter his age, doesn't adore to find his head between two generous and sensuous breasts? It generates feelings of warmth, protection, sensuality, sparkling desire, availability, motherhood, malice, just to name a few… I could stay in this position for hours if not days and still crave for more! Later, as I grew up, I understood that I inspired women to adopt a protective attitude towards me, maybe because of the tenderness of my own attitude towards them, since I would invariably imagine any woman I'd met as being in a sensual situation, and this would certainly be intuitively grasped by the vast majority of them, creating a certain radiance of complicity.

Hence, we would all sit around Theodore and listen to fabulous stories of battles, love at first sight, crazy sex, passion and so on, all of them spicy narratives witnessed by one or more of his lovers who would know of each other but would pretend total ignorance as a sign of respect to his seniority and… maybe his generosity! My father, at this point, would still be sober or almost, and would serve as Theodore's preferred witness to most of the stories. His preferred one was the one in which my father would explode the officers' latrines in sequence in order to attract them to the opposite camp hence allowing Theodore and his highly trained team to steal everything they could put their hands on such as the officers' food storage secret cache located under the sand of the desert! Then they would summon 'salesmen' amongst the troops that would go around the tents and offer fried eggs "à la minute!" at a hefty price, of course! Those would be fried on an old tin plate obtained by carefully cutting a sardine can, under which three candles would burn for as long as the avid customers would order the delicacy. Theodore was probably the only active combatant who was supposed to send money back home to his unemployed, penniless mom whilst fighting one of the bloodiest wars in History…

After lunch, of course, my father would have absorbed an unbelievable amount of alcohol to the point of throwing some of the guests out of the house, yelling frantically at everybody, among who Theodore, who at that point would have gotten on his nerve by asking him repeatedly to stop drinking. However, long before that sad epilogue of the weekend, Jeanne, who was always late, would show up after a languid night with Theodore himself who was an early riser, and would kiss everybody including me giving me the extra benefit of spying her tits from the top of her décolleté. She would bring 3rd class chocolates with a strange, faded taste probably well beyond their expiry date. Poor Jeanne… she was probably the only one who didn't know of Theodore's other affairs and was extremely proud of being the "one and only" as Theodore would very ably convince her.

All that exotic environment would help stimulate my first sexual impulses and sow the seeds of my adoration for women… their sensitivity and understanding, their ability to listen and to respond wisely, their smell, their looks, their taste, the voluptuous touch of their lips when kissing me, the furtive sight of their legs whenever they would sit in the right angle, not to speak of the occasional vistas of their tits, by far my favorite sight, were all more than a fair compensation to the extraordinary quirks of those wild weekends! All that would awaken in me an attraction, an insatiable curiosity, a passion and an admiration that followed me throughout my entire life. I did not become a Don Juan for the matter, but instead I managed to love all women in my life as if they were different facets of a fascinating single being, who offered me, in each and every encounter, a novelty which would stimulate me to explode my passion as a reflection of theirs and to renew myself in their infinite capacity to love. Those feelings and perceptions were partially innate, and partially acquired through an acute sense of observation and curiosity that were gradually developed in my psyche as a second nature and guided me inexorably towards those superbly inspiring beings ever since my early childhood!

I will never forget the day when one of my neighbors' aunt asked me to accompany her to the grocery store through a shortcut passing through the nearby bushes. Something sad or deceiving had happened to her, and I could sense it despite my young age. She was evidently showing signs of craving for understanding and affection…

Our neighborhood was crisscrossed by small stretches of forest but was very safe at that time. It was late in the afternoon, hence the night had started to fall and all of a sudden, after having been through approximately half the distance, she asked me to wait for her by the roadside while, to my surprise, she would quite naturally undress from the waist down in order to urinate.

Don't look back naughty boy! She would say loudly with a malicious tone in her voice.

I am not looking at all I would reply lying grudgingly, trying hard to distinguish her through the shadows of the trees, directing my attention towards the noisy torrent of her urine pouring and hitting the ground. The guessing of her intimate parts being exposed next to me, would flare up my imagination beyond any boundary, awakening feelings that probably were far more vivid and impressive than reality itself.

I will carry that utterly innocent excitement and highly arousing feelings in my memory for the rest of my life! It made me feel like a brave warrior full of tender feelings, ready to defend her, a vulnerable female against any potential attack of a dragon or any other kind of being, human or otherwise, that had the idea of hiding in the vicinity of those bushes! Luckily for me, no terrifying creature crossed our way during the very short time we spent together silently hand in hand on our way back home.

My enormous curiosity and sensitivity towards women and my constant craving for tenderness and affection would awaken my puberty in a rather premature way inflaming in my heart and mind feelings and thoughts of profound sensuality that would somehow permeate my attitude toward the opposite sex having, as a result, instilled somehow analogue feelings in most female individuals that crossed my life. As such, women would admire my emotional maturity and my capability to listen, feel and discuss intricate aspects of their own emotional life. As I once heard from Paulette, "talking to you about intimate things is like placing a seed inside your heart, knowing that it will quickly germinate to become a wonderful flower that will exhale a pure, powerful and exquisite perfume capable of placating any worrisome feelings as well as awakening my libido in a very powerful way". Indeed, I had developed what was probably an innate power that enabled me to reach incredibly deep levels of spiritual and psychological communion with women.

I must admit that my fertile imagination concerning females followed me throughout my childhood and into my early teenage years and that contributed greatly to a rather precocious maturing process. It was also a means to run away from all the horrors that were abundantly provided by a highly frustrated and drunken father who so cowardly would discharge all of his negative impulses on me, a defenseless boy, and at times on my sister and mother too. As awful as all of this was, I must say that it contributed towards adding some premature characteristics to my demeanor that would make me a pole of attraction to women, starting from a very young age. A simple way to put it is that I would constantly seek the security and the absence of violence in the opposite sex.

The saddest part of my upbringing was the continuous drama

that unfolded with no real reasons whatsoever! It was like a calm ocean all of a sudden subjugated by a hurricane that would bring all psychological structures to the ground, making me literally lose all possible references of a normal life, obliging me to start rebuilding my tenuous balance mildly resembling sanity all over again, until the next inescapable crisis and so on, in a diabolic and perpetually vicious circle.

I still vividly remember, with an unwarranted contrition in my heart, that horrifying afternoon when my old aunt who had survived her sister (my grandmother), went literally mad following a shouting match with my mother who had left for work, leaving me to deal with the 'aftershocks' of the crisis by myself. In a total state of panic, the old yet still energetic lady decided to drive me crazy by repeatedly suggesting suicide attempts by threatening to jump head-first from the upper bedroom window of our tiny suburban house. The process lasted at least an hour and there was no way on earth I could calm her down. She would shout at me, and her behavior would turn increasingly belligerent, abusing me physically each time I would try to hold her with my arms in order to calm her down. At one point she rushed and grabbed the main door key from the dining table and tried desperately to unlock the door shouting loudly, "I want to die and you will not stop me no matter what you do! I simply don't want to live with your bitch of a mother any more!" I grabbed her by the waist and held her back, not without being very stunned by her sudden acquired strength. I will never forget that seemingly frail old lady all of a sudden capable of confronting me, a healthy adolescent, with such might!

Another good half hour of horror ensued in a macabre negotiation for me to give her the keys to the house. I was feeling increasingly exhausted and disgusted by all the nonsense that was being thrown at me on behalf of my mother's mistakes and unjust behavior towards the old aunt. All of a sudden, she became even more incensed and started to loudly beg for me to give her the key.

"I will not live another day in this hell, so no matter what you do, I will kill myself today! You can get a rope and tie me down; as soon as you set me free I will either jump or get a knife or whatever! I am fed up, and I have the right to leave this inferno! Who do you think you are to stop me?" We had no telephone at that time therefore it was simply impossible for me to try to call the police or at least get some sort of medical assistance.

After maybe another hour, I handed her over the bloody key, crying loudly and begging her to take care and to come back soon... I have to admit that at that point I was myself acting out of sheer confusion, but still in a way betting that she would go for a long, brisk walk and finally come to her senses and head back home. Instead, a couple of hours later the police knocked at the door.

That was my third experience with death. The most traumatizing of my entire life, there's no doubt about it!

It took me years if not decades for me to come to grips with that devastating experience... I am not sure whether I will ever be able to objectively describe the torrent of conflicting feelings this experience created in me at that time, some of which still persist deep in my soul. All I know today, despite all the sufferance I went through as a result of this sad experience, is that no one has the right to expect another person to stay hostage to her life problems, no matter how difficult, trivial or intricate those can be. We are all inter-connected in this world, however, this doesn't necessarily mean that we are codependent or symbiotic! Freedom is an exclusive human concept generally used to define a total absence of restraint, which begs the question... restraint from what or rather, from who? From our often-absurd set of socially acceptable norms of conduct? Wild animals are free by definition, obviously until such time that we humans come into play by interfering and destroying their habitat or by enslaving them into our way of life so that they become what we define as pets! The meaning of freedom has perhaps more to do with its various antonyms, like those which define conformity to preestablished norms of conduct, which are once again defined by... ourselves! The human race has created behavioral conditions for an orderly and socially acceptable life that are often completely devoid of true spirit! Isn't that shocking to say the least?

My rapport with women is a story of an unconditional quest for real freedom, not of promiscuity as it may appear to the more puritan reader! I allowed myself to consciously follow my instincts so to speak, with the only self-restrains of not infringing the law or disrespecting a person's preferences. I gave myself permission to love independently and above all social conventions, rules, or preestablished canons. I followed my desire to get to know women and their fabulous inner selves in as much as it is possible for a man possessing enough feminine instincts and sensitivity. This appeal came to me naturally, possibly as a result of the rather peculiar circumstances during my upbringing, and I followed it consciously as soon as I realized that it could only add to my humanity.

My adolescence was quite a solitary and boring affair. The sheer lack of money would preclude me from having nice girl friends despite my good looks and early achieved maturity.

Instead, I would bore them with my insights and, as ridiculous as it may sound, the lack of a car, an essential apparatus leading to flirtation or even to sex, would only make things worse since riding buses in Brazil was definitely not a charming endeavor! As a compensation though, mature women would show their interest in me, but the problem then would be the potential breach of social conventions… I was still too young for any official or even recognized affair. And a hidden affair with a youngster represented some serious risks that most of them didn't want to run!

The only viable solution was for me to exercise my charm with prostitutes, whom I prefer to call professionals, a far less stigmatizing and deservedly respectful adjective! This is probably the reason why I have always respected them, whilst developing a paradoxical sense of trust and intimacy towards the latter. The lack of money would still be a problem, however, much more easily surmountable than with the 'comme il faut' girls of my entourage at that time. The reason for that was quite simple… professionals are after all women like any other, simply exercising a very tough activity often imposed on them by bad and sometimes terrible circumstances beyond their control. No matter how much one wants to stigmatize them, the fact remains that they deal with love or the lack of it continuously… My personal experience with them has been very enriching and often endearing. In my adolescence for instance, I have never paid for their services, which were offered to me graciously and on a complimentary basis. Paradoxically, the well to do girls of my very constrained social circle at that time were much more interested in one's socio-economic status than in anything else so much so that I would quite often become puzzled by the sheer contrast between the two categories of girls, and, invariably prefer the far more enriching company of the professionals.

My initiation happened with one of those women who used to work at a particular nightclub called 'Vagalume' (Firefly), located on the red district of the docks of the Santos harbor around fifty miles distant from the city of São Paulo. I would travel there quite often to hang out with friends and to "flirt" with the girls in between their professional rendez-vous… I used to love it! I will never forget the heavy smell of the surroundings, a mixture of cheap perfume, cigar and cigarette smoke, beer and at times even urine. The place was very dangerous, even more so than other harbor districts, due to the sheer lack of policing, which would make it a free-for-all zone where sex professionals, drug dealers, pimps, smugglers, underground sellers of literally everything one could think of like clothes, lighters, medicine, preservatives, etc. would share the available space and the potential customers together with cheap artists, musicians, sailors from all over the world, adventurers, creating at times quite conflictual situations that would inescapably end up in violence. All that would create, notwithstanding the evident dangers involved, a vibrant and excitingly powerful environment, simply fascinating for a teenager looking for adventure and trying to cope with the awakening of his sex instincts! My courage was definitely fueled by the strong feminine presence on the streets and at the bars, that did instigate in me all of my 'don Quichottesque' instincts of protection towards the sweet "Dulcineas" of the obscure, yet definitely exotic and enthralling Port of Santos's harbor zone!

One night I came across a very beautiful girl called 'Olga'. She was dancing by herself at the 'Vagalume' stage and as soon as I entered the place, she came down and invited me to join her on the dance floor. I walked towards her with a strange feeling of familiarity and took her in my arms as if we were old friends meeting after a long interlude. After a couple of slow dances, when her strong perfume had deeply penetrated my clothes and lungs, we sat at one of the empty tables and she asked for a soft drink... I was quite surprised since the usual order was a glass of cheap, fake and despicable 'Champagne', sold at the price of Dom Perignon, so that the club optimized its revenue. I always had enough money on me for a couple of shots since I knew very well that this was imperative for me to grant a lady's company for at least a good hour... and this was my idea of fun at the time.

"Why are you just asking for a Coca Cola?" I dared to ask. "Don't you want a glass of Champagne?"

"Because I know you are broke and since I find you nice and attractive, I don't want to rip you off!"

I was shocked albeit delighted by the fact that she had decided to spend some time with me knowing beforehand that I had no money! Even so I decided to play a little bit around her blunt reply as well as the very correct perception she had had of my pecuniary condition in such a short period of time!

"How do you know I'm broke... I mean, how did you guess?"

"Very simply by your attitude, your apparent young age despite your macho looks, and the way you dress... remember handsome, I'm a professional in the field!" she added with a loud and sensual laugh. "I can sense those things from a mile away!"

I was obviously convinced, albeit still a bit embarrassed, I must confess! I could now better understand the reason why my female classmates would give preference to the other boys at the end of the day, even when those were less attractive than me. "Bloody Wealthy Whores", I said to myself thinking about them and their 'honest' way to practice what amounted to a hidden and socially accepted form of just that…! prostitution! And I did not change that thought for a long time thereafter articulating it secretly in my mind every time I would entertain a frustrating flirtation attempt with my female classmates!

Olga and I engaged in a very lively conversation about life, beliefs, motherhood (her dream was to have a child as soon as she would be able to quit her work…) her profession, the why's and the who's, her livelihood, the heavy environment she had to bear and many other genuine subjects of interest. She was very emancipated and reflective and had very strong ideas about a vast array of matters by having experienced them under her skin in her short but very intense life. Finally, she decided to call the night off and invited me to her hotel, a filthy building impregnated with a strong smell composed of a mixture of cheap perfume and urine that would make any reasonable intended guest turn around and leave! Instead, I caved into my very strong sexual desire and libido and stubbornly followed Olga through a long corridor where one could hear a mixture of moaning, whimpering, sobbing and not always pleasurable crying coming from the closed doors.

We finally reached Olga's tiny bedroom composed of a double bed and a couple of very old, run down pieces of furniture where she would pile up the few clothes she had. There was a window leading to a dark alley followed by an old, abandoned warehouse and then an equally dark dock where a cargo ship was moored as if fast asleep waiting for the dawn when the charging or discharging work would once again begin. No wonder that port was so heavily congested since there was no night shift…

Olga sat at the edge of the noisy bed and started taking off her very light clothes and laying them carefully on an old chair, the only one in the room, keeping her sexy, red underwear on.

Her young body didn't show any signs of her reckless life style, and was still attractive and very sensual. She had pear shaped, very firm breasts with big nipples and glowing, dark aureoles that would transmit constant excitement... her skin was young and soft, and her belly region had a velvet like feeling, without a single wrinkle or fold, denoting that she hadn't bore a child yet, as it is commonly the case among young professionals.

She took me by the hand, pulled me towards her, and made me delicately lie down by her side pressing her warm body against mine, making me feel a tremendous heatwave running through my spine resulting in an uncontrollable erection that made her smile wickedly at me. "Wow, cool down baby, we have lots of time until tomorrow morning" she whispered in my ear not without reaching for my penis, being immediately contradicted so to speak by a high and long ship siren announcing the dawn shift was about to get started.

The set of feelings I had in that precise moment and in all the ones that ensued, aren't easy to describe since they are the result of a man's first sexual experience! Olga, being a highly skilled lover immediately understood the importance of those moments to me and made me feel like the single most important and desired man on earth! I felt like a champion of all sorts, a fabulous stallion, close to a beautiful princess—-mare, about to make incredible love to her! The tiny, filthy, run down room suddenly looked like the most beautifully appointed sleeping quarters I had ever dreamed of! All the nauseating stinks of the brothel now smelled like the most exquisite fragrance and Olga's cheap perfume made me crave for more especially after our first kisses and cuddles that would bring out her divine, natural body scents melding them together to create the most compelling bouquet ever! The following ship's siren made me dream and transported me to beautiful, exotic and mysterious distant citadels surrounded by splendid beaches, making me want to kidnap my lovely newly found princess to crown her as my queen and live there happily forever after! I was happy and fulfilled finding myself whole in those magic moments that transcended whatever reality was all about! In fact, reality is nothing but the total immersion of one's being into the present moment leaving the mind and its machinations behind! I could swear that Olga was in love without faking her feelings for a single second as is generally the case in those circumstances... and she probably was!

We made crazy, unrestricted love through the night and late into the following morning, and I must say that I shall always recognize in Olga someone who initiated me in a series of sexual, unique, unimaginable originalities that would mark my sexual exploits and discoveries for the rest of my life!

After that incredible experience, and around two to three months after what I considered to be a perfect initiation to my first carnal delectations, I couldn't stop daydreaming with that unforgettable night, wondering when I would be able to repeat it in order to, once again, reach Nirvana... I didn't dare return to the harbor or to Olga from fear that it would somehow spoil the perfection of what I had gone through with her. I have always been a believer that destiny has a way to present us with unexpected, perfect events that usually tie into one or several loops of our life in a given point in time... This is how on one day that looked pretty much like any other, the bell rang and, to my surprise, Paulette was standing at the door... she would very rarely come to our small apartment except when she was needing my mother's advice for something she could not cope with by herself.

"Are you ready to exercise your muscles young fellow? I am moving tomorrow, my husband is in Switzerland, your uncle, as you well know him, is totally unfit for the task at hand, and I couldn't think of anyone better than you to lend me a helping hand."

"No problem," I replied. "But if I heard you correctly, you are moving tomorrow?"

"Yes, yes you heard me well. But do not expect me to drive all the way here to pick you up at 6am… and the movers will be there pretty early, I can tell you!"

By that time my father came out of his room wearing his old and worn-out pajamas and declared, "Of course, you will go, and you will accompany this marvelous and defenseless lady immediately or else, you and I will have a serious conversation…" This was his way to try to charm Paulette, despite knowing that she was totally out of his reach… it was the Dr. Jekyll and Mr Hyde syndrome playing itself over and over again…

"Of course, I will!" my voice came out with a tone that could hardly hide my deep joy and excitement in the face of the unbelievable opportunity offered to me out of the blue to spend twenty-four hours or so with that incredible creature who was certainly, at least for me, the most beautiful woman on earth!

It took me seconds to gather two or three pieces of clothes and my toothbrush and out the door I rushed excitingly into the most incredible of all possibilities! Paulette, Paulette, Paulette, her name was the only thing I could think of, and it would occupy the totality of my thinking capacity…

"Did you like my strategy?" She murmured to my utter surprise, as soon as the doors of the elevator closed behind us. Now that I could finally sense her familiar perfume, her comment abruptly woke me up from the stupor I was immersed in.

"What strategy?" I asked naively as a response to hers... My question was the only possibility for me before jumping into embarrassing imaginary conclusions and causing a terrible misunderstanding with far reaching consequences...

"Well," she said, also hedging her bets while we reached the sidewalk. "I thought it would be very nice to spend some time with you, just you and I, so that I could have your undivided attention for a while... you know," she sort of resolutely continued after taking a long breath. "I saw you growing up and I must confess that I am intrigued by your sensitivity and depth towards what is really important, not to speak of the fast and precocious development of your intellect... and your physique I must say. There is something about you that we women want to explore but it is so hard to define just in words. However, each time we meet there is that crowd around us and everything gets lost with everybody talking at the same time as you know... and then there is Uncle Theodore... do you follow my reasoning?" She was groping for any signs that would show a receptive reaction from me...

"Yes, I do." were the only words I could utter before being able to try to interpret what I thought my ears had just heard... although still not trusting them at all...

"So, do you agree with me?" she insisted.

"Yes, I do." I was kind of mentally paralyzed, totally seized by the unbelievable magic of the moment and unable to exercise any control of my mind that would at least enable me to articulate more than two or three words in a logical manner...

"You know, I am the type of woman that can only communicate fully with someone like you, such a genuine and pure person, with whom I can not only employ my intellect but also my entire body, and when I say my entire body, I really mean it if you understand what I am trying to convey to you. My thinking has to be expressed physically in order to corroborate what I say or what I think you know or understand about me, otherwise it's like it's not really validated… what is your opinion about what I just said?". Now she had definitely decided to cross the red line and risk it all by taking the initiative since I simply did not display any signs of having even the most remote intention to do so in her place! We men, great cowards indeed!

"Well, I guess I fully understand you," I lied encouraging her to continue by calling whatever bluff remained in the conversation.

I had the sweet feeling of succumbing into some kind of exciting manipulation, a life-or-death sort of game to me who was trying hard to behave like a grown up, as if I was experienced in that kind of role, which was in fact shaping up as a totally unchartered territory to my teenage, almost complete inexperience in the field if it wasn't for Olga's fantastic initiation just weeks ago. Of course I had imagined the ensuing moments thousands of times and had rehearsed thousands of outcomes for similar or equivalent imaginary situations for quite some time, but now I was suddenly confronted with a reality that was potentially shaping up well beyond my fondest dreams… and I was at a complete loss as to how I should behave and not sound like a complete idiot… little did I know about what was at the very core of her attraction to me — precisely my innocence and lack of experience.

She was obviously mastering the whole situation while she was also exploring a new, unknown and unchartered possibility with an unexperienced youngster. Obviously, she was in full control and totally at ease to gradually express her feelings and desires leaving always a way out in case she spooked me. This being said, she had to cross a difficult initial stage first in order to define the rules of the game, guarantee the outcome and become able to delve into the exciting situation as naturally and spontaneously as she had envisioned it. She was therefore running a great risk in case I decided to give it all up and run away in fear of not being a la hauteur. Instead, I was totally charmed and craving for more of that new, utterly exciting game but my own insecurity made her feel that she had to dig further just to make absolutely sure that the playing field was clean and entirely hers to be explored... obviously that unnerving cat and mouse game debut had a highly exciting side by itself and would play quite deeply into her female hunting instincts.

- "Are you sure you understand me? I can sense some hesitation in your reaction... Give me then some kind of signal to convince me that all is clear in your mind too. After all, I am taking practically all the initiative here, while you are just nodding your head and giving me very short, telegraphic answers. Usually, you are much more eloquent when you are interested in a given subject. If this is the result of your nervousness, which I fully understand, we can deal with it together so that you feel at ease with the situation. Do you at least find me interesting as a woman, by the way? I mean attractive enough for a young man like yourself?" She was firing all her guns at once now in what appeared to be the last raid before finally taking the entire fort!

That question reached me like a bomb! She was increasing the pressure maybe out of impatience or sheer excitement or probably both. It was like a checkmate taking place literally before moving a single pawn from the chessboard since the game, as far as I was concerned, and despite all of its still incognito parts, was just beginning! I was at a complete loss as to what I should do next and all the love stories that I had read or watched in the movies were playing frantically in my head while I tried to figure out what the hell somebody deeply immersed like I was in that moment and in that situation, should do to counter or rather encourage even more that disconcerting invasion into my intimacy. I was loving it and was struggling to stay afloat whilst groping for ways to embolden her to continue. The experience with Olga had been a direct and overwhelming assault so to speak straight into my most intimate instincts, while this was a subtle, albeit also resolute foray into my deepest intimacy unveiling the longstanding feelings I had been nurturing for Paulette since I laid my eyes on her... I could feel my hands sweat and my mouth was getting so dry to the point that I felt I would probably be unable to articulate an entire phrase without sounding stoned. I also felt victorious and privileged for having been chosen by such a fantastic female to what seemed to be a prelude to a complete sexual experience that would probably take me well beyond the wild yet still unskilled sex I had with Olga, or the furtive kisses I managed to steal from the girls my age at the few school parties I used to attend on Saturdays before they figured out that I was completely broke in spite of all my promises granted by my good looks... they would certainly enjoy my practicing the caresses I would have learned and usually exchanged with the professionals that I would at times meet at the end of their working nights and that would be like a purification ceremony for them and a sexual enthusiastic exploration for me...

We finally reached the car and she asked me to drive it. She knew I did not have my license yet, but she also knew that I was an excellent driver and that I loved to drive like most adolescents.

Besides, it was rush hour hence it was highly unlikely that we would be bothered by the traffic police. I took the wheel and, before starting the engine, the question fell like a fatality...

"So, before we depart, do I deserve an answer? Or did you forget my question?" She asked impatiently.

She had gently rested her hand on my thigh, and I could feel a burning sensation that would radiate through my entire body, as a result of that furtive contact. All the romantic movie's crucial scenes I had watched in the past came back into my mind and very hastily I tried hard to choose the outcome or the phrase that would best adapt to my own situation.

Finally, after moments that felt like an eternity, I turned and kissed her in the mouth with such eagerness and passion, that she moaned deeply out of pleasure. I started the engine and moved away swiftly through traffic trying to avoid her eyes that were looking at me with an expression of languid anticipation... I was levitating towards heaven!

We finally arrived at Paulette's elegant home a couple of hours later due to heavy traffic, and a light meal was on the table set for two as if everything had been planned in advance and details taken care of. That reassured me in a very funny way by erasing any feeling that would eventually make me feel guilty for the seemingly improvised course of events... as if that was in any way possible given my inexperience and young age in the face of her sexual maturity and command of the whole situation!

Paulette was married to a rich, ruthless and hardnosed Belgian individual called Bertrand who had made a fortune by providing gardening decorative services at a time when it was easy to make money in Brazil since the country was growing fast and literally everything was on demand. They had built a gorgeous house in one of the poshest neighborhoods of São

Paulo, where both lived alone since their young son was studying in a boarding school in the UK.

Why don't we have a good drink and leave dinner for later darling? I became instantly aroused by both ideas and especially by the fact she would call me darling... the same tender word she would use to address Theodore! I thought I was day-dreaming!

I agreed and reached for what was probably a triple dose of scotch poured into an elegant glass. We toasted and I gulped the whole thing in seconds...

"Are you nervous?" she asked me like a cat playing around with what she now certainly viewed as a sure pray. Then she went on and unwittingly, yet intentionally, touched my penis as if to test things...

"Wow!" she murmured kind of jokingly, I guess you approve of me, right? By then, I was obviously excited beyond measure, and it showed...

"What is your guess?" I finally reacted, surprisingly without any embarrassment thanks to that magical malt concoction now totally gone from my glass!

"My guess is that you will make me very happy..." she whispered while I could feel her warm and extremely soft tongue practically penetrating my left ear...

She then started to undress slowly, with a radiant expression on her face, full of expectation and excitement. Every piece of clothing that she pulled from her body, would unveil a superb white, soft, yet firm, piece of skin and her unbelievably sex appealing intimate parts... Her breasts were firm and full like a full moon with enormous nipples, rather rare for a blond. Her sex was protuberant probably full of hormones ready to burst into an explosion of fertility. Her lips were humid and meaty in sheer anticipation of all the pleasure that was about to reach us both.

Her natural blond hair would cascade on her back in waves that would softly caress her silky skin as she moved her head. Her demeanor was feline, and all of a sudden, she climbed on a chair and as she reached the dining table, lied down on it, as softly as a feather. Then, she turned her head and stared at me with those marvelous blue eyes, shinning as if full of tears… I had the clear impression that she was crying out of sheer pleasure!

"Are you OK?" I asked her in order to fill the silent void that would make me almost lose track of the chain of events.
I am very well my love. Come closer, I want you as close to me as possible.

I approached the table and kissed her passionately in what was a long, interminable embrace. I was discovering pleasure in every gesture, in every touch, in every smell that would emanate from that warm and vibrating body, now offered to me with such grace and surrender that would make me feel totally at ease and abandoned as I was now to my wildest instincts, far from my earlier feelings of nervousness, in what I could categorize as my second initiation ritual in just three months or so apart… She sat up on the table facing me and, in between avid and languid kisses, started to unbutton my shirt and my trousers so ably that the next thing I vaguely remember was me being totally naked and kissing and licking her tremendously sensual upper body. She then pressed my chest against her magnificent breasts whilst kissing me and licking my mouth with such passion and desire that I simply lost all reservations and let my instinct dictate all gestures that ensued as if in a kind of intimate and well-known script based on everything I had imagined, in endless sessions of masturbation inspired by Paulette herself. I felt my penis slowly penetrating her wet vagina whilst my mouth ardently licked and nibbled her now very hardened and enormous tits. We came together in a torrent of pleasure that made us both laugh loudly out of pure delight and abandonment!

We made love several times that night with passion and total carnal devotion but also with warmth, tenderness and with such an affection that it was a true act of adoration between two beings who seemingly desperately needed each other in order to overcome every preconceived divide and embrace a loving unity. She had given me a sense of belonging that I couldn't possibly feel in any other way than that pure, profound and all-encompassing experience of love!

I will never understand or accept the cultural walls, taboos and preconceived ideas that surround most issues related to sex… even the word itself often evokes a forbidden, stained and misleading perception or even a sin. I was never able to sense dirt, sin, forbidden barriers or any of the negative concepts that are commonly associated with love making… making love and love are so intimately intertwined in my view, that they are indeed the same thing! 'Making' love or having sex as we have regretfully vulgarized the act, is nothing but the materialization of the feeling of love, nothing more, nothing less. We have, as a human society, however, usurped all true meaning of such natural, human (and animal), instinctive, God blessed act that we have ultimately created huge distortions to the extent that the negative concepts that have been adopted by different cultures simply became self-fulfilling as a result of the widespread acceptance of the distortions themselves… As a result, sex abuses and even worse, sexual crimes, paradoxically proliferate in every cultural or religious environment no matter what precepts of love and understanding exist as the very foundations of those cultures and religions. Our minds have the undeserved power to project whatever we believe in, which should in fact serve as a base to build loving and benevolent societies based on compassion and humanity... Instead, we frequently project our ire, fears and greed which often attract similar sentiments from whoever we interact with.

We were very close to New Years' eve which falls right in the middle of the summer in the Southern Hemisphere, and Paulette confided to me that Theodore was going to travel with one of his new conquests At that point Paulette and I had met with a certain frequency, at my friend Jeanine's cozy apartment which was usually available in the afternoons when Jeanine was at work. Jeanine was a divorced mother of two, very open minded, and especially cheerful of my love affair with Paulette and very curious about it and its unforeseeable outcome. Some years later we ended up having a short-lived love affair of our own, particularly designed to satisfy Jeanine's curiosity which had originated from the relatively high frequency of my meetings with Paulette at her place...

The problem concerning the New Year's Eve date was that Paulette's home was going to be busy with a couple of Bertrand, her husband's, friends whom he had invited to stay for the holidays despite the fact that he was planning to be away as well. Jeanine's home was busy too since she had invited her friends for a New Year's celebratory dinner, which in the end left us with practically no option besides celebrating the date in a hotel room, a rather sad project!

I had a daring idea but was not sure at all whether Paulette would go for it. It consisted in simply going somewhere in the woods that surrounded the city, more specifically in the outskirts of a small village called São Roque and celebrate on our own under the stars. At that time Brazil was a relatively safe place and this was perfectly doable from a safety standpoint!

Paulette agreed immediately! "All I long for, all I crave for, is for us to be together, and I really don't care where you take me as long as we celebrate the start of the new year making love to each other!" Needless to say, I was obviously thrilled with such an exciting prospect!

On December 31st, late in the afternoon, we met in our usual designated place which was a supermarket parking lot and left for São Roque like two teenagers in love! Upon arrival, I decided to make a quick stop at an Italian restaurant where we used to frequent with the family often on weekends and was immediately recognized and welcomed by a small crowd who were already celebrating the year's passage. I could see a huge amount of delicious food and several bottles of wine being passed around to each other over the table and, as I came closer, they pulled me to a chair and tried to convince me to share the meal with them! Typically, Italian! As soon as I gently declined the invitation telling them that I had someone waiting for me in the car, they handed me a bottle of Champagne, another one gave me a nice Italian red, two empty glasses and to my amazement a well wrapped package with a delicious smell coming out of it!" These are the Gnocci de la mamma! You've never eaten anything like it!" a young man whispered in my ear while handing me the warm package.

My insistence to pay fell on a series of deaf ears so after greeting them and wishing all a Happy New Year, I walked out and entered Paulette's car.

"I was starting to worry, my love!" she whispered and immediately went on to say, "Wh-what a terrific smell!" I quickly explained that incredible situation and the huge generosity of those nice people and then we went on to look for a nice clear spot right in the middle of a small, tropical forest.

We finally found what appeared to be an appropriate, quiet, clean spot at a good distance from the closest lights which could hardly be perceived through the tree branches hovering above us in the dark of the night. Paulette jumped out of the car and pulled a small camping pad out of the trunk extending it on the soft ground covered by dead leaves. Then she suddenly undressed, literally taking off all her clothes which made her look like a fairy tale princess, a blond luminous and delicate beauty coming straight out of a dream, in sheer contrast with the moving shadows of the majestic tree branches, the sole apparent witnesses from the surrounding forest. She would then perform ballet movements and her able turns and twists allowed me to admire her sculptural forms from a variety of awesome angles with her firm and big breasts hovering around in prodigious, alluring movements… Then she came close to me half breathless and delicately took off my clothes saying jokingly, "You won't need these well until next year baby!" and threw them carelessly to the side…

By that time, we were approaching midnight, I opened the Champagne bottle and poured a generous dose between Paulette's wonderful breasts down her velvet like tummy, and finally dropped a good dose onto her generous vulva and in between her fleshy inviting lips… then, I licked all the Champagne slowly before handing her the bottle and enticing her to do likewise to me which she obviously did with a dazzling ability!

Suddenly, the sound of a not-so-distant thunder announced a summer rain which started falling upon us just moments thereafter. We were totally oblivious of the fact that we became drenched in a matter of seconds, such was our excitement and blinding passion towards each other! Our love making became even more ardent by the sheer contrast between our warm bodies and the cold rain that somehow added to our overwhelming sense of pleasure. We came together in consecutive ecstatic orgasms and Paulette's soft and quivering body was like a passionate, humid and tender flying carpet taking me far away into pleasurable, infinite fields of soft, placid bliss and harmony.

We stayed there for quite some time, holding each other tight until the rain subsided and the stars once again invaded the vast sky upon us. The wonderful fresh smell emanating from the wet dead leaves beneath our naked bodies gave us a tremendous sense of serenity and a certainty of definitely belonging to that environment… to nature!

My affair with Paulette lasted until she left to go back to Belgium, and I owe her practically all the mastering teachings of a rather fallacious definition of what one could call physical love. She was a true lover in the deepest physical meaning of the word. Her affirmation addressed to me at the very beginning of our rapport namely my thinking and my feelings have to be expressed physically" was exactly an accurate description of what she was, in fact: an instinctive, physical master of the art of love making! I will obviously always keep a very tender soul connection to Paulette and the importance she represented to my development as a man. She definitely contributed significantly to my ardent and passionate attraction to a woman's body and soul.

Sophia was a totally different being… she was complex and complicated, profound and extremely perceptive. In fact, and despite all the misunderstandings, fights, and a half-broken relationship with Theodore, her husband, they would still live together, and one couldn't do without the other. She was Theodore's 'eminence grise', some kind of consiglieri for all matters be it business, his lovers (yes, he would consult with her about his lovers!), his health, his decisions in life, and so on… she, in her turn, would receive from him a strong sense of protection, money, a definitely spicy existence, culture (music, theatre, mythology, philosophy, history, etc.). They would both strive for control and as such would try to manipulate each other with the mantle of victory falling invariably onto Sophia… I was always intrigued to observe their contest for power watching Theodore, a man at times greater than life, with a huge array of life experiences in his luggage and an excellent penchant for philosophy and psychology succumb to Sophia's insightful awareness. She would command their discussions with such mastery that Theodore's encyclopedic knowledge would be gracefully neutralized like a powerful boa immobilizing a bird through hypnosis on a branch in the middle of the jungle. My relationship with Sophia had been extremely intense since my early childhood years, and our complicity would create a solid barrier to whoever dared to interfere either by curiosity, jealousy, or disbelief that such a mature and sophisticated woman would spend hours in the company of someone who was initially a boy and then turned into a teenager, no matter what his maturity. The truth was that we would both feel absolutely free together, with no restraints or limitations whatsoever that could preclude us from approaching the most intimate of subjects. She would trust me and, most of all trust my capacity to understand her and put myself in her shoes. Such strong affection would make her therefore disarm and plummet pleasurably into her true nature devoid of her usual defenses. We would spend entire days together whenever Theodore was travelling which happened quite often. On one of those sunny, brisk winter days, what was supposed to happen, happened with the fury of a contained barrage that finally relinquished its resistance to the indomitable strength of the water.

We were on a farm, some kind of a health spa in which Sophia had enrolled for a three-day treatment. She had proposed to the family that I accompany her so that she wouldn't feel lonely and would have someone to chit chat during her free time between treatments. Our love was far from being the physical ecstasy I had experienced with Paulette but instead was a tight and cozy meeting of the spirits and a perfect marriage of our minds. The physical aspect of our rapport was somehow secondary, although still great since Sophia finally came across as a superlative lover and a particularly sexual and sensitive woman! The most important part of our relationship though was our tender understanding yielding a very rich dialogue and the unforgettable lessons she patiently and lovingly taught me about female instincts and mind power. Phrases like "don't offer, let alone give love to anybody who is not open or receptive to it" or, "nobody ever changes really, all we can do is learn how to live better with the perception we have of ourselves... and that perception evolves as we grow older." Just to mention two out of maybe a dozen citations of hers that will stay with me forever. Sophia would go through life as someone who had built an emotional roadmap out of an existence filled with utter psychological sufferance that sieved through her being to become pure wisdom. That wisdom would serve its purpose which was to provide her with some kind of a protective gear against the great vicissitudes of her perilous and dramatic life. Her story was filled with sad and dramatic events. She was thrown out of her home at the age of fourteen by her father who would despise her probably because of his own tortuous character and upbringing. She would then wander for years being repeatedly harassed and exploited by unscrupulous men who would take advantage of her vulnerability... The time we spent together was for me like an intensive course in emotional intelligence as well as a balm for my own spiritual wounds. Sophia definitely marked my life and awakened my curiosity towards women's different ways of coming into this world, all of them though essentially and inherently equipped and fit for life so to speak, the result of the fact that the latter are indeed born ready as opposed to men, who will go through life in a never-ending learning process with highly debatable results or achievements to say the least...

Unfortunately, our relationship ended in drama, with my mother discovering and distorting what amounted to be something much more significant than a mere love affair, to all those who wanted to project their own frustrations into a blind condemnation of something they simply could not understand! That precipitous attitude resulted in a family schism with unforeseen consequences that would change everybody's feelings towards each other in a complete, irreversible and permanent way!

From my part, I innocently offered Sophia to marry her and to adopt her two small children, but she obviously and wisely declined.

My only alternative to look for love subsequent to that period, not only from a physical standpoint, but also, and mainly from an emotional one, was to go back to my well-travelled road with professionals — once again an erroneous, offensive, unjust and plainly wrong definition of the latter! — and so I did go back to my dear professionals in the art of love!

The price I ended up paying in the end however for my trust and tenderness vis a vis those creatures, those masters in the art of love, was dear I must confess... I ended up being ill and under severe medication for almost two years, out of which six months of those were spent in bed in order to get rid of a grave pulmonary tuberculosis, one of the major causes of death in Brazil at that time…

Like everything else in life though, and as the Chinese define it beautifully, a problem also means and indeed brings opportunity, and as such, my convalescence brought me the necessary time to think things over and to ponder about some obscure aspects of my life… not that I made any earth-shattering decisions about my existence that would engender immediate results, but I employed practically all the free time I had available to undertake an inner voyage that would point me towards better solutions hence easier choices for my life's endless and intricate intersections. That attitude would in its turn offer me some positive guidance enabling me to bravely continue ploughing into my unusual albeit unknown destiny.

Luckily, a couple of exquisitely devoted and caring women presented me with their undivided affection during that particularly trying period, which helped me cope and finally rescue myself from the sheer misery I was immersed in as a result of the ravages caused by that terrible disease. And so, the first of those true angels made her first quick yet courageous appearance right in the height of my lung infection, when I was still very contagious, fighting a persistent 42° Celsius fever that stubbornly wouldn't go away despite the very strong antibiotics I had been prescribed. She was a fellow university student named Patricia with whom I had a short flirtation period before the disease… it turns out that Patricia had fallen in love with me despite my poor life conditions, given the fact that I had shown empathy for her psychological problems and had really tried hard to help her overcome her depression by showing compassion and understanding towards her intricate predicaments. I must also point out that she was born into a filthy rich family, hence social status and possessions were definitely not what she was looking for… she came for a short visit, keeping a prophylactic distance from my bed and we had a short conversation remembering the days we had recently spent together at her farm. Then she left promising to come back soon.

Patricia suffered from deep depression to the point of staying for several days in bed without being able to harness the necessary strength to stand up and simply live life! On those sad occasions, I was quite often the only person she would allow in her room simply because I would make her laugh and somehow, for short and furtive moments, make her transcend her sufferance. I would defiantly mock her condition and ridicule her somber self-projections that would spring like the heads of a Hydra all the way from the depths of her depressed self. One day that I will always remember, roughly a month before getting ill, she had invited me to her elegant farm in the outskirts of the city and, during one of our nice walks through the fields, a summer storm abruptly announced its arrival with gale force winds which had the effect of literally paralyzing Patricia who became all of a sudden rigid and absolutely motionless, refusing to move a single step ahead, even with the first drops of rain starting to fall on our heads… I took her hand, told her to close her eyes and to keep them closed no matter what, and started telling her a tale where a dauntless and indomitable heroin had to battle horrifying monsters that would invade her body appearing suddenly from the abysses of the earth and paralyzing her movements in order to devour her little by little. Finally, as I continued improvising, after putting up a considerable fight with the assailants, the heroin dominated the intruders by discovering and using an incredible, newly found inner strength which forced them to leave her body and run away in total disarray, bouncing in desperate ripples towards the abyss they had originated from... I then cuddled Patricia warmly and caressed her head and her long, thick hair telling her that all was fine and that the storm had no power whatsoever over us, like the monsters in the tale. She then finally started to move very slowly following my lead and listening to my words as if the storm rumbles and growls were unable to reach us like the inner creatures of the tale, totally exorcised by her now newly found inner will.

Patricia kept on thanking me for what I did to her on that occasion for a long time subsequent to that episode... It is indeed interesting to ponder about how much we can give lovingly to a neighboring soul, so effortlessly, just by letting our instincts and loving feelings take the helm for a while.

That evening we nestled together and kissed each other repeatedly like two castaways who, precisely because of being together and helping each other, had overcome a terrible storm, an inner one in the case of Patricia... and in a way, definitely my own storm too! We didn't make love properly speaking, because we wanted to prolong the newly found feeling of cohesion and camaraderie prevailing between us.

About a month later, late at night, right after having been diagnosed with pulmonary Tuberculosis, when my high fever would make me have crazy hallucinations, my mother came into the room with an elegant basket containing fresh red salad which I loved, a rarity at that time. Its seeds came from Italy, and could only be found at Patricia's farm...then, in addition the basket contained three fresh eggs coming straight from the ass of the chicken as I would joke about, a selection of fresh fruit, a red rose and a note saying, "You will beat the monster inside you too, the same way you taught me to beat mine the other day! Just follow my thoughts which are with you all the time and trust your inner strength as you taught me to trust mine, and… eat the bloody eggs! They will give you strength! Talk to you tomorrow! With love, Pat."

I cried like a child since suddenly I felt wanted… loved… remembered… important… all those good and essential things that make us feel that life is still worthwhile after all! How critically vital it is when someone expresses love towards us on certain occasions when we suffer and consequently feel vulnerable and lonely! I fell deeply asleep with no more hallucinations for the rest of the night!

The baskets kept on coming daily, always at the same time; in the evening! Always with a rose, each time with a different variety of delicious, fresh food and, most importantly, with a sweet and encouraging message of love! A week later, the antibiotics finally kicked in and my fever abated. After a couple of days and following her request, I gave Patricia a call to tell her that according to my doctor, I was no longer contagious despite my very weak state. His recommendation was for me to stay in complete repose for at least a month until the huge number of pills and daily injections I was taking would start their healing effect. The daily injections and the intensive care the disease required in those days had forced me to take shelter at my mother's home where she managed to spare one of the two existing small rooms for my healing process. I had suggested to the doctor to send me to a sanatorium, however, according to him, that presented the risk of delaying my remission due to the fact that people often get used to the sanatorium's cozy routines and unconsciously delay the healing process of the body despite all the care and the prescribed powerful drugs! How quickly are we able to spiritually adapt to a sense of safety and protection even if fictitious!

After my call, Patricia showed up on the following afternoon, however this time around she was carrying the basket herself and delivered it directly to me.

"What about the nice little note? I got used to it and I must tell you that it has done marvels to my daily mood," I said kind of jokingly.

"I am here to deliver it to you personally…" was her answer with a naughty expression on her face while closing the room door and locking it twice with care.

"Can you finally fuck now?" Was her absolutely unexpected and stunningly shocking question thrown at me just like that, without any hesitation!

"Nope, unfortunately my doctor wants me to be in a complete repose… but, maybe…"

"Sorry to interrupt you Axel but there are no buts or maybes in these circumstances, my dear friend! We must follow your doctor's instructions to the letter! That doesn't mean however that we cannot have some fun, right?" She finished the phrase while starting to undress like a stripper before my incredulous eyes!

That was definitely not the scared and vulnerable young woman whom I had to liberate from all those terrifying ghosts during the storm at her farm.

Standing in front of me was a resolute, self-assured, divinely and deliciously naked female with a strong desire to experience physical pleasure in any of its possible forms in the face of the circumstances… I guess she wanted to put herself in a dominant situation vis a vis me, her redeemer from that terrible inner storm, now at her entire mercy, totally subjugated and hopelessly weakened by the disease… That dominant position coupled with the vivid memory of that kissing session filled with tenderness at the farm, had finally awakened her instincts and her sexuality, long dormant in the face of her depressive condition.

Patricia sat on the single chair available next to the bed and started masturbating herself with such a voluptuous expression while exuding heat waves of desire, that I got an instantaneous erection after a long period of time without even realizing any more that I had a penis notwithstanding that soft kind of abscess that I used in order to urinate from time to time...

She then started caressing her tits and her areoles caringly with one hand and her clitoris with the other, and finished squeezing and chafing them so vigorously that I thought she would end up hurting herself in the process... That would excite me even more resulting in my entire body suddenly waking up from its long torpor and becoming highly excited and sensitive!

Within minutes she reached an orgasm, then another one, before sitting quietly on the edge of the bed while caressing my dick now about to explode out of extreme excitement. She then caressed its head with her soft lips, took it in her mouth and gave me the best fellatio I ever had in my life. From time to time, she would look at me and murmur the words "take it easy and relax, remember the doctor..." Patricia definitely knew exactly how to drive me crazy within the circumstances by sucking and licking the most sensitive parts of my penis and its surrounding areas in a hellish crescendo that made me reach a long and fervent orgasm much sooner than I would have anticipated.

She then stood up quite abruptly and asked me several short questions bearing a guilty tone in her voice..." Do you think that was OK for you to do this? How do you feel honey? Are you too tired? I hope we didn't totally disrespect your doctor's instructions after all babe..."

"I am in heaven my love! And I am sure this is the best possible cure of all, certainly better and more effective than all the drugs combined that I have been taking! "I murmured still feeling the pleasure of the contact of her skin now that she was in bed literally encroached on me like an octopus!

Two days later my doctor categorically forbade me to have any kind of sexual intercourse or activity for that matter, which obviously Patricia and I disobeyed not without exercising a certain amount of restraint... Our newly discovered source of mutual pleasure somehow filled our lives and brought us a world of goodness, greatly relieving my sufferance from the Tuberculosis and restoring some of my self-esteem, whilst relieving her depression that was now practically non-existent!

Six months later that felt like an eternity, I was allowed to get out of bed and to resume normality on a very gradual basis since I still had a good year of medication ahead of me at the very least! I shall never forget the first week of my renaissance so to speak, a real awakening marvel thanks to Patricia's all-encompassing and caring love. She had asked me to prepare a small suitcase with enough clothes for a week and on a beautiful sunny morning passed by to fetch me very early as planned.

The weather was one of those brisk cool days and as soon as we reached the highway, Particia disclosed the destination.

"Guess what! We shall spend a week together at the Toriba hotel in Campos do Jordão!" The place was located in a quaint and small town up in the mountains at about three hours from the city. It was my favorite spot although all I had ever experienced there had been a day tour with friends and a short sneak visit to that uniquely exquisite and private boutique hotel inspired by Swiss Alpine resorts... It was managed by a Swiss hotelier who used to run the place with even more rigueur than his Swiss counterparts, hence the very high standard and consequent hefty prices charged to the elite that used to patronize this distinctive, high ranking hotel.

"Wow, I yelled, but you well know that I can't even afford the coffee they serve on their terraces," I muttered without hiding my joy and excitement at that unbelievable prospect.

"Well, you can stay on and wash the dishes if you wish to pay for it… lots of dishes, I must warn you by the way…! Or if you prefer, you can forget about that disproportionate pride of yours for a while and accept my invitation with grace and enjoy every bit of it! How about that option…? Sounds better, right? This is what I plan to do anyway, regardless." She finished by giving me a perverse glimpse with the corner of her blue and very expressive eyes.

"Your option sounds amazing!" Was all I answered before making her stop the car in order to kiss her passionately. Life was good again for sure!

We spent a memorable week at the Toriba Hotel where we definitely bothered and annoyed a lot of people besides raising lots of eyebrows with our constant love making which was all but silent let alone discreet… I shall never forget this very special woman who probably loved me like no other ever would and knew how to express it so sweetly and poignantly. She was my savior at a time when I desperately needed love and affection, when life had lost its zest causing me to go through that terrible disease that I had no doubt contracted out of sheer solitude and despair…

I knew deep inside however that Patricia was not going to be part of my life for the long haul, and I was right. She was simply not prepared to risk spending her life next an unstable individual like me given her own emotional disarray… I was desperately searching for meaning through love and affection which were plentifully offered by Patricia; however, I was definitely not ready or even able to recognize and seize the opportunity to settle down at that relatively young age with a single companion. I still had to go through a long process of inner search and self-fulfillment before entertaining the idea of marriage and forming a family... And most of all, I still had to submit myself to my almost obsessional attraction to women's mysterious sensitivity that somehow mirrored mine, and for the compelling attraction I had not only for the latter but, perhaps even more importantly, for the quest of my own feminine inner features. That innate curiosity and the unearthing of such identification, would end up creating an instinctive demeanor resulting in the strong attraction I, in my turn, would exert upon them. At that particular time, I felt strongly that I had a long way to go before being able to fully satisfy a woman and her true expectations of a true man and all his attributes! Hence, after some months together, Patricia and I decided to part ways keeping the unique feelings towards each other that we both knew would be carried forever in our hearts.

At that point in time, I was totally healed from my disease, however I was kind of stuck and directionless as if lost in my own life vicissitudes, without knowing really what I wanted to do in order to give myself some sense of purpose. I felt I needed to get back to some kind of action with a view to find at least one reasonable and potentially fulfilling life objective that would propel me forward and eventually lead to new, unexplored horizons. I dreaded studying yet finally I managed to, quite painfully, finish and get a bachelor's degree at a well renowned business school I used to hate along with most individuals who would graduate with me, excluding quite a few honorable exceptions! I was consistently placed among the worst grades of my class, however somehow most teachers nurtured a paradoxical respect for my views maybe because of my courage to express my thoughts and feelings with honesty, and often bringing innovative and challenging opinions to the fore. As a matter of fact, I despised almost all the executives I had met throughout my fairly young existence, notwithstanding the fact that I was prepared to become one myself. There's nothing more intellectually arid, in my humble opinion, than an executive's life. The business environment generally reflects ruthless competition at its core, coupled with utterly disloyal behavior, which is commonplace in most organizations, resulting in disastrous consequences in one's character, psyche, attitude and quality of life. That ends up reflecting into the executive's environment thus irradiating stress, anxiety and sufferance in everyone around. I definitely do not recommend this kind of career to anybody wanting to keep his or her sanity intact.

AMAZON REGION I

I was therefore looking for some kind of a professional activity that would at least allow me to earn my living, when I finally stumbled on a job offer posted in one of the local newspapers. It was a French trading company long established in Brazil, that was searching for a young and energetic candidate to be in charge of their Tropical Trading department. The activity would basically consist of sourcing crafts, medicinal herbs, gems and tropical timber from the Amazon region to be subsequently exported and sold in North America, Europe and Asia. The company was fully compliant with the rather loose environmental regulations and requirements of that time and had all the necessary licenses and permits allowing it to exercise its trading activities in the Amazon region. I have to point out that the environmental awareness of today was simply non-existent at that time, for nothing else but the scarcity of solid, proven scientific evidence!

My predecessors on the job had simply not been able to develop the activity either by sheer incompetence or because of its huge challenges in terms of being able and available to travel sometimes for weeks to extremely remote areas of the Amazon rainforest with all the inherent risks involved in the undertaking, not to speak of the highly questionable intermediaries involved in that kind of trade from a moral or ethical standpoint. What had happened, as a matter of fact, was a real business mess exceedingly difficult to disentangle at that point in time due to the fact that the company had hastily granted significant cash advances to all sorts of peculiar characters, most of them foreigners who were fugitives from the justice systems of their own countries hiding in the middle of nowhere… The significant amount of cash that had been granted for expected deliveries of everything one could imagine, ranging from fake tribal crafts manufactured in Manaus (the capital of the Amazon state), to timber, to semi-precious gems without even asking for samples beforehand to be duly analyzed and authenticated, let alone signing the necessary legal documentation… The job was showcased to me as an exotic activity full of challenges but also enticing travels to distant lands worldwide since I would also be visiting distribution points and customers scattered all around the world, and exclusive attractions given the diversity of products, markets and so on… Thanks to my language skills, I was hired practically on the spot despite my young age not before a couple of long interviews that seemed more like a test of my survival skills in lieu of an attempt to gauge my technical capabilities and academic background… I would understand that twist some months later when I realized that I had to travel almost monthly to the 'Alto Solimões' in the Amazon close to the Peruvian border to highly primitive places lacking all and every sense of comfort, where the great river acquires different denominations before joining the 'Rio Negro' and then becoming the almighty 'Rio Amazonas', the largest in the world in terms of volume of water.

One of the most intriguing events of my entire life and one that I have experienced repeatedly during the period I spent working for that company, was the relativity of travel time… time itself being by definition a relative and highly subjective notion anyway. In fact, I would board a then brand-new Boeing 727 jet in São Paulo to find myself some four and a half hours later in the city of Manaus, the state capital of the 'Estado do Amazonas' some 4,500km from São Paulo. That is the largest Brazilian state and covers a significant part of the so called 'Amazonia legal', in other words of the Amazon region as defined by its legal geographical boundaries. To put that fantastic region and its dimension into perspective, suffice to consider some numbers such as its huge territory of seven million or 2,700 thousand square miles that encompass the Amazon basin, comprising territories belonging to nine nations. 5.5 million square Km or 2.1 million square miles are still covered by the rainforest which is equivalent to about 50% of the planet's remaining rainforests. Biodiversity speaks for itself since one in ten known species in the world are originated in the Amazon rainforest. And still, despite all its might, biodiversity, and size, a 2009(!) study found that a mere 4% rise in global temperatures would wipe out 85% of the Amazon rainforest along with its indigenous peoples that depend on that highly fragile ecosystem for their own survival. The majority of the rainforest is contained within the Brazilian borders. The cultural heritage of the Amazon tribes is fantastic, still relatively unexplored and I must say, almost unbelievable… Just to cite a single fact, the linguistic diversity is simply astonishing! There are thirty-four language families listed in the Amazon basin against a single one in Europe (Indo-European) and twenty-one in Europe, Asia and Africa combined! This is a result of around 11,000 years (Yes, eleven thousand years !!) of human settlements…

Coming back to my travel exploits, I would then hire a small single engine 'sort of' plane that would fly for about three hours to land in 'Tefé', some five hundred and fifty km upriver or west of the city of Manaus. I would then hire one of those typical river wooden boats quite common in the Amazon region with two or three hammocks hanging from some kind of wooden poles that also serve to hold the roof that protect the passengers from the often-cataclysmic rain showers which frequency would vary according to one of the two yearly seasons — the rainy one and the dry one! The rainy season also known as the flood period, would coincide with the thaw of the Andes resulting in a literal deluge that would submerge all the lowlands of the huge basin thus allowing a significant variety of animals such as snakes, crocodiles, turtles etc. to regain their original habitat in order to procreate. That event would also allow loggers to move the dry season's fallen trees one by one manually through the forest in a herculean undertaking that could last several months and be a life-threatening activity since all the work is performed with half of one's body literally underwater... Then the logs are tied to one another and transported by flotation towed by barges until the sawmills on a trip that can last from one week up to two full weeks depending on the availability of the logs at a given time in the various collection points. Then they are finally delivered to the numerous sawmills some of which are located in unbelievable places with very difficult access. Most of them were nevertheless scattered in such a way that access to narrow, dirty roads would allow their haulage by old, rickety trucks.

The justification given at that time for that kind of quite primitive, low impact, timber extraction activity (a justification still widely accepted nowadays), was that only very old trees would be harvested before rotting while still standing, giving place to younger, stronger ones to grow, in what was considered a forestry sustainable management enterprise as opposed to sheer mechanized deforestation... I must say that the argument holds water if practiced with scientific zeal and in full respect of each species' particularity, region, soil, climate etc. In fact, this would be tantamount to 'gardening' the rainforest as opposed to the modern huge mechanical behemoths built specifically to deforest and destroy huge swaths of land in one go in what is called productivity gains… Nevertheless, it has to be acknowledged that the main causes of deforestation in the Amazon basin are human settlements and clearing of the land for agriculture and cattle raising. The deforestation in those cases is usually criminal and based on slash and burn methods.

The relativity of time imposed by the drastically diverse means of transportation would gradually permeate my mind throughout the journey and, as a consequence force me to adopt a radically different rhythm myself. I could notice a significant change in my thinking process which would become calmer, more pondered, and less anxious as if that full immersion in that fantastically natural, unexplored and mysterious environment would make me feel an intrinsic part of it thus generating feelings of insertion and serenity. As time went by for example, I wouldn't feel the usual and familiar pressing need to impose my point of view or to sway anyone with my preconceived assertions. The personages I encountered in my different journeys to the Amazon region were so unbelievably different and surprising that I could write a book on every single one of them without repeating a single trait in each description. On the contrary, the variety of features and personal attributes was such that no reader would run any risk of being bored.

I would undertake one trip a month on average, and by the end of the first year or so I had changed my ways in innumerous aspects ranging from my dressing code to my views towards modern western societies and their culture or, should I say, often the sheer lack of it. My manners toward my fellow women were also evolving, keeping pace with my new life experiences. I had become a far better listener and a more observant individual and those were attributes generally appreciated by my female friends. I would judge less and understand more their motivations and reactions, thus generating a higher degree of confidence from their part vis a vis the honesty of my intentions. This in turn would enhance their curiosity (definitely a woman's feature) towards me, as well as my now numerous stories about my riverbank experiences in the Alto Solimões and its effluents... those would range from love stories with professional lovers, my meetings with tropical aquarium fish smugglers like Angelina, or rural union leaders like Veronika.

Angelina was one of a kind! She was born in Chicago and owned a small, however, powerful and brand-new single engine plane whose only cargo consisted of a huge aquarium ingeniously installed right in the middle of the cabin. She would spend weeks in a row catching exotic small tropical fish underwater with a set of small metal grids and specially built nets assembled in a kind of multi-faceted mesh that she would manipulate with extreme skill. She would seek to catch the right and most valuable multi-colored fish some of which would be tiny yet extremely valuable for aquarium fish collectors back in the US. Quite often she would dive into murky waters and resurface a couple of minutes later with a valuable catch, making me wonder how on earth she had managed to see the often-minute fish before catching them so ably. I recall that her favorite fish was called Discus which apparently could fetch very high prices in Miami, or in New York, her usual trading markets. She was a real beauty queen, tall and blond with a demeanor of a Hollywood star. She couldn't care less about her dressing code, a fact that would make her appear even more sexy, giving her the looks of some kind of a modern Mata Hari. That was especially true and even more evidenced whenever she entered a man's bar with her unperturbed yet disturbing presence, or whenever she had to land in far-flung villages for fueling her plane. Strangely enough in the face if her risky activity, Angelina was a highly cultivated individual, and later I would learn that she boasted more than one post - graduation degree...

We were introduced incidentally by Jérôme, the French craft and semi-precious stone supplier who tried hard to charm her on different occasions with no success whatsoever. Much later he confessed to me that it was as if he knew beforehand that our first meeting would sooner or later result in a love affair but there was nothing he could do, to preclude it from happening, since Angelina and I would cross paths quite often. And I must give him the credit of being right...

Our passionate love affair started in one of those unique, starry, moonless nights distinctive to the Amazon that have no equal anywhere else in the world... The magnetizing feeling is that one is definitely observed by creatures existing somewhere between the stunning falling stars and the myriad suns, planets and asteroids... There is no doubt in my mind that all those countless worlds in constant motion, progressing eternally and ethereally in their obfuscating trajectory, so bright and intense, certainly contain other forms of life, perhaps not like ours or abiding by our scientific definition or precepts, but definitely some form of intelligence, hopefully superior to ours... My favorite thought when gazing at all those wonders, is that there are certainly multiple forms of intelligence maybe far superior to ours up there, only waiting for us to achieve a higher level of consciousness that would finally enable them to establish contact with us... and rescue us all from what appears to be our dramatic, self-inflicted destiny! In an earthlier assertion though, I must say that our dear planet earth, or should I say the whole universe, had been kind and generous to me on that specific day especially conspiring to create the unique circumstances that contributed to my encounter with Angelina...

Angelina was spending a couple of days in Tefé, a small town upriver on the left bank of the Solimões and was readying her plane in order to fly to a remote village located on the banks of a tributary river, the Jutaí. Jérôme and I were coincidently also in Tefé and were supposed to rent a boat and navigate for four to five days upriver to the same destination with several stops planned along the way where we were to buy stones and crafts. The day before our departure however, Jerôme received a radio message requesting him to go back urgently to Manaus to deal with a health emergency involving one of his two wives... yes, he was married twice concurrently, and the two ladies were living a couple of miles from each other without even suspecting of the others existence let alone of their shared husband!

Jérôme was a hell of a character. An outlaw from La Rochelle, a seaport town in western France, he had arrived in Manaus abroad a cruise ship where he had been engaged as a magician... and a magician he was! An adventurer by nature, Jérôme was one of those individuals that one could drop off in the middle of the Gobi desert without clothes only to find him a couple of weeks later enjoying life in a desert village, maybe engaged to the richest heiress in town, hired by her father to trade, a respected friend of the entire population, with plans to start up his own business activity sometime later... wherever he went in real life, he was received as a distinguished guest and his presence would magnetize everyone's attention. This was his nature, a superb storyteller who seemed to tread through life effortlessly and managed to get things his own way most of the time.

Well, the moment Jérôme had been informed of the radio message requesting his presence in Manaus, Angelina and I had just been introduced by a common acquaintance who introduced me as a very close friend of 'Mr Jérôme' and Angelina as the 'most skillful and beautiful airplane pilot in the world!' I could feel the electricity in the air later on, when Angelina naturally proposed to give me a ride on her plane that could accommodate only a single passenger due to the space occupied by her big aquarium. "Jérôme is a big boy", she told me, "And he can join you maybe a week later upon the completion of his affairs in Manaus, while you can get on with the business you have to conclude. "Alternatively," she said smartly, "I could fly you back to Manaus in a week's time since I'm supposed to be there to inspect some new equipment I ordered from the US." Of course, Jérôme simply could not make himself available for so long hence could not rebuff the offer for me to fly with her first despite his evident jealousy of my luck… To make a long story short, Angelina and I took off very early in the morning to what was for me an exciting journey into a totally unchartered territory.

Whoever flies over the Amazon jungle, is usually stunned by the same impression. As soon as the plane takes off, all references seem to suddenly disappear to give way to a green ocean with no visible boundaries whatsoever! The radio receiver during those years was practically useless due to the absence of enough ground transmitters which meant that the pilot skills and his prior acquired knowledge of a couple of occasional and very scattered visual references constituted the only navigation tools which were of course paramount to the voyage. Angelina seemed to master the art of flying under those difficult not to say quasi-impossible circumstances, and her assertiveness was just incredible! She would circumvent huge thick clouds loaded with electricity and thousands of deadly ice balls the size of a baseball with the ease of a lady serving afternoon tea to friends in an elegant British style living room... I was literally in heaven flying over the Amazon jungle with an unbelievably beautiful woman so exotic in her demeanor, so mysterious regarding her life story, and at the same time so courageous and determined, that I felt warmly secure and in full trust to put my life in her hands... A tremendously charismatic and interesting woman such as Angelina has indeed the power to instill confidence to the point that I wouldn't really care to crash and depart this life in her company! In fact, all my fears of flying a small plane were left aground and I was enjoying the trip greatly in anticipation of all the interesting and exciting moments I was about to spend in her company in the middle of the jungle... a jungle that suddenly, as the trip progressed, was starting to develop incredible tones of familiarity certainly induced by the conduct of my fantastic pilot!

I could not avoid glimpsing from time to time her firm and well-formed breasts, which would appear through a discreet and possibly intentional opening of her shirt left partly unbuttoned as an accidental negligence that, following some of her movements, would reveal sensual parts of her body. She was obviously aware of that as are, usually (and deliciously), all women in similar circumstances. Her expression would betray her in a very disguised, almost hidden way that was simply enchanting! Our staring at each other became more and more frequent and her expression sweeter and inviting, as was mine too... The weather was good and the air currents quite stable, which is not the norm under those latitudes. Angelina reached out to the controls of the cockpit in what appeared to be a well-rehearsed operation that was performed routinely.

"I am setting the automatic pilot," she explained, breaking our silence.

"I see... that means you become superfluous right?" I asked jokingly not without a hidden intention to trigger her reaction... which came immediately.

"If there is something I never become, that something is called superfluous my dear chap... in fact I am always essential to everybody whom I come to love or respect. And quite often I even end up becoming essential to complete strangers who come to cross my path... depending of course on the circumstances. Just consider my responsibility towards both of us right now while I'm piloting this plane. Does it look essential to you or not?" she stated with a discreet smile as if to define things outright...

"I guess I understand what you mean, I sort of murmured foolishly, dodging the question, trying to compete with the constant purr and vibration of the engine.

She was listening to my short replies quite attentively, as if groping with a complete unknown situation, probably pondering whether it was worthwhile to explore that terrain further or not after all... Her attempt to bring the dialogue to a more personal level bore fruit however, and finally made me focus on the exchange.

"Well, you see," I said trying to erase my elusive replies and grab her interest. "What I meant to say is that you become superfluous to the plane so to speak... But never mind, that was a simplistic reaction, an automatic one if you know what I mean... I was simply trying to break the silence... This being said, I take it that the fact you are listening to me despite the noise and the focus you have to keep to fly the plane, makes me feel that you are interested in my views even though those end up being rather superfluous… I guess this is far from considering me essential to the dialogue but…"

"But what?!" she interrupted me abruptly, "of course you are essential… and you know why? Firstly because of pure logic… there's no possible dialogue without an effective exchange, a meeting of the minds if you like! — Dialogue comes from the Greek and means 'two elocutions' — hence, without the speaker and the interlocutor there's no possible dialogue! And secondly, because I feel that there is a communication between us that goes beyond words, meaning that there's an understanding between us at an instinctive, silent but very meaningful level… An electricity, if you prefer, and this is far more powerful, and therefore more essential than any verbal dialogue… words usually spoil the idea, the communication, not to speak of the feelings that are there to heighten the passage of emotions which is the most essential aspect to any valid dialogue…"

I was surprised by her intellect as well as by her aptitude in articulating elaborate ideas out of a simple provocation on my part. If on the one hand my strategy had worked out in terms of causing her to come forward, I was still very thirsty in terms of getting a more complete picture of this intriguing lady and the apparent paradox between her tropical fish smuggling activity and her intellectual level that uncovered a sophisticated, most probably a very well-educated mind!

"Tell me more about this, it sounds very interesting." I said in a speculative tone. I wanted her to dive completely naked into the conversation, revealing her true self, leaving all hesitation and insecurity behind…

"Look", she reacted in a balanced tone, "now you are trying to play games with me, and let me warn you that this would be a big mistake since we could end up losing the connection that is being established between us and that could end up hurting each other instead of approaching us. My feeling is," she continued, "That you want me to expose myself entirely so that you get an option, like a hedging so to speak which would enable you to relinquish all responsibility for the events that may or may not follow between both of us, right or wrong?"

"Well," I started hesitantly, feeling a mounting excitement by mentally projecting the possible events she had so ably infused into the conversation…

"Right or wrong?" She interrupted me abruptly, almost in an authoritative way.

"Right! God you are smart and a tough cookie too." I almost shouted making myself very clear over and above the engine continuous reverberations.

She stared at me and as I was readying myself to continue, she crossed her index finger on my lips to make me silent. I spent the following few minutes observing that impressive and captivating woman, full of knowledge, self-reliance, beauty and sensuality! There was something in her that was difficult to define or even to grasp, something such as a secretive existence, one that would help her hide away from her true self for reasons that would definitely not be made available to the first newcomer, thus avoiding any unnecessary exposure… She certainly felt my curiosity and as if reading my thoughts, expressed it by a malicious, furtive smile filled with mystery. We stayed silent for a good hour and my feeling was of an electrified atmosphere, very dense, full of meaning. Interestingly enough and generally speaking, in those kinds of circumstances we tend to hit a stumbling block out of our highly stimulated emotions that leaves us speechless, desperately searching for something to say that falls nowhere short of being remarkable or at least out of the ordinary in order to impress our interlocutor!

As such, thoughts were galloping through my mind at a lightning speed, running too fast for me to halt at least one of them in order to break what appeared to me like a critical moment, an impasse waiting to be cracked by something big, meaningful and unanticipated.

I dare to affirm that most men have, at least in some rare and cherished occasions in their lives, faced a secret instant where they fall helplessly in love with a woman they've never met before. It happened to me more than one time and the great lesson I've extracted from those stealthy, highly emotional experiences, is that despite all of our conceivable hesitation, lack of courage or plain fear to connect even through a simple conversation, it is always preferable to dare and engage in whatever possible exchange or communication in order to overcome the very fear of probable yet not ultimate defeat! This is definitely better than facing a setback for certain as a result of not even trying… which is tantamount to the most atrocious of frustrations!

Daring in a way eliminates every uncertainty and placates the possible defeat that eventually ensues whilst creating the possibility of rectifying the situation and still seizing the opportunity of materializing that magical moment against all odds… As such, kissing those alluring red lips and starting a love story suddenly becomes the ultimate prize of the gambler…

I finally grabbed her shoulders, turned her delicately towards me and kissed her languidly… and she corresponded eagerly!

I can't remember of any kiss that lasted for such a long time especially considering the woman being a pilot flying the airplane! My guess was that we kissed each other again and again in an almost uninterrupted mode for at least another good hour that seemed an eternity! Her lips were the most inviting, sensuous, intense and voluptuous lips I had ever kissed! It was like making love with our mouths so ardently as we were suddenly possessed by an intense and feverish passion for each other!

"Time for us to land," she murmured softly into my ear as I slowly came back to consciousness and tried hard to distinguish any opening amidst the dense jungle that would resemble, even remotely a landing strip... The plane started its abrupt descent despite my anxiety, and all of a sudden, I could see a tiny clearing between the tree canopies, and this is where Angelina performed a superb short landing, finally bringing the plane to a halt right before almost hitting an enormous mahogany trunk...

A group of no less than thirty kids appeared instantaneously from nowhere and surrounded the plane displaying expressions of curiosity and sheer disbelief.

"Some of them are already familiar with small planes, others aren't," said Angelina, trying to reassure me whilst disembarking and inviting me to do likewise. She then reached for some kind of an old leather bag and started distributing candies and other sweeties to the small crowd who followed her immediately, gathering around her like a group of small chicks, away from the plane.

"If I don't do this," she explained, "they will stay here forever and I cannot trust that they won't touch some sensitive parts of the engine or even damage the flaps... and then, we will be in real trouble my friend... or should I now say my boyfriend?" She asked me in a malicious tone.

"Whatever makes you feel better, my arousing beauty! How about that eh?" I exclaimed whilst holding her by the waist.

"Oh, isn't this lovely? Coming from your mouth of course, otherwise it sounds completely ridiculous... You are so romantic, my love, and I love it!" and she quickly kissed my lips.

I felt particularly proud to be called "my love" by such a terrific woman within such a short period of time! Her taste was still in my mouth and the texture of her generous lips was still alive in me. It nonetheless crossed my mind for a moment that all that time spent with such an intriguing woman in what had probably been for me fairy-tale like works of destiny, was for her a mere encounter like so many others or even worse, a silly pastime that made her trip feel less dull… probably my low self-esteem expressing itself!

She dragged me out of all those insidious thoughts as if reading my mind yet once again whilst grabbing my hand in a reassuring way and kissing me quickly before saying, "I will give you a taste of the true Amazon, of what it really means for someone like me to be here by pure choice, if you allow me to do so of course! You will understand why I fell in love with this place and its wonderful people! By the way, you should know that I never offered this to anybody…"

"Of course, I will allow you… as a matter of fact I will allow you to do whatever you want with me," I replied, piercing her eyes with mine and feeling much more reassured and confident by her words which transmitted comfort and trust especially in those circumstances. Indeed, those words were expressed so convincingly by that intriguing creature that I could all but rely on them completely. I now sensed the true lady in her, an amazing woman who couldn't possibly be defined by just a bunch of words anyway… The fact was that I was feeling increasingly dominated by that gorgeous creature who, amongst all her still unveiled qualities seemed to know her way so assertively within that strange and almost hostile environment, that it was as if our roles had been reversed… I was indeed invaded by a vulnerability that was quite feminine and, the more she sensed it and felt her ascendency and dominance over me, the more she seemed to enjoy it. We men are often blinded by our conditioning that forces us to behave in a manner that exudes strength and projects what we believe is masculinity but deep in our souls we are much more vulnerable, and weak, than most women, especially when confronted with unknown, challenging emotional situations.

After a thirty-minute walk through a winding path that made us stumble every now and then by hitting the enormous roots, that had not been removed or damaged by those who built it, we arrived at our destination. The presence of all those roots gave me a clear impression that the magnificent surrounding trees had been preserved hence the environment had been reasonably and intentionally respected! The place we arrived at consisted of a big cleared square plaza, where maybe fifty indigenous people had gathered in order to welcome us. Angelina seemed to know each one of them by their name and her greeting gestures were immediately and profusely reciprocated by all. We were shown into a small straw bungalow that had obviously been prepared for our arrival, or for someone else's... ahh my low self-esteem knocking at the door all over again!

"This is my usual guesthouse," Angelina said with a smile on her face. "As a matter of fact," she continued, "This will be the first time I will share it with someone... You should feel proud and perhaps in a way even honored!" She said, with a malicious smile on her face.

"I definitely do," I replied caught by surprise. She was one of those persons that would instantly rock one's confidence by being so direct and assertive that any answer would sound stupid and often devoid of true meaning anyway...

I had noticed that the verbal communication between Angelina and the villagers was very short, always complemented by signs.

"In what language do you communicate?" I asked.

"Well, it is a mixture of Jivaroan, a native language mostly spoken in Perú, Spanish and Portuguese. As you have probably noticed, they are all from Indian descent although they have all suffered influences to a greater or lesser extent of a mixture of Peruvian and Brazilian cultures."

They were very athletic and quite tall which was a rarity among most indigenous people of the Amazon basin. Their archetype denoted purity despite the influences they had suffered from other cultures which made me believe that they had struggled to avoid mixing excessively with other ethnic groups in order to keep their origins quite intact.

Each time I would glance at one of them, I would get a radiant and reassuring smile back that would make me feel welcomed, and would infallibly make me smile back at them as well… why is that we, smart and so called 'culturally emancipated' westerners, are so incapable of smiling at each other spontaneously like those 'primitive' people? Why the hell have we lost every sense of grace, loveliness, and should I say elegance towards each other in the name of words devoid of any true meaning like objectivity, efficiency, productivity, speed, professionalism, not to mention harassment of course, and I could go on indefinitely. Was it due to the development of our survival skills? Well, those people go through the same amount of danger or probably far more than us who live or rather survive in our messy and big agglomerations. The differences are more subtle than meets the eye in the sense that we have to struggle in order to avoid being crushed by menacing, merciless, speedy machines or even worse, sinister people that have gone inevitably astray driven to the sidelines of our glacial societies that simply cannot admit any insertion other than what is conventionally accepted as being 'normal' by the majority. Well, the main difference in my view is that the indigenous peoples are much better educated and prepared than us to face the vicissitudes of their lives, in the sense that their initiation rites and educational processes are directly focused on survival skills and conviviality whilst ours are not! It is very simple indeed to corroborate this assertion… just observe a middle-class child belonging to any western culture lost in a shopping mall in one of our big cities: what is the most pressing danger incurred by that toddler? Well, it is dreadfully present everywhere and emanates almost exclusively from his equals, not from a wild animal like a passing snake or a jaguar that happen to share his vital space with the toddler's in any given moment. Our children are far more in danger of being kidnapped, raped, tortured and ultimately killed by no reason whatsoever except for sheer madness of their own "tribalmembers" if I may say so! The resulting societal reaction, instead of being one of revisiting our fundamental values and correcting our life-styles, accordingly, is one of self-restraint based on fear that forces us into losing more and more of our spontaneity as well as our communication skills! Moreover, it is sad to recognize that those social deformations affect not only the spontaneous act of smiling at each other but even our eye contact! Isn't this unbearable? And what is worse, all this doesn't seem to put our children on safety grounds so much so that horrifying crime rates towards defenseless children are anything but rampant! In conclusion, I guess that indigenous jungle toddlers are indeed safer than our 'civilized' children despite all the snakes, spiders, crocodiles, jaguars, venomous ants and piranhas they have to learn how to avoid or neutralize in order to survive… and those threats make them stronger!

Angelina finally broke my deep thinking by asking, "Don't you need to wash away the day? Would you like to join me for a swim in the river?"

"What about piranhas?" I asked without hiding my genuine concern…

"Nonsense! Piranhas are simply not present on this side of the river," she replied with a devilish smile. I knew that it was better for me not to insist on the issue and either follow her to the river-bank or simply give up and face her disdain for the rest of the trip… I decided to have my initiatory river baptism whatever the gamble, and reached for my backpack in order to grab a pair of shorts.

"Don't bother," she said nonchalantly. "Everybody will be naked and if you swim in any kind of attire, they will tease you which will make you feel even more undressed than their complete nudity!"

A wave of excitement and anticipation ran through my spine, and I gently followed Angelina with no more questions asked.

When we reached the river some 20 minutes later, I understood what she had tried to convey to me regarding my concern with my swimming dress code. There were about twenty to twenty-five individuals in the river, swimming, diving from the bank, splashing water onto each other, yelling, screeching out of sheer joy and amusement, calling each other by their impossible-to-articulate names… and, virtually all of them were completely naked, displaying their superb body forms perfectly modeled by nature itself, looking like a heavenly inspiration of an ultimate sculpture masterpiece crafted by Rodin himself! I couldn't take my eyes off of those splendid forms intertwining with each other as if in a tremendously perfect choreographed ballet borne from the confines of the cosmos! The most interesting aspect about their nudity though, was that it was so spontaneous, natural, expected, and most of all, fully accepted by all, that there were no displays, let alone attempts of any malicious gestures or vicious conduct towards each other, contrarily to what would probably happen in a public swimming pool in any big city anywhere in the world, so much so that nudity is simply not allowed in the vast majority of public swimming pools around the world!

I felt immediately contaminated by that spontaneity and was invaded by a sense of security that made me swim along the bank as if I was in a swimming pool with the surveillance of a lifeguard. The water was transparent and ethereal which made it feel almost insubstantial. It was just at the right temperature and would slide through with my naked skin offering almost no resistance to my movements, and the feeling was one of belonging to that exuberant, fantastic nature! I felt a sense of wholeness and of extreme peace and stillness whilst gliding through those calm and transparent waters... Nothing seemed capable of spoiling the serenity of those unforgettable moments. The splendor of the superb, lush forest surrounding us, added to the quality of the moment made me feel an inner joy that I had never experienced before in my entire life. My guess was that I was close to experiencing a superior degree of consciousness! All of a sudden somebody grabbed my leg underwater and emerged at my side... it was Angelina, gorgeous and welcoming, who had appeared out of the blue, having probably swum quite a respectable distance underwater in order to reach me without being detected. She was radiant with a glow in her face. She would definitely rock me out of my inner balance with her determined attitude and most of all with her disturbing beauty and feline femininity. I could sense that she was indeed attracted to me, after all. I tried, as it was still often the case, to evoke my next gesture by reviewing the unfolding scene in my imagination but this mental progression did not happen fast enough. She kissed me passionately and her body spiraled around mine in a delicate but strong grip that made me feel the firmness as well as the extreme embrace of her voluptuous forms against mine. It was as if a boa had exerted her deadly encirclement on one of her defenseless prays with the difference that despite my feelings of total subjugation, I did not want to set myself free from that blissful grip... We stayed there for maybe one hour or perhaps two, making love to each other in the river, with such passion that it was as if the earth had stopped its spin out of respect for our own cadence, tempo and ultimate thrill. Her love making was wild like her demeanor hence she would take the entire initiative, notwithstanding her loving care of gently guiding me through a succession of sexual exploits that I had never dreamed or imagined before. She would make me feel a total immersion in that wild yet so wrapping environment that, in some specific moments, I was feeling a total loss of consciousness, as if my entire being would be engulfed by the river, only to reemerge moments or even minutes later to that sweet and precious reality that I knew quite well and to my deepest despair, would never play itself back again. We can only enter the same river once, as the sages have so wisely observed.

Angelina was a totally singular being, out of any norm, a fabulous and unexpected drop out, an independent and free spirit that had learned to extract the best out of every moment without trying to retain anything from the past or to project the future in any shape or form... She was probably a clear demonstration of inner strength and determination, rarely seen in a woman even less so in a man for that matter. Obviously, her femininity and superlative beauty would blend into those characteristics which would result into an extremely attractive woman that would use her instincts to captivate the world in any given circumstance. This would most certainly explain the reason, still a mystery to me, why she would make her living out of smuggling exotic fish from the Amazon into the U.S. In her mind, there was nothing fundamentally wrong in doing so since she would bring joy to all her customers, especially the lonely ones who would find delight and also an occupation in caring for those splendid, rare, yet extremely fragile creatures. Environmental consciousness was not a big issue in those days, so she would not really care about it. She would certainly pay her taxes, according to her own saying, if she could declare her 'professional' activity… Well, all this was very debatable and quite frankly, I knew that convincing her of the contrary would turn out to be an impossible task. This was Angelina! Either you loved her and accepted her at face value, for what she was, or you'd better leave her alone like those colorful, highly venomous yet extremely attractive spiders that all you can do is observe them, keeping a distance of course. Her dominant character would place me in a very comfortable situation where, for the first time in my life, I was not expected to behave as the 'dominant male' but could instead relax and simply be myself without caring much for what she would think of me. What would be perceived as a gaffe in different sets of circumstances, was totally ignored by Angelina who seemed to go straight to the essence of things without really caring for their form. I felt good by her side.

"Do you know what I dislike the most in any human being? It's mediocrity. This is a despicable feature in my opinion," she continued as we walked back to the village at dusk which would make the trees look like guardian giants monitoring our steps, "That bothers me a lot, maybe because it is probably the most common feature among people nowadays. You see? I can no longer sit in front of someone and listen to his or her annoying stories usually about money, children, jobs and bosses, spouses, houses, cars, vacation, illness, marriage and divorce, or worse, sexual fantasies that never come true simply because those same people never dare to change! Life is change in its own essence... if you don't follow the changes, you miss life's dynamic reality and end up getting stuck in the same place forever having as your only solace... mediocrity! Of course, there are honorable exceptions to that rule, but I must confess that those are becoming more and more rare tending to extinction! They are usually individuals that fall out of the curve and end up being marginalized by society."

"Aren't you generalizing a bit too much?" I questioned her. "I know quite a few interesting and definitely not mediocre individuals that aren't marginalized at all... on the contrary, they are usually leaders in their social groups exactly because of their uniqueness."

"There's no question about that," she retorted looking me straight in the eyes. "But they were ostracized and excluded from all groups before redeeming their leadership or influence within a given society. And there were those who simply didn't bother with that and chose instead to never look back. You see," she went on, "most social groups, at least those which are recognized as such, act in what we can call a herd behavior. It all boils down to a matter of acceptance of a leader's opinion who has the ability of conveying any given message in a timely and opportune fashion. The essence or the truth contained in the message is not so important really. Business empires as well as governments have been built just by following and exploiting that simple technique and widely recognized, universally accepted methodologies have been developed based on it and are taught in the most prestigious of our universities… we call it marketing by the way. Just to give you an example, I am a Harvard educated person destined to be a filthy rich heiress in the Midwest of the United States and to assume the command of a very prestigious group of companies, but as I grew up, I felt that I simply did not belong to that mediocre environment where money plays the most important role of all by far, and dictates all kinds of rules in almost all relationships. This has become by the way such a powerful and engrained universal value that if one wants to live by a different set of rules, that individual will ultimately have no other option but to drop out from what I call mediocrity or plain society if you will, unless that same individual can bring revolutionary change into a given business organization or government… which is exceedingly hard to achieve, believe me! It is like abandoning the beaten path and entering an unknown jungle. I mean it in the figurative sense here" she concluded with a malicious smile on her face.

I was so intrigued by Angelina's revelation that I simply lost track of my next argument. So, my Amazonian Mata Hari was even more fascinating, mysterious, and surprising than I first thought! She had simply abdicated what appeared to be a huge fortune in America only to become a single engine airplane pilot flying on the fringes of the law, in the middle of an almost totally unexplored swath of the Amazon jungle! And she was doing that just to keep herself faithful to her own inner beliefs that life is only worthwhile if we keep truthful and faithful to our own viewpoints whatever those are, and no matter what judgment others make of it!

We arrived at the hamlet to find a big fire burning, with everybody gathered around it, in what seemed to be a celebratory ritual. A barbecue was taking place at the edges of the fire where some burning bushes would be set aside for cooking. The specialty of the day looked like some kind of hare and the ones already cooked smelled very good and seemed quite appetizing from what I could distinguish in the darkness of the night. Angelina approached me from the back and asked me mockingly and defiantly, "do you like barbecued monkey?"

"What did you say?" I almost shouted, making some heads turn towards us wondering what was going on... "Monkey? How come you assume that I will eat monkey for heaven's sake?"

"Well," she continued very coolly, and slightly ironically, "in that case let me check with the chef what are the options in today's menu... I'm afraid however that the hunters brought home the very best of all choices, probably in our honour and let me tell you that monkey is one of their most coveted delicacies," she murmured in my ear. "Therefore, I doubt that there are any alternatives available tonight..." she then kissed me and whispered with a very calm tone, "you will enjoy it darling... it's very tasty indeed! Besides I guess you are hungry enough to forego some of your exotic preferences and indulge in the special of the day..."

Time flies, and much sooner than I would have imagined we had to wake up from that dream like reality, and start our return to the place we were supposed to meet Jérôme...

As we reached the airstrip, I confess that I felt greatly relieved to find our plane intact, at least in its appearance... We flew for less than one hour before landing on yet another impossible-to-land airstrip but Angelina definitely knew her business!

I spent the following days travelling around driven by a local, in a very old Jeep, crossing very rough terrains and visiting semi-precious stone suppliers who would also try to offer me all sorts of different commodities such as gold, silver as well as different kinds of handmade crafts. Most of them were Jérome's usual suppliers and would treat me with great respect, some of them even with reverence since they sensed that I ultimately represented their most significant flow of cash. I was supposed to choose the merchandise without discussing prices since that was Jerôme's exclusive prerogative as a supplier to the company I was working for. Angelina had stayed with yet another tribe, this one more 'civilized' notwithstanding the total paradox of the term and was supposed to wait for my return there as soon as I would have finished that short expedition.

Finally, after six days of hard work where I managed to draw down a list of products I would be willing to purchase, we drove back to the village where I met with yet another tribe and obviously with Angelina whom I missed greatly… I was received with smiles and warm expressions by the tribe members and got a long sought loving kiss from Angelina. After a quick bath at the small cascade that would serve as a shower for everybody, we gathered around the fire for a session of song and dance followed by dinner which was composed of boiled cassava mixed with corn and some kind of meat I would not dare to ask the origin of.

I was starting to feel at home in the jungle so to speak, although quite saddened with the prospect of our departure that had been planned for the following morning. Those extraordinary people made me feel as if I was one of their own without having to articulate a single word. Everything was done with gestures and facial expressions that would definitely mean much more than an infinity of words given the spontaneity of their expressions. I was immersed in those thoughts, totally oblivious of my surroundings, when a strong grip grabbed my shoulder breaking my isolation at once. As I turned around, a solid figure looking more like a bundle of muscles than anything else stretched his arm and handed me a dark concoction in a shallow bowl.

"What is this?" I asked Angelina, not without a repulsive expression in my face. This was in fact a mere academic, fact-finding question, in the face of my resolute feelings telling me that I would most certainly dislike whatever was in the bowl...

"Listen to me, now," she practically shouted at me with an authoritative tone in her voice that I had never encountered before. "If you expect me to become the decipherer or worse, the escort-bodyguard to some kind of stupid white male who vacillates at every obstacle, like a city sissy, which is something that deep in my heart I definitely know you are not, forget it! In that case, I would rather be in Chicago hosting one of those stupid dinner parties' side by side with a foolish industrialist who would call me his dear spouse thinking that that kind of absolutely idiotic status would give him certain rights over me!"... and she walked away disappearing into the small crowd.

I finally grabbed the bowl from the hand of Patahy (that was his name as I would learn afterwards) and brought it to my mouth, drinking the whole thing at once... The liquid went down my throat burning me from the inside out as if I had swallowed gasoline. Angelina reappeared suddenly and, with her usual malicious look congratulated me profusely.

"Bravo! You just went through one of the most important initiation rituals of this community. My rather coarse attitude for which I apologize, was designed to give you the courage to swallow it at once with no further questions. By the way, do you know what you just drank?"

"I don't have the slightest idea," I replied with my guts literally on fire... not so sure I want to know either..." I felt as if I was being literally corroded from the inside.

"You just drank a mixture of blood extracted from one of the most venomous snakes of our planet while she was still alive, with a very strong alcohol beverage distilled from cassava plus a juice from a secret root that they ferment in order to boost the immune system. Just wait some thirty minutes or so and you will feel energized like never before in your life! And not only that... forget colds or flus for at least a decade not to speak of other infections or insect bites such as scorpions, spiders etc. against which you will become practically immune for quite a long time."

I finally understood the reason behind her aggressive attitude... it was indeed designed to encourage me to drink the snake blood without further questions or hesitation...

Her prediction proved to be absolutely correct and some minutes later I felt a tremendous energy like an invading wave of fire running through my entire body. I grabbed Angelina by her waist and threw her in the air sensing a lightness as if her perceived mass was a fraction of what it really was! She laughed loudly and I could clearly hear the crowd laughing in the background. They had gathered behind us in order to watch our interchange in what was certainly a distinctive altercation between a man and a woman. They also wanted to witness my reaction to the brew I had just so courageously swallowed... I felt exhilarated and was ready to ask for more of the awful cocktail when Angelina who had seemingly read my thoughts said...

"Don't even dare to drink more of it right now… maybe in a couple of years…"

"Why is that so?" I asked, intrigued by the assertion.

"Because if you drank more, you would simply die! The quantity you've just swallowed is enough to kill you had it been injected into your blood stream instead. By drinking it, it achieves the benefits I've mentioned to you before, whilst all the toxins are subsequently eliminated through your urine. This being said, they know exactly how to balance the mixture keeping it just below the lethal threshold, so that it doesn't kill you almost instantaneously."

I was fascinated by the subject and felt very privileged to have been given the opportunity to taste that seemingly incredible beverage.

Minutes later everybody went to their respective huts for the night. We did likewise, however I felt restive and very excited by that tremendous female lying by my side, who seemed to be insatiable in her quest for tenderness and physical contact. Her breath was exhaling a smell that only women in the pursuit of love or at the point of having intercourse have… her eyes had an expression of sweetness, elation and tenderness and their expression translated into a welcoming invitation to pleasure…

"My superman," were the only words she murmured before lying over me breathing heavily out of desire…

We had sex repeatedly, and to my surprise I performed almost like superman indeed thanks to the potion I had been given some hours before. Her desire was fervid and passionate and her gestures so sensual that I candidly lost all references of space and time, while she would put me into an enhanced state of carnality and ecstasy. At times she would guide me, whispering words like "slow down" or "yes, baby" into my ears.

I could feel her abundant sweat run through parts of my body mixing with her intimate fluids which would create an exhilarating smell so stimulating that I would reach sheer exultation and delight... I could sense the strong and fast beating of her heart each time she would come like a gazelle in the heist of her heat. She would then glide her vagina rubbing it like a soft brush on my chest, neck and face, leaving her intimate scent all over me, like a wild animal posting her territorial boundaries on her ultimate property. She finally laid down by my side breathing profoundly out of satisfaction and kissed me repeatedly while pulling my hair murmuring "oh boy, that was so gooood." We fell asleep shortly thereafter cuddled against each other despite the heavy heat. The tenderness we felt was so overwhelming that we didn't bother at all with the very high temperature of the Amazonian night.

Sexual attraction which obviously has to do with our own sexuality, is definitely more than a mere physiological set of neuro-transmitter impulses that science struggles to define and to categorize and dictionaries can hardly find a coherent definition towards the real sense of this expression that has been so unfairly used by science, literature, psychology and so on. It has probably to do also with dream stuff, imagination, and a mysterious exchange of a specific current being probably originated in some part of our cortex or within our solar plexus. Regardless of the precise definition of the term, reality is that all cultural, religious or societal boundaries in any given sexual relationship, which is in fact and very often a pure expression of love, conspire against the most sublime of its aspects which is the attainment of ultimate intimacy, excitement and climax by two human beings who set to discover each other's pleasure by exposing and exploring their own. This is nothing but love, and as such should not be stonewalled or evaded from the latter... Otherwise why on earth God or Mother Nature would have given us the capacity to feel and seek pleasure and the ability to bypass all or almost all social or religious obstacles in order to achieve full intimacy vis a vis another being?

Angelina had the power of eliminating literally all barriers to reach total and unrestrained intimacy. Being with her was the pinnacle of pleasure so much so that I would simply lose myself in the process together with all my barriers, preconceived ideas and inhibitions. I would likewise lose all my reserves and reticence only to dive into that blue, diaphanous sea of bliss that had one and only one name... Love!

We left very early the following morning and were greeted by the chief of the tribe who posted a stain of what seemed to be charcoal or some other vegetable powder on our respective fronts. "This is designed to protect us from all evils," explained Angelina taking me tenderly by the hand. The entire tribe walked us to the airfield and greeted us with a monotone song that, as Angelina would explain later, meant farewell. The aquarium had been replenished and was full of multi-colored fish which seemed to swim in flocks changing directions swiftly, following the abrupt movements of the aircraft while taxing on the shaky airfield. Seven hours later we landed in Tefé to meet Jerôme who was waiting for us on the tarmac.

He was simply furious and even before greeting us appropriately, went on asking with an uncompromising tone, "Where the hell were you for heaven's sake? I have been waiting for you for three days on top the date we had agreed to meet! Angelina dismissed him with a laughter telling him, "Well, it seems that now we have a guardian angel who controls our timing in a place where it is notoriously impossible to keep up with tight, let alone precise schedules!" The fact of the matter was that Jerôme was simply crazed by jealousy since upon our arrival he immediately realized that my relationship with Angelina had crossed all boundaries he had unilaterally chosen to depict in his mind...

He drove us to our quarters which were located in an old and quite dilapidated small building and left quietly looking extremely frustrated, not without promising to pick us up later on for dinner. The place was one of those typical old constructions from the region and had served as a brothel when French adventurers such as Jerôme would come to the Amazon in herds looking for gold and precious stones. We could still see an old and faded sign where one could read 'Sheileene', an improvisation for 'Chez Helène', the latter probably being the pimp or rather the 'madam' of the once highly sought yet probably not so highly attended bordello...

"We have only one air-conditioned room," the corpulent, sweaty lady tossed as if we would fight over the privilege... unless you want to share it, she continued with a malicious grimace on her otherwise impassive face.

"Give it to the lady," I volunteered, concerned about Jerôme's reaction in case he realized that we were sleeping together in the open...

"Don't be silly, intervened Angelina as assertive as ever, we have nothing to hide from that idiot my love!"

The lady finally opened a generous, acquiescent smile that would allow us to see through her lips into her big, toothless mouth.

I couldn't agree more, since as far as I was concerned, I wanted to give Jerôme a lesson anyway after all he had cheated on me more than once as far as business was concerned.

When we reached the room, we immediately realized the true meaning of the word 'unpretentious'. The furniture couldn't be more modest and succinct and the worn down uncolored walls were guaranteed to have witnessed the most unbelievable scenes and situations... including the remains of the slaughter of hordes of mosquitos seemingly killed in different eras since the decrepit paint seemed to have bravely withstood the passage of time. I reached for the air conditioning button and to my utter surprise I realized that it was nothing but an old fan installed in the wall in such a way that it would expel the already rarefied air from the room into the Amazon torrid atmosphere, instead of at least bringing in renewed air from the outside... the damn thing was simply reversed! I immediately turned the device off before literally suffocating! The shower was a rusty pipe hanging out of the bathroom wall and obviously the water was coming out naturally warm at all times...

Angelina had a quick shower and laid down on the bed without even drying herself... she was magnificent! Her forms were simply perfect, and the shiny moonlight would pierce the night with its high humidity and enter through the wide-open window to finally create mythical dancing reflexes on her ivory skin as if caressing it. She knew I was watching her, and she obviously seemed pleased about it judging from her carefully planned sensual and slow movements. I was in heaven, greatly enjoying the scene and surrendering myself completely to those precious moments... I will always be amazed by the serenity a woman can instill in the soul of a man no matter what the circumstances. I guess the warmth that emanates from a female will always connect a man to the familiarity of his origins and lend a sense of protection and spiritual shelter to the latter. Women have definitely the power to insulate men from all evil by bringing them back home... and God knows how far away from home most men are, contrary to their frail certainties or beliefs...

My languorous thoughts were abruptly interrupted by the strident sound of Jérôme's horn, loudly announcing his arrival. We both dressed slowly so we wouldn't drench in sweat and went down the stairs in an unhurried and lethargic rhythm, awakening slowly from our dreamy state, as if from a trance, whose images we were still carrying and sharing only to be interrupted quite abruptly at the sight of an obviously jealous Jérôme...

The dinner was delicious, composed of fried fresh fish and beans, yet quite uneventful. My guess was that Jérôme had decided to leave the fight at least for a while, sensing that he'd lost it even before its start. He certainly was fully aware of his advantage of being quite often much closer to Angelina, which would give him several opportunities to re address the issue... And he was stupid enough to believe in this, grossly underestimating Angelina's class and human caliber. We then were driven quietly back to the 'Sheileene Grand' and obviously could not sleep without making love first, despite the excruciating heat. The fact we would part ways the next morning was suddenly so disturbing for both of us that we simply could not afford to spoil the opportunity to love each other for what could well be one last time...

Angelina had to leave early, so did we. I was suddenly possessed by a feeling of abandonment and it was apparently visible, so much so that Angelina whispered in my ear after kissing my lips softly and tenderly, "I am sure we'll see each other again soon... all this has been very meaningful, and way too good but it was definitely too short to end like this my love..." Minutes later I could hear the roar of the engine propelling the plane and swallowing the runway at full speed while Jerôme and I were approaching the opposite side of the small airport for our flight to Manaus. A few hours later, after a short connection in Manaus, I boarded the aircraft to São Paulo not without some stubborn tears rolling down my face… I would miss her dearly.

The day following my arrival in the big city started with some rather exciting marching orders. I was supposed to prepare myself for one long trip or maybe two to our main markets, namely France and Japan. My boss announced it to me as if it were a huge bonus which in a way it was indeed in the face of my long tours in the Western Amazon region. I confess I was thrilled despite my unremitting thoughts about Angelina and our passionate love story hence could hardly wait the weeklong I would still have to patiently spend in São Paulo, a city I definitely did not enjoy to say the least, before departing for Tokyo. In spite of my excitement with the incredible news — it was not usual to send such a young chap to what at the time represented a costly and important mission, the prospect still would not eclipse the fact that I was missing Angelina and that slow paced but very genuine life in the Amazon jungle, which I had come to appreciate. Both in their own ways had given me a great sense of detachment from my day-to-day concerns and from material stuff in general. The fact that that incredible woman had chosen that kind of life, despite her origins, education and possessions was mind boggling to say the least! She was certainly a paradigm of detachment and determination in the face of her inner search for the true meaning of existence. Yes, she was quite unique, and I was a very lucky guy to have been given the chance of that fantastic, very enriching albeit extremely short relationship amidst those fabulous people and surroundings. I had acquired a reassuring feeling that she and I would meet again sometime in the future, hopefully to resume our wild and unparalleled love story. Needless to say, by that time I had lost all interest in those often-superficial metropolitan girls who conversely would immediately lose interest in me as soon as they discovered my simple tastes and my penchant for the esoteric and the extraordinary. They were instead searching for the typical Brazilian — empty — minded — but — rich — candidates who would pave the way towards a solid marriage that would generously represent a grant for their material needs for the rest of their even — emptier — lives. I would therefore lock myself at home in the remaining evenings before my departure, saving my energies whilst anxiously looking forward to my parting day whilst day-dreaming about the mysteries that lay ahead for me to discover.

JAPAN

Finally, my waiting came to an end, and I was only too happy to board my flight to Tokyo with a two-hour time connection in Los Angeles. The arrival at Narita airport is usually a tiring experience despite the impeccable Japanese orderliness, tidiness, cleanliness, and organization. The reason for the fatigue is due to the jet lag resulting from a twelve-hour time difference vis a vis São Paulo, and this, after an exhausting thirty-five-hour journey... not forgetting the subsequent two to three hours plus spent in a bus to one's hotel in Tokyo! When a reasonably healthy individual reaches the check-in desk of the hotel, a certain amount of effort is required to remember one's own name... fortunately there are passports to make our lives easier in those circumstances!

My hotel was a correct 3-star establishment located in Roppongui, one of Tokyo's bohemian and bustling neighborhoods. My room was located at the back of the building hence away from the noise of the nearby numerous bars and night clubs that proliferate in the area. I was exhausted but starving, so I decided to go to one of those fantastic small Japanese restaurants...

"Dômo arigatô gozai maschtá," greeted the chef together with his small but impeccable staff behind the counter. A not less impeccable hostess took me to a minuscule table at the back of the small dining room, but I had grander ambitions...! I hesitantly pointed towards the counter, and she immediately took me there with a discreet laughter that would hide her shyness... The most formidable aspect in travelling to radically different cultures in my opinion, resides in trying to decipher the hidden signs that are expressed beyond the articulated, spoken language. In this regard and to a certain extent, the language barrier becomes an advantage since it obliges the usually curious and interested foreign visitor to make an effort in order to grasp the non-verbal communication which often is richer and far more interesting than the plain-spoken language. I could spend years living in a place without understanding a single word and communicating through signs, but the trouble is that the human mind is so trained into learning how to speak a foreign language that after a while the exercise simply becomes impracticable... we start to speak thus destroying the infinite possibilities of a far more sensitive and subtle kind of connection with others.

While I was absorbed by those considerations, the chef came closer from behind the counter and asked me in broken English with a wide smile on his face... "Purifer some sake or biru sir?"

To which I replied, putting on my most polite tone, "I'd rather like some beer thank you." A small bottle of tremendously cold Asahy beer was poured by the hostess into my likewise frosty glass with just the perfect amount of foam... "Arigatô," I murmured which had the effect of lightening her sweet and radiant smile. "Oh... speak Japanese?" she asked me with the extreme politeness generally employed towards a new customer who in his turn, had probably used the very same ruse as thousands before... "Oh, no, no I..." I quickly replied returning the smile. Her face blushed and she went away certainly embarrassed by my evident interest in triggering some kind of communication despite the language barrier. The short and innocent exchange had been so intense that I felt a sense of belonging despite being 17,000 miles away from what I used to call home. The chef brought a succession of fabulously prepared dishes that seemed to be served just in the perfect order thus allowing the palate to adapt and enjoy each one of the exotic and delicious tastes without mixing them to any of the previous ones. A perfect, well thought, deliciously cooked gourmet dinner!

After maybe five or six Asahys plus a couple of cold sakês, I realized how exhausted I was and got ready to leave the place. The entire restaurant staff greeted me effusively and the hostess who was standing at the door, handed me a red, fresh rose with her beautiful smile greeting me with the sweetness and spontaneous innocence that only eastern women are capable of expressing without appearing submissive at all, contrary to the wrong, generalized impressions we have about the latter in the west...

I walked back to my hotel in the brisk night and fell asleep instantaneously. I slept for seven hours or so and was woken by a wake-up call dialled automatically from some computing device with a strident and mechanical voice giving me the precise time repeatedly until I hung up. A quick shower and some time spent to put on a tie correctly plus the time to quickly enjoy half of a marvellous Japanese carefully grown melon got me to the lobby some 20 minutes later where our local manager was impatiently waiting for me.

We spent the day visiting customers in a succession of boring meetings like in any typical business trip stopping only to grab a sandwich despite my adoration for the Japanese cuisine... a real and terrible waste dictated by money! Dinner took place in a sophisticated restaurant which was far from the quality let alone the vibrations I had received the evening before in the small yet highly special place I had dinner at. I promised myself to go back there in the first available opportunity.

Back in my hotel room, I could not avoid reading the sign displayed on the small desk, "DEAR AND HONORABLE GUEST: GET A RELAXING MASSAGE AND LEAVE ALL YOUR TROUBLES BEHIND," followed by a number to dial. I nonchalantly dialled the number and a busy voice replied hastily answering my questions about prices, times etc... It turned out that one of the masseuses was immediately available as a result of a last-minute cancellation. I booked the time and the lady who had answered my questions, somehow nervously asked me, "are you aware, Sir, that our masseuses are all blind? Our hotel participates in a charitable foundation that teaches physiotherapy techniques to blind ladies... if this is not acceptable to you, we can cancel it..."

"Not at all," I replied immediately while thinking that a blind person would certainly have developed extra sensorial abilities that would certainly contribute to an even better massage...

Finally, after a ten-minute wait, the door-bell rang, and I couldn't retain my astonishment when I perceived an incredibly graceful silhouette standing at the door holding a small bag probably containing creams and other necessary accessories for the massage session. I pulled the door wide open, and she stepped into the room as if her eyesight was better than mine. Her "good evening" accent was impeccable, and her demeanour was supple and refined and so agile that I had a great difficulty in accepting the fact that she was blind. She showed me the bed and to my surprise, asked me to undress. I took off my clothes except for my underwear and laid down. She then started a fabulous massage session, so professional that it made me discover some of my muscles and nerves that I had never felt before. Her hands would slither all over my body and her touch was as soft as silk yet at the same time firm and strong whenever she would touch the right nerve. After about an hour she stopped, and I was feeling literally renewed.

"It was, OK?" she asked me softly as if trying not to bring me out of the almost dreamy state I was immersed in.

"It was fantastic!" I replied. "Do you understand the meaning of the word "fantastic?"

"Oh, certainly sir! It means very good right?" her English was definitely above average signalling that she had certainly studied the language.

"Much more than very good, I can tell you! Can you come tomorrow at the same time?"

"Oh, almost certainly, Sir," her "almost" assuring reply made me feel somehow less lonely in that new and totally unexplored environment.

I reached for my wallet and handed her a generous tip." Oh no, no sir, "She immediately retorted with an almost vexed tone. "The bill will be added to your room"

"I know" I replied with a polite tone, "but this is a tip for your very professional and nice massage."

"Oh no thank you, Sir, but no tips!" she answered with a conclusive gesture with her two hands.

"May I ask your name please"? I asked hesitantly, afraid that a continuation of the dialogue could end up frightening her...

"Oh, my name is Keiko." That sound came out of her lips as sweet poetry, a romantic one-word song, a word that pronounced by such a delicate, beautiful and sweet creature would instigate an immediate sense of empathy... I knew by then that some kind of special connection was taking place between me and Keiko...

She then left the room as swiftly as she had come in. Upon her departure I was invaded by an excruciating feeling of loneliness that I could not understand or explain. Was it because I was suddenly left alone after such a close contact with such a beautiful and intriguing creature? Was I transferring my rapport with Angelina to that almost furtive yet intense contact with Keiko? Was I falling back into adolescence and to my still unabated thirst for tenderness as a compensation for my lack of self-esteem? Was I doomed to become one of those very frustrated men who adopt a stupid, Don Juanish kind of posture throughout their existence in order to hide their own frustrations vis a vis their empty life? Unlikely, since my life was rich enough after all, and my rapport with women had nothing to do with the one of a Casanova. So, what the hell was going on with me? Was I simply acting immaturely? But then, if it was all about maturity, did that mean that I would have to dismiss all those fantastic opportunities coming my way just to feel mature and inserted into a frustrating social paradigm of monogamy? Whatever the explanation, the reality was that I was simply and purely falling in love at first sight with every attractive or special woman that would come my way... and, to make things worse, they were somehow instinctively detecting my feelings which, in their turn, would spark their own curiosity and sense of attraction, as a magnet attracts its own opposite magnetic pole... Maybe we were all dealing with the same unfulfilled thirst for true, non-judgemental love, and were desperately looking for it by falling in love, or rather having the impression of doing so with different partners who at the end of the day would prove unable to fulfil our expectations... thus denying the notion of true love altogether? That mental assertion, a self-defeating sentiment that only contributed to worsen my feelings, made me think that I was perhaps lacking coherence, or that I was immersed into a state of confusion... I was also feeling anxious by simply not knowing what was going on the other side of the globe. Was Angelina still attached to me or was she enjoying the present moment with someone else, as she enjoyed the moments she had spent with me? Maybe with an individual much better looking and more mature than me... maybe even with Jérôme? Oh no, not Jérôme! That would simply be unbearable! Why was that so? After all, why do some tribes accept polygamy both for men and women and who are we, the so-called civilized world to criticize them? Why can't we accept the fact that it is probably OK to fall in love regardless of our mental chains which make us feel attached to a series of pre-defined cultural and social concepts or even imaginary standards that deep in our souls do not serve their purpose any more? In any case, I was not practicing polygamy! Angelina had left it quite clear that our short rapport was just that! A short adventure somewhere in the Amazon where nobody could formulate any kind of judgement about it, since the cultures we were in contact with were so distinct from ours with their own set of rules and maybe even their preconceptions. Well, the persons we had been in contact with were really totally diverse from us culturally speaking as well as in terms of our thinking processes that we felt accepted instantaneously by them. A highly comforting and liberating feeling I must say! Nevertheless, when it came to Jérôme we would confront an entirely different ball game. It was quite intriguing to say the least that a single individual would have the ability, just by being present, to pollute this state of affairs only to sadly remind us of our so-called cultural values — the good and the bad ones — ending up by propelling us back into that same cultural hell that definitely had no place let alone any significance in the Alto-Jutaí — Western-Amazon region, somewhere close to the Peruvian border! Something was wrong in all those paradoxes and, with all those contradictions dancing in my mind, I fell asleep not before portraying Keiko in my fertile imagination one last time... Oh boy, wasn't she gorgeous?

I woke up abruptly at five a.m. with a single thought in my mind... Keiko! The name sounded like music running through my brain. It was simply painful to wait until seven a.m. when the guest service department would open for business. Finally, after two interminable hours, at seven a.m. sharp, I dialled that unusually long number as they often are in some hotels and hastily confirmed a series of five consecutive daily massage sessions with Keiko, all at seven p.m. At least I was guaranteed to see her every evening for the next 5 days. That certainty calmed me down, and then after that I said to myself, I would play it by ear depending on the development of the circumstances. Circumstances? What kind of circumstances was I expecting? The question was quickly erased from my mind giving place to a sweet feeling of self-doubt coupled with her image that stubbornly wouldn't leave my thoughts. For now, all I needed was just to see her again and let my soul be caressed by that velvet like voice...

My day went on as boring as ever. The meetings were endless and uneventful as most business meetings are, with all due respect to all the frustrated executives of this world who spend their entire days agonizing in front of a screen, or in a meeting room, putting on a purposeful expression on their faces in order to convince their bosses and their peers that they are not trying to desperately kill time, when in fact they are counting the seconds for the clock to finally reach their time to go back home to their loved ones or even to fall numb on a comfortable couch in front of a TV.

I diplomatically declined all dinner invitations for that week, alleging a light health discomfort and managed the timing of all meetings — quite a challenge when confronted with the endless back and forth of the Japanese language translation — in such a way that I could reach the main lobby at six forty-five p.m. max! On that specific day, the lift was packed and took forever to reach my floor making me feel as if everyone in it had booked a massage for seven p.m.! Finally, I reached my room shaking out of excitement and anticipation…

The bell rang punctually at seven p.m. and I simply felt thrilled to open the door to that exotic, elegant and discretely perfumed creature… yes, I immediately noticed not only the perfume but also her beautiful new hair style as well as the more elegant kimono compared to the one she was wearing, the night before… Keiko had obviously prepared herself for the massage session! It probably meant that she was trying to please me! I felt a sense of praise and assurance.

"With all due respect, I must say that you look gorgeous," I stuttered with emotion…

"Oh, thank you very much, Sir. You are very kind to me." That melodious and sweet voice filled the atmosphere as a soft embrace. "Are you ready to suffer again with my hands?"

"It is not suffering at all, on the contrary it is a great pleasure, and to be totally frank with you, I waited the entire day for this moment to arrive." I could hear my stupid voice over and above my heartbeat mentioning those words like an adolescent on his first date. I felt totally dominated by her delicate demeanour and completely insecure as to how to behave myself!

Keiko was indeed gorgeous and beautifully dressed. She then suddenly took off some sort of tiara and her bulky, black and silky hair came stumbling down her back in delicate, almost imperceptible waves coming to an abrupt stop at her waist. She then turned her head towards me as if 'looking' for my approval, her eye lashes shining in contrast to the soft light of my bedside table. Her expression was full of life and irradiated flashes of energy and emotions that would explode in a nervous, short laughter like cherry blossoms in the early spring... I felt a compulsion to take her in my arms and never let her go but retained myself out of fear that any precipitous attitude could make her run away forever. She started the usual preparation of creams and her home-made special concoctions while indicating the bed with a gentle motion of her left arm. I laid down motionless and tried my best to concentrate on the massage. Her hands felt like delicate petals caressing my skin and when she asked me to turn around to face her, I could see her blushing with an almost embarrassed expression in her angelical face. I had to make a huge effort to keep my focus on the massage instead of following my inner impulse of grabbing and kissing her all over that delicate and appealing naked neck and shoulders that seemed more like made of malleable porcelain than of flesh and bones. The sensation of being touched and sensed by somebody without any eyesight, generates a powerful feeling of being totally invaded by a whole host of hidden senses that transcend sight, hearing, taste, smell and even touch... it was as if, all of a sudden, I was accessed by a profound and pungent perception exercised by another being with highly developed humanly unknown senses. Those mysterious hidden senses which originate from nature's way, or should I say from the universe's way to compensate for the deficiency of one or more of our five senses, are certainly governed by different sets of laws, much more encompassing, profound and precise than our familiar five senses... and that makes us feel totally exposed and vulnerable to that other being...

This is precisely how I felt facing Keiko and her very meaningful expression despite her blindness. In fact, Keiko was looking at me or rather through me with a much higher degree of perspicuity than anybody with a perfect eyesight. She seemingly had the power to discern my inner feelings and reactions whereas I had to find solace in my superficial observation restricted to my cramped five senses and to my imagination — this one representing perhaps one of the less developed hidden senses present in the average human mind?

The massage ritual finally ended, and I felt renewed and relaxed as I did the night before. Keiko stood up ready to leave but I delicately stood close to her... she felt my presence, raised her head in my direction with a firm, yet sweet facial expression and whispered. "Please, let me go... this is not possible... I am working..."

I immediately stepped out of her way and mumbled, "Oh, I am very sorry... see you tomorrow, same time please?" I felt relieved to hear "OK" coming out of her mouth before she went out the door.

That night I couldn't fall asleep for hours thinking of Keiko and the irresistible attraction I had developed for her in just two massage sessions. In fact, there isn't a rule for falling in love or for feeling the enthralment I was so strongly experiencing towards such an appealing and fascinating human being. I believe there must exist a series of invisible electrical or maybe sub-atomic particle exchanges between two individuals within a pre-determined set of circumstances that probably create waves of mutual attraction... those in their turn eventually influence brain cells as well as other parts of the body such as the heart for example which finally, through a certainly complex pathway of chemical reactions, elicit passion...

It then occurred to me that maybe or rather almost certainly, she was the one taking the entire initiative in a subliminal manner leaving up to me the inglorious task of going through the tortuous path of figuring out how to turn all those feelings and electrical impulses into deeds of love without offending her or acting like an idiot... it finally occurred to me to wonder why the hell did I have to scientifically try to justify my own feelings of passion towards Keiko? Most likely to assure myself of her corresponding feelings towards me as well, especially considering the huge cultural divide that separated us... Finally, amidst those quasi-dreamy considerations, I managed to fall asleep till my punctual yet irritating wake-up call at seven a.m. sharp...

Fast forward, since there was absolutely nothing really remarkable for me to describe concerning that long and boring third day with the almost identical and interminable business sessions. To my joy and relief, my doorbell rang at seven p.m., almost as punctual as the start of my waiting anxiety that lasted just minutes before seven p.m. but appeared to be interminable nonetheless... There she was, as beautiful as the day before, exhaling a tremendously good and appealing scent, with a coiffure that would enhance the beauty of her masses of hair, however with a significant difference... she wasn't wearing a kimono but instead was dressed in western fashion wearing an elegant light blue dress that would show off the delicate and sensual forms of her voluptuous body. Her entire being was as delicate as a petal of one of those oriental exotic flowers which made me think that as long as creatures like her exist, the world makes sense and life is worthwhile after all. Keiko would transport me into her own world of infinite and undefined senses just by standing there and being present with her sensitivity that would fatally claim possession of the entire environment around her and all that was in it physical or otherwise, me in particular...

Wow! I almost screamed out of uncontrolled emotion. "You look tremendously beautiful! Where are you going tonight?"

"Tonight, I was invited to join my friends in some sort of a Hen party... you know, one of our long-time friends is going to get married next week so this is like a farewell to her bachelorette years... only ladies," she swiftly volunteered as to assure me of the innocence of the occasion. And she almost did!

"But where do you go to celebrate?" I insisted, only to really make sure of the good intentions behind the idea.

"Well, we will take her to a strip tease bar in Roppongui!"

I felt my legs floating devoid of all support including the ground they were standing on seconds before. It was a strange possessive feeling towards her with whom I had literally exchanged no more than perhaps fifty words or so. How could I be so concerned and jealous of her planned evening amongst her female friends?

"What do you mean by strip tease?" I couldn't resist the question.

"Oh no, it is not what you think... those are girls that simply volunteer to participate in those sorts of outings in order to make them more interesting. They are usually very beautiful and the strip tease ends before they take off their underwear... then, they can offer advice to the bride ranging from dressing codes, postures, honeymoon night attitude as well as questions that can or cannot be asked and so on... the whole idea is to put the bride-to-be in a comfortable situation and to make her discuss her first night with all of us without preconceived taboos thus allowing her to relax and possibly start enjoying the whole situation..."

I finally gave up convinced that my beautiful oriental

princess would not meet any prince at least during that evening.

"Massage?" she asked, pointing delicately to the bed.

"Yes of course," I replied resigning myself to yet another wonderful massage session.

That night I was left literally without any further initiative perhaps so inebriated was I with Keiko's beauty and her 'at ease' demeanour... That definitely contributed to my perplexity and surprise when Keiko turned around before leaving and asked me gently, "Tomorrow is Friday, and I will be going back home to Osaka for the weekend. Do you have plans for the weekend? If not, would you like to come with me? I can show you the city and we can have the best Tempura you ever had." That invitation had the sweetest taste ever and resonated in my ears as the most harmonious melody one can possibly hear.

"I would love to join you!" I immediately replied without any hesitation. "But I thought that you would be around since I booked another two massages with you for the weekend..." I stupidly argued in order to fill the void in my voice.

"Well, I know, and I was going to advise you that one of my colleagues would come in order to replace me" she replied not without a subtle malicious tone in her voice. You see, this weekend is my free one and in case I miss it, I cannot recover the two days off. But, if you prefer to stay and have your massage, no problem, I can tell them that you agree with the replacement masseuse." This time around, I got the impression that she was pulling my leg!

"Never," I unwittingly almost shouted this time! "I definitely prefer to come with you to Osaka!"

I could not remember the reasoning for a six-thirty a.m. bullet train — the first scheduled for that day — but I reached the station at six a.m. sharp and there she was waiting for me holding the tickets. The train left punctually at six-thirty a.m. and I simply don't know how long it took to reach Osaka — maybe a couple of hours, maybe more, maybe less. My only realization upon arrival was that the passing of time at Keiko's side was a totally ethereal, unearthly experience. I dare to say that her blindness would give me the strong impression of being transported to or rather forced to join her into her highly sensitive dimensions... My imagination was galloping ahead and filling me with excitement and anticipation for what a full weekend in the company of such a captivating woman would feel like!

In fact, and this is quite intriguing, scientists estimate that tangible matter makes up just four per cent of our perceived universe. Dark matter makes up twenty-three per cent and is perhaps at the origin of all gravitational forces that hold stars and galaxies together, whilst the remaining seventy-three per cent is composed by a "repulsive", non -gravitational mysterious force called dark energy. The most flabbergasting of it all though, is that even those scientific estimates are limited by our still incipient science and obviously by the very limits imposed by our own imagination as well... they solely constitute an attempt to define the unreal possibly existing beyond the imaginary limits of what we call 'universe', still a finite and highly imperfect concept of existence per se...

My perception was that Keiko, by force of nature but also by her innate inquisitiveness, let alone her sensitive receptivity, had developed such a strong extra sensorial ability to the extent that it would possibly allow her to navigate and to 'feel' the universe maybe within far reaching extraordinary dimensions simply unattainable to most humans. This feeling was evidenced to me by her intriguing attitude present most of the time, which translated into a perfect command of everyday life despite her handicap, not to speak of her extreme intuition and extra-developed instincts probably enhanced by that same handicap. It is in fact astonishing, to say the least, that ancient sages have established quite similar conceptual ideas of existence perhaps much more comprehensive and all-encompassing ones simply by breaking the barriers of the known, through esoteric experiments and discoveries. This way, they established a close relationship between the macro-cosmos and the micro-cosmos thus enlightening the ones who were prepared to receive the notion contained in the knowledge that God is all and everything and in fact resides within each one of us. We are therefore a living expression of God, and the only reason we find ourselves incapable of tapping into this infinite field of energy, is because our fear has been consistently lying to us and we chose to trust that traitor instead of challenging it with all our might!

Keiko's blindness had in fact developed a high level of inner energy that would in turn radiate a very advanced yet gracious interaction with whoever was receptive, or should I say privileged to receive it. The ensuing plenitude that she would irradiate, created a highly uplifting and reassuring feeling of such a quality that one would simply forget the fact that she was blind hence lacking the most important of our five senses.

We arrived at her tiny Japanese style home in the outskirts of Osaka still mid-morning and as she unlocked an old padlock and slipped open the fragile door, I immediately felt I was entering a very special living space. The floor covered by a tatami was so clean that I took off my shoes as if it was a very obvious thing to do. The furniture was modest yet warm and welcoming. A low-level table surrounded by cushions made me wonder whether Keiko would cook and entertain people despite her condition... the answer came without a question since she was probably reading my mind yet once again.

"I invited a very nice couple of friends to join us this evening for a homemade Tempura... as you probably already know, Tempura is a Japanese speciality invented in Osaka... Now we have to go to the fish and vegetable market to buy very fresh ingredients for the Tempura... then we can have a light lunch — some soba (Japanese noodles) for example, and then we can go for a walk so I can show you some interesting points of my hometown..."

And so, we went first to a very colourful fish market next-door where Keiko seemed to know literally everybody! The fishermen were there themselves personally making sure that customers would get produce to their full satisfaction. All Keiko had to do was to mention the word Tempura and a couple of other words which seemed to indicate the number of guests, and the right variety of shrimp, squid, fish, vegetables etc... would be immediately packed and inserted into her shopping bag. The entire process didn't take more than thirty minutes or so and to my embarrassment, I could notice some persistent glances of surprise and curiosity directed at me as we went from one stand to the next. After all, it was still quite uncommon in Japan to see a Japanese woman accompanied by a westerner especially considering such a beautiful creature bearing such a special condition... To my relief, we shortly headed back to the house in order to place the fish into the fridge and quickly savour some Soba graciously prepared and served by Keiko. I was very impressed by the total trust that Keiko bestowed to all who took her money and handed back change. She later explained to me in a reassuring tone that, being herself a native of Osaka, it would have been simply unimaginable to even conceive an act of dishonesty from the part of those people! The following couple of hours were spent hopping in and out of buses and subway trains, walking around old and new, reconstructed neighbourhoods and after a while I was literally taken aback by Keiko's ability to move around a city that size with such ease. Back home she pointed towards the bathroom and suggested that I have a relaxing Japanese bath to get ready for the Tempura... and so I happily did. The single bedroom was equipped with another floor tatami, with vivid colours and I couldn't help speculating about how we would sleep that night without sharing it... For now, Keiko insisted that I had a nap while she finished the preparations for dinner.

I had maybe a good hour of a deep and restful sleep and, at the very end of it, I plunged into a strange dream of a terrible storm in the upper Solimões that finally woke me up drenched in sweat. I knew I had dreamed of Angelina since her portrait was very vivid in my mind, but I couldn't recall the scene. The disparity between the two environments was so stark that made me ponder the incredible luck I had of being able to visualise and compare such radically different universes and contrasting cultural environments in such a short lapse of time. I guess this is a privilege that very few human beings can accomplish and most of all, comprehend the phenomena with their minds and especially with their souls. Suddenly I realised that I was sitting on Keiko's Tatami somewhere in Osaka — Japan having had vivid, almost live impressions of places maybe 20,000 miles away, located in the heart of the largest tropical rain forest of the world! Had I, be it for a single moment, been in reality at the two places at the same time? Maybe what we call dreams are nothing but our ability to travel through dark energy in a no-space-or-time dimension, finally interrupted by our own, self-imposed boundaries of fear of the unknown? That thought brought me a sense of detachment and freedom for a few moments.

Keiko entered the room whistling an old American song and, as if she didn't bother with my presence, entered the tiny bathroom and closed the sliding rice paper, almost transparent door that separated it from the room and very delicately, with sensuous movements undressed herself in order to enter the small Japanese "Ofuro" tub with the grace of a Bolshoi ballerina. She was tremendously feminine and absolutely perfect in her forms which reminded me of famous sculptures like the Venus de Milo, which is exposed in the Louvre Museum in Paris. There is ample debate about the sculptor (presumably Alexandros of Antiqua…) but all those who saw the masterpiece agree with the fact that it incarnates femininity in all its splendour! Well, my host easily fitted the analogy since she was very much indeed one of the most attractive and delicately perfect females I had ever seen!

She finally got out of the "Ofuro" with the demeanor of a sleek gazelle and quickly dried herself with a very small towel that obviously could hardly hide her impeccable forms from my extreme fascination and this despite the almost transparent rice paper door which separated us…

"Are you ready for the Tempura?" she asked nonchalantly. "Are you hungry?"

"Yes," was all I could stutter out of my bewilderment.

"Well, I just need another fifteen minutes and it will be ready… our guests should be here at any moment now."

A few minutes later the bell rang, and I had the pleasure of being introduced to an incredibly charming and communicative couple — Hamakko and Hideo. She (Hamakko) was a nuclear scientist with several international degrees and published articles in some of the most prestigious international scientific publications, and Hideo was an anthropologist besides being a famous lecturer who would disseminate his knowledge all over the world. I couldn't get enough from that highly educated and interesting couple in a single night in terms of knowledge and fascinating information and was equally very pleased and honoured to be questioned myself about the scattered information I had gathered about the Amazon region and its people during my trips to the region.

I noticed however that the most important aspect of a constructive dialogue does not reside in the quality of the answers or the technicality of the details of what one knows, but rather on the emotional dynamics of the exchange especially on the genuine curiosity and appraisal of those asking the questions. I also noticed that it goes without saying that nothing can replace direct experience, nevertheless the circumstantial lack of it can be minimized if the receiving party has enough interest and living background to be able to interpret the message in an accurate way. To that end, I was definitely facing a couple of highly sensible and mindful individuals...

Keiko was the perfect host and a highly trained Tempura cook. Being a chef in Japan is no trivial matter and extensive training is paramount if one wants to master any of the several classical Japanese specialties. Learning can take several years, and the candidate must endure a true ordeal "behind the scenes", which translates into endless hours a day training in a kitchen for months on end or even years in a row, perfecting and sharpening what we, in the west, consider to be simple or mechanical chores such as cutting vegetables. There lies the secret however, what is supposed to be simply a mechanical motion has to be repeated endlessly until it becomes an art... Keiko's art was greatly enhanced by the fact that she would not be able to see the food and its cooking, but would instead simply sense the right timing, mixtures, and its complex and detailed preparation in order to have it cooked to perfection… amazing indeed!

After a nice couple of hours of a highly interesting debate ranging from world affairs, environmental issues, to humanistic topics and esoteric extremely interesting exchanges, Hamakko and Hideo greeted us profusely, making me promise that I would be back soon, before heading back to their next-door prefecture in the suburbs of Osaka.

Keiko closed the door softly and turned her head towards me with a sweet and sensual expression.

"Are you tired?" was her tricky question.

"Not at all," I replied. "Don't forget that I had a good hour's sleep in the afternoon. "How about you?"

"I'm not tired either, but I would like to simply lie down and chat with you if you wish."

"I would be delighted," I replied being now reassured that the tatami would be for both of us to share.

"This being said," she went on jokingly, "Sorry but no massage today, since it's my day off…"

I was so pleased with all that spontaneous behavior, certainly owed in good part to the excellent beer and sake we had generously consumed with the exquisite Tempura. This being said, I felt confused, unable to read through the different signals she was explicitly as well as subliminally conveying…

Keiko finally broke my hesitancy, abruptly ending my vacillation by taking me by the hand and guiding me into the bedroom.

"Just wait for me, will you?" she murmured, disappearing inside the small bathroom.

She came out wearing a light silk kimono that enhanced her forms, exuding a subtle scent of Jasmin that would fuse extremely well with her delicate figure. All I had in order to make myself sexy and appealing despite her impaired vision, was my unfashionable 'Jockey' underwear and all I had to do to eventually get ready was to pull off my trousers and take off my shirt. Keiko knew my body quite well since she had massaged it several times, which in a way reassured me.

"What do you expect from me?" she asked bluntly taking me by total surprise. She was surprisingly very calm and in full command of the entire situation.

"Well," I started hesitantly, and she stopped me abruptly...

"Sex? A short adventure with a Japanese blind lady to add to your hunting trophies? Or maybe just a way to spend a more agreeable time in Japan instead of visiting Tokyo and Kyoto by yourself getting bored in the end and collecting a huge number of meaningless pictures that would end up in the garbage sooner or later?"

"More than that," I cut her short. "I am very curious to better get to know a very special and extremely interesting, sensitive and beautiful woman with whom I'm afraid of falling in love with... and I don't want to suffer or to make her suffer as a result of it... In fact, I feel extremely attracted to you not only as a woman but mainly as a very special and elevated soul that makes me feel at home whenever you are close. It is hard for me to define this feeling using words, since those have a very limited scope by definition. I prefer to sit here and listen to you no matter what you feel like telling me..."

"You know," she spoke with a very sweet tone, "I was born blind, and that on the one hand allowed me to compensate that handicap by developing my other senses extraordinarily but on the other hand gave me a terrible psychological handicap while I was growing up, especially during those age brackets where peer pressure becomes acute and the acceptance you get from the group where you belong represents a highly critical measure of your own success. I therefore had to compensate my handicap by struggling to stay ahead of the game vis a vis my peers. That lofty target obliged me to use my sensitivity in order to quickly understand and gauge the opposite sex in order to protect myself whilst establishing special relationships that would again compensate for my blindness. I think all that resulted in the development of a veiled communication process that can only be reciprocated by someone who understands and captures what is going on and, most of all, appreciates the subtleties of such a relationship. My feeling is that you are this kind of person and that makes me feel extremely good and comfortable when I'm close to you. It is rare to find a man with those hidden attributes hence I really don't care at all what name we will use to define our rapport as long as we both understand that the affinity we have for each other, must be treasured no matter how long we stay together or under which circumstances. In fact, it is my view that this affinity will subsist forever even if we live separately at opposite sides of the globe. Life is too short for us to impose preconditions on each other in any circumstances. Maybe my blindness gave me the ability to surrender to the present moment instead of sacrificing it in the name of a future that simply, and by definition, does not exist!"

Keiko turned her head towards me as if she could see my reactions and stayed silent for a while that seemed an eternity… she then dimmed the light from the lantern placed at her tatami's side low table and took me by surprise by kissing my lips softly and tenderly. We were both almost naked, our bodies compressed against each other, cuddled in a tight embrace. We stayed in that position for quite some time as if we wanted to perpetuate those moments of pure tenderness, anticipation and attraction. She then pushed me away softly, and took off her kimono in a slow and voluptuous motion, unveiling her magnificent and exciting forms... her breasts were impressive with huge nipples and a dark, protuberant areola that instantaneously enticed me to kiss, lick and suck them with passion which, as I could feel, excited her, hardening them even more as a result. Her not less hardened sex would touch my thigh leaving a delicious trace of her intimate nectar, a sign that she was at least as aroused as I was...

She acted as if she knew my body perfectly well which in fact she did, and that gave her a clear advantage in terms of being in full control of the situation. She seemed to enjoy exerting her power of domination. I loved the feeling of being possessed and made an effort to retain my impulses and keep myself in a passive mode letting her indeed take the entire initiative. Her inventiveness knew no restrictions as a result of her highly developed senses as well as her professional skills, hence she had multiple orgasms even before any penetration. Her mouth and tongue had no boundaries either and made me reach the apogee of pleasure more than once, which resulted in an arresting state of indulgence that made me literally lick and slurp her entire body slowly, like a wild animal in the pinnacle of its passion. Her taste and smell were so welcoming that I simply could not stop doing it... She came again and again making me wonder how a woman could have so many orgasms...

Then, very softly, she put herself on top of me and after having carefully separated the outer lips of her sex performing small circular movements with the head of my penis, introduced it very slowly into her vagina, increasing the rhythm gradually until reaching a wild and seemingly uncontrolled speed that made us come together in full ecstasy. We were sweating and breathing fast like two sprinters at the end of a marathon... finally, she laid down by my side, drenched and bearing an expression of sheer pleasure and satisfaction.

We were so happy and delighted to be there leaning against one another, with no restraints whatsoever, that in variable intervals one would entice the other for an encore! It was as if our desire knew no boundaries and grew stronger as the night progressed! Our smells were mixed into one and when the morning came, we simply did not feel like separating our now very intimate bodies, let alone getting up from that marvellous tatami that was now stained all over with the marks of our passion...

Finally, late in the morning Keiko got up trying not to disturb my state of relaxation and came back some time later with a perfect Japanese breakfast composed of fried noodles, dried fish, eel, green tea, and a refreshing algae salad.

She made me sit by installing a bunch of cushions against my back and fed me with chop sticks or at times simply with her mouth like a bird-mom feeding her small, making me feel the softness as well as the sexy taste of her meaty lips...

Here we were, two individuals from diametrically opposite cultures passionately making love after knowing each other for barely a week... shocking? Second thoughts? Guilt feelings? None of the above for sure! On the contrary, we were simply two adult individuals behaving heavenly, surrendering to our ardour, respecting our instincts and our genuine feelings of love towards each other which are and have always been an intrinsic and sublime part of us human beings! All socially imposed rules and baseless principles in this regard are worthless and obsolete in the face of the transcendent communion between two adult individuals in love! If we, as a human race could deeply understand and for once accept such precepts, maybe the world could be in a better shape with far less rapes, forceful and at times insane unions or marriages, not to speak of a vast array of sex crimes resulting from the systematic repression of our most sacred impulses. Obviously, some broadly accepted, truthful and genuine principles should be put into place mainly through education (totally lacking in most societies which is appalling) and scientific means such as birth and disease control among others. Needless to say, we should be equally very conscious of the risks and dangers of over-population hence birth control should be broadly instituted through education and prevention and through correct medicine availability amongst other means! We must recognize that all the potential risks of a freer and more loving society, pale in the face of the presently adopted alternatives — sheer repression in the name of insane so-called traditions, with its disastrous results — in lieu of pro-active and intelligent education! Love in all its manifestations, including what we call quite narrowly 'sex' or 'physical love' should never be considered a sin by any social, religious or cultural precepts, period! And this, simply because love is the answer, the only way out allowing us to escape the disasters we're heading into precisely as the result of lack of love, never due to the abundance of the latter! But there's a catch here, love cannot be qualified as good or bad, accepted or rejected, elected or condemned! Clearly, I am referring to universal, encompassing and genuine love amongst all beings and needless to say, excluding all of its sick, deviated forms which obviously aren't love really, but often the consequence of the very absence of it!

Sunday evening came much faster than it should and marked the end of our idyllic weekend. Our journey back to Tokyo was silent most of the time. We didn't need to talk to each other since our communication was now mostly taking place without the encumbrance of words… we held hands all the way like two young students who had fallen in love for the first time in their lives. From time-to-time Keiko would kiss my lips assuring me of her allegiance to our newly found passion… Upon our arrival, she surprised me by saying that she had taken two days off in order to be able to stay with me for as long as she possibly could before my departure for Paris. I was simply thrilled and immediately started to imagine ways to free myself from the boredom of my customers meetings. I had a full agenda for Monday and also for Tuesday! Obviously, we couldn't stay together in my hotel room since Keiko was well known by the entire staff as well as by some of the patrons still hosting there and who had had the privilege of experiencing one of her miraculous massages.

I have always been blessed by what are commonly known as happy coincidences or synchronicity that in fact are a convergence of universal forces that conspire in order to bring abundance and joy to a given circumstance. The secret behind this conviction, resides in believing in it and actively expecting the best in life… Deep in myself, and notwithstanding the almost unsurmountable obstacles I had to occasionally face in order to survive, I have always been a believer that life is in reality a good deed as opposed to a fatalistic tragedy. Even in the most difficult of times, I was privileged by what I would call a deliverance impulse that would present itself in different forms but invariably came to my rescue or to the encounter of the deepest of my desires! This often occurred as long as the latter were pure and genuine, contributed to my well-being as well as to the one of my human mates and were devoid of greed or egotistic ambitions.

Well, the universe was apparently conspiring to the

fulfilment of our desires since as I left Keiko at her tiny apartment next to the hotel and arrived in my room, there was a message with a terribly hoarse voice coming out of the messaging machine from Taketo, the local manager announcing, "Alex, I am so sorry, but I am in bed with high fever hence won't be able to work at all tomorrow, maybe Tuesday… I suggest you take it easy and have some rest and I will call you tomorrow in the evening hopefully to schedule our Tuesday meetings. Our customers have been advised accordingly, not to worry… Have a good night…" I couldn't believe my luck and it took me literally two minutes to grab a couple of clean pairs of under wear and a shirt before rushing out the door and making a quick stop at the reception desk to advise them that I would not spend the night in my room. That was necessary in my view for safety reasons.

I then reached the almost empty street which was normal for a Sunday night like in most big cities, and ran like a kid who had been given the key to a candy parlour…

Keiko opened the door with a concerned expression as she saw me totally out of breath…

"Are you OK?" she asked me with her sweet and melodious voice.

"I am in heaven!" I replied telling her the story about Taketo's fortuitous condition.

"Poor Taketo," she mumbled unconvincingly. "But… this is really marvelous," she went on, bringing her hand onto her mouth in a sign of self-incrimination… "What do you want to eat my love"? This was the first time she called me "my love…"

"You! Lots of you my loving princess!" I replied taking her into my arms in a very tight embrace and kissing her avidly…

We made love right there, on the floor, like two thirsty nomads who find a source of fresh water after a long and exhausting desert crossing. By then I knew that I would carry forever, deep in my heart, the feeling of her body against mine and the taste of her tender lips... Keiko, Keiko, oh Keiko! She made me exceedingly happy and gave me the most precious of things... her loving and unblemished tenderness. Obviously, the question I still ask myself from time to time is why didn't I abandon everything right there and decide to stay in Japan, a country and culture I simply love and admire, to share my life with Keiko... Well, in hindsight I understood that I was simply not ready for such a commitment as of yet... neither was she. And she knew it! The woman who had been predestined to me was waiting for me somewhere and likewise the right man was waiting for Keiko somewhere else... and she definitely deserved the best!

The following morning, we went out to see the cherry blossoms, so beautiful in Japan during springtime! To my surprise, Keiko was as thrilled if not more than I was, simply by smelling and sensing their presence...

"You see, this is nature telling us that there is always a new beginning, a new rebirth!" And she went on as if trying to convince herself, "Hence, one should never get anxious or depressed by death or decay, since those are absolutely necessary in order to give way to a renewed and refreshed life. Besides, souls don't break... they bounce! In this regard, we, humans, have distorted reality by virtue of an almost infinite set of misunderstandings of the laws of nature, in favor of our own interpretation of reality based on the mirage of materialism which obviously is totally false!"

"I fully agree," I quickly replied to her wise observations. It translated a thinking process coming from someone that had undoubtedly spent a significant amount of time observing life, nature and understanding its wonders…

"I don't see you coming back to Japan," she suddenly exclaimed, while holding my hand firmly.

"How can you say such a thing?" I reacted grabbing her by her waist. "Of course, I will come back, if for anything, to come and fetch you!"

"Oh no, I shall never leave my country! This is where I want to spend the rest of my life!" she replied without hesitation.

"Well, in that case, my only remaining alternative is to learn Japanese and try to find a job here in Tokyo!"

"I told you already… you will not come back. I can sense it very clearly. This is not where you belong! You would feel unhappy living in a place where you do not belong… and this has nothing to do at all with the fact that you don't speak Japanese. This is relatively easy to learn especially for somebody like you who enjoys so much our culture therefore would absorb it and would become part of it very soon. The reason I think you do not belong here, is simply because you still need to explore the world… I can feel your thirst, so go ahead, fasten your belt and just do what you have to do!"

"And where do you think that I belong?" I challenged her to continue.

"Well," she started, "you belong to the stars and to the universe like all of us… now, if you want me to tell you where I believe that you would feel better on this planet while spending your short and transitory time over here, and after all the places you still need to explore before settling down somewhere, my reply would be, far away from what is called civilization, somewhere that you could immerse yourself in nature. You are a rebellious soul, a wild being by nature and I simply do not feel you leading a daily routine and a boring kind of life in a big city…"

Once again Keiko gave me that familiar feeling of being capable of transcending human boundaries and seeing beyond. Time would eventually prove her right since life events would in fact and regretfully preclude me from ever returning to Japan…

Our last night together was simply terrifying since we both knew that our separation was imminent and that it would be a long one not to say a definitive one. We avoided making empty promises that would sound like lies and instead spent most of the night holding each other tightly, in silence, broken only once quite abruptly by Taketo's apologetic call telling me that he had no choice but to say goodbye over the phone due to his still very high fever. As soon as I hung up, we embraced each other tightly again trying hard to tame the angst that had invaded our hearts. I couldn't sleep at all through the night, and I guess Keiko couldn't either. Very early in the morning she prepared her delicious Japanese breakfast and time literally flew till the moment that the taxi arrived to take me to the hotel for my check out before heading for the airport.

Her last words were, "I guess we loved each other from day one, and we will always communicate through it and be able to feel the love we now have for each other no matter where we are." I could notice a couple of stubborn tears coming out of her eyes and rolling down her cheeks, and I kissed her without being able to hold my own.

"I am sure we'll be seeing each other soon my love," I said unconvincingly before jumping into the impeccable taxi that had been patiently waiting for me.

The Narita airport was crowded as usual, yet everything would function close to perfection, given the Japanese penchant for order and discipline. Impeccable police officers wearing strikingly clean white gloves would guide huge crowds without losing control and keeping their balance as if performing a trivial ritual that would drive any western police officer crazy in similar circumstances.

The 'All Nippon Airways' flight was rigorously on time, and I was welcomed by a smiling ground crew lady holding a sign with my name in capital letters on it…

As I reached her, the young and smiling lady wearing an impeccable uniform bearing the name 'ANA' for 'All Nippon Airways' on her lap, approached me and after having courteously and gracefully inclined her body in a distinctive sign of reverence and respect, asked me "Mr Mavromatis San?"

"Yes," I replied with some perplexity by being so distinctively treated by such a delicate and considerate creature…

"Mr Mavromatis San," she went on delicately, "you have won our ANA special contest and have been awarded an upgrade to our first class." I recalled quite hazily having filled out some kind of an airline questionnaire while still on my inbound flight many days ago… "Would you please be so kind to follow me to our first-class lounge, while we take care of your luggage and check in procedure?"

"Of course," I replied, while stepping into a small and perfumed elevator that took us both to a luxurious lounge filled with excellent food and selected beverages. The following two hours allowed me to read all sorts of western newspapers in order not to think of Keiko, whilst my check in procedure took place as swiftly and invisibly as possible. Boarding was uneventful and I wouldn't be able to recall the number of times that the highly trained on-board crew, mainly composed of exceptionally beautiful young Japanese ladies, bowed as soon as I approached any of them… my seat was huge and extremely comfortable —

in those days, airlines hadn't yet invented the flat beds that one sees today in most business and first class cabins. As soon as I sat down, an equally beautiful and attractive blond haired, blue eyed Caucasian flight attendant dressed in a Japanese kimono like all the others, came towards me and asked me in an impeccable French, "Je vous mets les pantoufles, Monsieur?" (should I put on your slippers for you, sir?) I was at first embarrassed to be offered such a service by such a stunningly beautiful creature, but obviously accepted the offer if not for anything else, at least to keep her as long as possible close to me. She went on and gracefully took off my shoes and with a series of delicate and precise movements put on a pair of flashy red slippers bearing of course the 'ANA' logo in golden embroidery. Her hands inadvertently touched my feet, and I was surprised to discover the same finesse in her touch as the one displayed by Keiko whenever she would touch my body. In that moment I realized that the memories of the rather short period of time we had so deliciously spent together in Tokyo and Osaka would never leave my mind and soul...

The supposedly 'French' flight attendant then left, not without giving me an evocative smile — ah women, such delightful and perceptive creatures... Keiko came immediately once again to my mind as if censuring my reactions, and at that very moment I started missing her voice, her touch, her tremendously attractive smell, her sweet smile and soft expression full of love and tenderness. The 'French' flight attendant disappeared from my sight not without leaving me with some sort of guilt feelings of neglect in the face of my involuntary and intuitive reaction to her beauty and grace... After all, I had practically left Keiko's tatami as well as her sweet embrace just some short hours ago! But hell, this is how things in fact work in real life! Even though we have a great deal of difficulty in admitting it, we simply are just as loyally devoted beings as is dictated by our feelings, period! At least in respect to the spontaneous reactions emanating from the depths of our nature, our instincts. We can deny them, try our best to control our minds and body in order to convince ourselves of our false moral values, but if we are one hundred per cent honest with ourselves, we cannot deny our nature and our genuine feelings and the laws of attraction! Yes, I admit that I was young and determined not only to enjoy life as it presented itself to me, but also to get to explore the feminine side of my spirit by surrendering myself to those extraordinary creatures — WOMEN — that I knew so little about, yet I felt so strongly identified with and attached to.

The aircraft took off powerfully in the darkness of the night and flew smoothly in the pursuit of an elusive sun that had left Tokyo hours before, heading swiftly towards the West. The dining service was just perfect and I couldn't let the Krug Champagne as well as the "Grand Crus" Bordeaux selected bottles pass by me without trying them... all of them! Over and over again! In a couple of hours after takeoff, I was feeling quite tiddly, yet extremely happy with myself!

All I recalled when waking up, besides the image of Keiko, was that her name was Florence and that she had laughed a lot at my stories until I couldn't keep my eyes open any more...

A gentle Japanese male flight attendant came to see me and offered me breakfast. "Don't misunderstand me," I said, "but where is Florence?"

"Oh sir, I see she is now taking a quick nap. Japanese air regulations for long, intercontinental flights, please kindly understand sir?" he replied very politely and a bit embarrassed by my request.

"Yes, I understand," I mumbled short of any available option in my favor... half an hour later we had started our descent towards Paris and finally Florence appeared fresh as a spring flower attending to various requests from the other passengers.

We finally landed and she disappeared from my sight during the taxiing procedure until the plane came to the usual halt at the gate. I took my carry-on luggage and headed towards the door when suddenly she appeared in front of me with a magnificent smile and said, "ça a été un vrai plaisir de faire votre connaissance" (It has been a real pleasure to meet you). I felt frustrated with what sounded like an emotionless greeting despite the word 'real', and stopped right there in front of her, staring at her, speechless, with what must have been a totally stupid and incomprehensible expression. Finally, I could stutter the first question that came to mind, "shall we see each other again perhaps in Paris?" The answer came back like scissors cutting deep into my feelings and tearing open all my expectations." Sure, most probably on your flight back to Tokyo."

I greeted her quickly, and rushed through the open door, amidst the protests of the other passengers who were waiting patiently for the first-class ones to go before them.

PARIS

After the usual customs procedures, I grabbed a taxi and headed towards what remains in my memory as one of the most charming hotels I have ever seen in my life. It is discreetly nestled at the 'Place des Vosges', right in the heart of the 'Marais', a very romantic and bohemian Parisian neighborhood. The 'Place des Vosges' consists of a perfectly symmetrical, large square enclosed by century old historical buildings which house intriguing museums, contemporary as well as ancient small art galleries, bohemian restaurants, librarians selling old and sometimes very rare books, and so on. On Saturdays, as I recall, there were very interesting and richly improvised shops, where one could buy affordable yet wonderful art, books, and a variety of curious and intriguing objects coming from all over France and the world... The ambiance transpired a mixture of sober yet simple elegance, with a smell of oil paint blended with a wide variety of aromas emanating from the cuisines of the small restaurants that are mainly placed at the corners of the square. Such a poetic environment creates a willingness to stay and stroll endlessly without ever leaving the square or its surroundings which are also quite charming. I was offered a small but very cozy room with a tiny but well-equipped bathroom, which is not an obvious assumption when it comes to French hôtellerie... many three-star hotels in France have rooms without a bathroom which is commonly located at the hallway and serves several guests. The hotel in question is a four starred hotel hence all of its rooms are in fact apartments. After giving the doorman who brought up my bags a nice tip (mandatory in Paris if you want to be treated at least decently during your stay…), I closed the door to find myself in an oasis of perfect silence! Interestingly, most small hotels in Paris are located in calm streets, or small plazas full of charm, which assures a totally quiet and discreet environment. The time difference with Tokyo was seven hours and I decided to call Keiko. She was having dinner at home and her voice came through the wire as sweet as usual, making me immediately feel the familiarity of her very feminine way of speaking.

"Did you arrive well, my love?" she asked me in an assuring tone, as if she was my long-time companion or wife.

"Yes, I managed to sleep during most of the flight," I replied.

"Good! That means that there were no beautiful ladies sitting next to you?!"

"Not at all, just an old gentleman," I replied sincerely hence convincingly. "Darling," I went on, "Please understand that I will not be calling you too often, since the company controls all of my calls, OK?" I sort of hedged myself as if having some sort of a premonition of what was about to occur in my life…

"Oh, never mind! This call was quite a nice surprise to me since I was not expecting you to call me at all!"

We blew kisses through the wire and said goodbye to each other. We both knew deep in our hearts that it was highly unlikely, to say the least, that we would see each other again. As awkward as it may sound, my short yet very intense relationship with Keiko was as close to perfection as one can aspire to reach in such a short period of time. Maybe this was due precisely to the very little time we had to spend together, therefore leaving simply no space for misunderstandings or unrealistic expectations which are usually at the core of most failures in rapports between two individuals in love.

Love is everywhere since it is all encompassing besides being representative of life itself no matter what shape or form it takes, hence it is up to us to uncover it through every single moment of our lives. It is in a blade of grass, in a summer afternoon's bird song, in the sweet expression of a child making simple yet astonishing discoveries, in the joyful sound of dolphins playing in the sea, in the wind, in the blue and turbulent skies, in the ocean and its fantastic nuances and changes of mood, and of course in two individuals who decide to let love carry them through, no matter the social precepts that try to dictate how a loving relationship must be in the context of a given culture, tribe, or even in what we call civilization! Lucky are the ones who succeed in dropping all those pre-conceived chains and decide to live a life made of love, letting it permeate all levels and moments of their existence.

It was Saturday and still quite early in the morning, so I decided to skip the shower and instead take a long walk through the lovely neighborhood of Le Marais and its surroundings. There was a marvelous aroma of freshly backed croissants in the air and I sat at a tiny table of a small but welcoming coffee shop, one of the dozen options offered by any of the Parisian boulevards or streets. The croissants were baked to perfection, crispy on the outside and soft in the inside... ah, I said to myself while sipping a delicious freshly brewed Parisian 'café au lait', and biting the delicacy with a carnal pleasure... this is happiness! The morning sun was already caressing the old tin roofs of the city, but the traffic was still slow, as it is the norm on a Saturday morning in Paris. I was immersed in my thoughts, deep in my galoshes, pondering on how reliant I was on all the women I had met and the ones I was still supposed to meet in my life... In fact, every single woman a man gets involved with represents a path to the unknown and as soon as one decides to undertake it, it surely becomes a lifelong exploit encroached forever in our memory, no matter its extent in time! Each and every woman, no matter the ethnicity or her origins, or her life story, has invariably a beauty of her own, sometimes obvious and apparent, sometimes perfectly disguised behind veils as if expecting its turn to explode releasing an infinity of mysterious and perfumed flowers that somehow, by pure accident, stayed hidden in the confines of her spirit during most of her existence… One can focus on the forms, skin, smell, demeanor, expression, sensitivity, sensuality, tone of the voice, hair, way of looking or staring, teeth, and I could go on forever… the fact of the matter remains though that there is always a poem to be deciphered in every single woman of this world! So, how can a man resist so many enticements whilst keeping his sanity? Impossible! God made us this way for some reason! And the reason is simply our natural inclination to love!

All those thoughts running through my mind made me completely oblivious of the environment and the people who would come in and out of the café endlessly. So, I was very surprised when I felt a hand poised delicately on my shoulder and a melodious and almost familiar voice pronouncing my name…" Axel, this is more than a coincidence… I would rather call it fate…"

"Florence!" I almost shouted jumping out of my chair and out of the torpor of my divagations. "It's such a pleasure to see you again!" I went on, feeling perplexed but extremely lucky as if my number had been called first in a tombola charity night. I pulled an empty chair from the table next to mine, not without raising the eyebrows and noticing an upset look from the fellow that was sitting next to it. "Je m'excuse monsieur," I mumbled without even bothering to look at the individual.

His reply was a vague "hummm," but quite frankly I couldn't care less!

Florence sat next to me, and her stimulating perfume immediately penetrated my nostrils and filled my mind and body with an indescribable sense of happiness and delight... she had obviously taken a shower and looked as fresh as a wildflower bouncing back and forth under the effects of a spring cool breeze.

"Well, tell me about coincidences!" I said. "I confess that I was pondering about calling ANA and asking for your coordinates..."

"Oh, they would have never given them to you... it's all about flying regulations, you know, and the Japanese are absolutely strict about it! Unless you had a serious complaint about me, in which case I would be made aware of it and of course of your identity, we would never again be able to connect through the airline, that's for sure!"

"Therefore, we may call it fate, indeed!" I replied without hiding my emotion, quite noticeable from the tone of my voice. "What can I offer you?"

"Well, just a café crème and a croissant. They are fabulous in this place, don't you agree?" She went on while I called the waiter to place the order. "Oh, definitely," I replied, mesmerized by her impressive looks.

I could now look at her straight in the eyes without being interrupted by anyone else like I was in the airplane. It gave me a certain sense of control, of finally being able to have her undivided attention! I was indeed a lucky bastard I must confess!

She was stunningly beautiful with lively and expressive big blue eyes, firm breasts that one could admire just by staring at her almost transparent blouse that would generously unveil the protuberance of her generous nipples surrounded by big rosy aureoles… her naturally blond hair looked like silk and would move in harmonious waves each time she would move her head. Her teeth, perfectly aligned and shiningly white, would almost obfuscate the onlooker and contribute to her tremendous charm. Literally everybody in the café would turn their heads at least once to stare at her for some seconds, as if finding refuge away from all the evils of the earth in that angelically attractive creature. Her skin, soft and tanned to perfection would irradiate some sort of golden luminosity mirroring a healthy and vibrant being. Yes, nothing happens without a reason, I almost murmured to myself…

"So, what are your plans for the weekend?" she asked me with a smile.

"Well, I must confess that I was planning on doing nothing, just take it easy and enjoy this lovely day by strolling wherever my legs would carry me thru this splendid city. This being said, and now that you have appeared, I feel like spending eternity with you!" I simply threw it at her without trying to retain my emotion…

"Are you always as impulsive with every woman you meet? Because if that's the case, you will probably need more than one life to live through all of your conquests," she asked sarcastically but not without a malicious smile revealed through her meaty lips.

"To be frank with you, the answer is no. I mean, I'm usually not the one who takes the initiative. As a matter of fact, and please don't take me wrongly, with me it is usually the woman who makes the first step… then I may feel encouraged to reciprocate… I am rather shy, and introvert believe it or not."

"Yes, I do believe you, but this is definitely not obvious!

Well, I have some errands to run since there's nothing to eat at home, but if you are patient and feel like it, I would gladly invite you for lunch. Have you ever been in a good Parisian street-market before?"

"No," I said... but I would be more than happy to accompany you and to accept your kind invitation... under the condition that you let me pay for everything you need to buy since I shall be eating it after all!"

"Oh, finally a gentleman 'à la ancienne'," she replied vibrantly without hiding her satisfaction.

Every Parisian 'arrondissement' or administrative neighborhood, has its own street market which usually takes place once or twice a week. The variety and quality of the food is second to none, especially seafood which comes to Paris daily by trains, called 'trains de marée' (tide trains) and arrives at every market strikingly fresh if not literally alive, at the early hours of every single morning. The markets are very colorful, and one can find virtually all kinds of food such as excellent cheese, fruit, vegetables of every sort, grains, meat and poultry and of course exquisite seafood.

Florence was of course extremely popular among the street vendors due to not only her good looks but also her communicative skills and ability to talk to those rough and tough guys as if she was one of their own. Not one would resist throwing at her what would be otherwise construed as a rather abrasive comment, however said in such a way that it sounded simply as a spicy compliment...

She would move through the infinity of food displays with ease and the grace of a princess in a fairy tale, stopping here and there to the delight of the vendor, who would instantly start offering her deals in order to keep her close to his display for as long as possible. One of them who seemed to have known her for long time, would tenderly call her "mon petit crocodile" (my little crocodile), which would betray his self-contained and unforgiving impulse to grab her and take her away with him forever... an impossible dream indeed...

I was greatly amused by the vivid scenes I was witnessing and mainly by the emergence of a myriad of extraordinary, uncontained reactions and feelings that Florence would inspire in those folks. Desire, craving, joy, lust, envy, and even nostalgia, were some of the expressions that were exposed either in an obvious and unequivocal manner, or in an implicit way but nonetheless revealed through expressions and surreptitious yet highly exposing glimpses.

Finally, Florence seemed satisfied with the two big bags now totally full of mouthwatering delicacies and we headed to her tiny car parked on the sidewalk as it is common among Parisians especially on weekends as if there was a tacit gentlemen's agreement between the shoppers, the vendors and the traffic police force...

Her small but extremely well decorated, charming apartment was located in Saint Germain, a well-known Paris district inhabited by artists of all sorts and home to art galleries and elegant shops. Cooking was very efficient and in less than one hour a delicious two course seafood lunch was ready to be served.

We started with premium champagne (Krug. please!) and Iranian caviar! I was impressed by the rather expensive value and sophistication of our 'appetizer', but the explanation came fast... "With the compliments of ANA," she was quick to justify the extravagance! "You see, as a first-class flight attendant we are entitled to some fringe benefits from time to time... and I love sharing it with nice people like you!" she went on while suddenly leaning towards me and in an entirely unexpected motion, kissed me languidly in the mouth! Her mouth was like soft velvet and her kiss was warm and wet, very intense and full of eagerness probably an anticipated intention from her part... I was taken aback by the surprise but evidently reciprocated allowing her to kiss me several times with increased sensuality between sips of Champagne whilst caressing her generous forms and gorgeous breasts with their enormous nipples already hardened out of excitement.

Florence's bed had the feel and the touch of a female lover... This is hard to explain with mere words since it is something that one not only has to sense but essentially to connect to past, poignant sexual experiences where similar references have been established...

The linen had an alluring scent that would remind one of Florence's perfume without being the same fragrance though. The mattress softness was just perfect and would create an irresistible sensation of coziness and a feeling of engaging expectation... when she lied down close to me, her perfume melded with the linens to create an extremely captivating smell only disrupted by the smell of her stimulating body nectars and of her young hormones abundantly exhaling through her skin. The clear sensation that invaded my mind was that she had gone through the same ritual maybe dozens of times with several partners. Was I 'à la hauteur' or at least capable of contenting her obviously highly developed sexual senses!?... was a persistent question insistently hitting my mind, so much so that suddenly I felt so nervous to the point of losing my erection completely!

Instead of showing surprise, frustration or even rejection, which is quite common in those circumstances, Florence took me into her arms in a tender embrace as if to protect me from my rather insane and intrusive thoughts. "Oh, my love," she murmured into my ear, "this shows that you are a very sensitive and a potent male." Her breasts were squeezed against my chest, and I could feel the pressure of the hardened tits/teats ? massaging my skin each time she would make a move. Her breath was short and the smell coming out of her voluptuous mouth was exhaling pure excitement.

"Can I caress you without reserves and without any compromise? You see, I feel very excited with a real man like you suddenly feeling vulnerable and abandoned by what you, stupid men, praise the most… a simple erection which is nothing more than a stream of blood stuffing the cavernous parts of your penises. Well, you should know that I love it when it becomes soft and tender, because then we can extend the pleasure and the experience becomes richer… we have nothing at all to prove to each other here! In case I do not come to an orgasm, so be it, I shall come next time, or maybe the following one! The same can happen to you… you don't have to fuck me at any cost today! We can see each other tomorrow or even the day after! In the meantime, we can have lots of fun like this and get to know each other better. After all, we just met yesterday, and I know absolutely nothing about you! And before you ask, no, I usually wait for a long time before going to bed with a man… now, let's play together."

Her words somehow calmed me down and all of a sudden, I could feel her mouth literally swallowing my penis with such a lust, that it started to slowly react to the extremely tender and experienced movements. Her vulva came very close to my face, and I could sense the strong and extremely sensuous smell exhaling from her wet vagina. I grabbed her clitoris with my lips, which made her sigh loudly and slipped my tongue down to her hot, open vagina licking it softly and caressing it with my avid lips which instantly triggered in me an immense sentiment of pleasure! By that time, I had finally recovered my full erection and Florence would make love to me in literally all possible positions for hours... Her vagina was pretty narrow, which would give me an extra pleasure in each of her movements which would have the effect of contracting it even more, making me feel as if trapped into her wet and hot embrace. We both reached several orgasms with her obviously hitting a much higher score until late in the night... finally we slept in a soft and ecstatic embrace feeling the tingling of our nerves as we released our energy and with it our anxiety and stress, surrendering to feelings of calm and plenitude that are only possible when two bodies and souls encounter each other in absolute abandonment.

It was around eight a.m. when Florence laughed loudly. "What is the matter?" I asked her, still half asleep.

"Well, do you realize the tremendously good sex both of us have been having for hours? I confess that I was not expecting this to happen so soon, I mean today... and... where does all this tenderness of yours come from? I have never met a man with such a tender attitude, and this took me to heaven! I never had so many orgasms in one single night before..." The way she spoke while caressing me all over made me feel so warmly welcomed, that I felt I could stay in that bed literally for as long as eternity! "Are you hungry, amour?" she asked me with a sexy voice.

"I am starving... for you!" I shouted while grabbing her unbelievably firm breasts from behind with my hands, turning her around abruptly and kissing her lips that were red and fleshly swollen as a result of our never-ending, wild kisses...

God gave us desire and sexuality as a gift not only to ensure procreation but also to allow us a profound, meaningful and legitimate expression of love, pleasure, and a way to reach complete intimacy whilst ensuring releases of contained, sometimes trapped energies through our orgasms. All this is essential for us to disconnect momentarily from the crazy world we live in and really abandon ourselves to our primordial traits. Indeed, the profound intimacy that only sex as an expression of love can bring is key for us to return to a primal sense of being, that brings down all defenses that at times corrode our daily lives. Carnal love, no matter how vulgar and rough it may be characterized by society, IS nothing but love! It is definitely not the aberrant and dogmatic distortion that society made out of this pure form of lovely connection in order to instill fear with the purpose to exploit its deviant forms, often to ultimately generate profits out of it! Sex is love and love is sex period! But, sexism, which is often used to describe and exploit sex is definitely not love! And as such, love can never be construed as a sin or as something dirty or evil for that matter. Throughout my lifetime, my own sexual liberation has played a critically important role in terms of developing my capacity to understand the other better, to connect assertively, to develop both my masculine and feminine sensitivity, in short to love in a freer and more profound way. But all this does not come with inertia, on the contrary, it requires conscious work and perseverance since one's path is totally unknown beforehand, and one can only discover it by decisively traversing the unfamiliar.

Florence carried a mysterious and extremely attractive scent of sex even right after the shower, which melded with her perfume to create a highly stimulating odor. That night we were invited for dinner at one of her closest friends — Marie-Christine — who happened to be married to a complete jerk called Maurice who had insistently yet furtively harassed Florence through the years despite her close friendship with his wife. On our way to their house, as we jumped out from the ROR (Paris express subway) there was a dark alley we had to cross before reaching our final destination. Florence grabbed me by the neck and gave me languid kisses whilst guiding my hand under her silk dress into her panties which made me feel her wet clitoris hard as a tiny penis. "Let us make love right here, I won't be able to wait until we get back to bed which is where we should have stayed in the first place!" She murmured in a hesitant and excited tone. I was aroused but concerned with the possibility of being interrupted by an eventual passerby when all of a sudden, an old lady showed up at the end of the alley. We immediately recomposed ourselves not without bursting into an uncontrolled laughter.

"C'est ça mes amours, aimez-vous tant que vous pouvez, car la vie passe vite… très vite! (this is it, my beloved ones, love yourselves as much as you can, while you can because life passes fast… very fast!), said the lady as soon as she reached us, without staring at us or even stopping by. What a nice thing to say, especially coming from a person two generations older than us. We couldn't avoid getting into an imaginary effort aimed at figuring out her love life which had probably been rich yet maybe short given the social precepts of her time… We continued our walk and reached the couple's door soon thereafter.

Marie-Christine was older than Florence and was a tremendously observant and sensitive woman according to the way she would stare at me throughout the entire dinner. I soon understood the reason why Florence was quick to accept the invitation despite her declared preference to have spent the night in bed. It was mainly because she wanted her approval or even her blessing with regards to me. She was a good listener and would not hesitate to ask peppery questions whenever she felt curious about some of my accounts concerning my story. Maurice was exactly what Florence had anticipated… an utterly idiotic being who wouldn't take his eyes away from Florence and her cleavage and would just utter some stupid and senseless interjections here and there in the hope of grabbing her attention. At one point he whispered loudly enough so that I could intentionally hear, "God, you smell good tonight." Florence gave me a quick glance and I had to stand up to go to the bathroom in order to hide my laughter. If he only knew what that terrific smell was made of!

We left past two a.m. and Maurice had no choice but to drive us back to Paris in his black Porsche. Florence took the front seat but only after yet another tasteless joke namely, "Axel, I must warn you that men never sit in the front seat in my car… this is reserved for beautiful women,", and I squeezed myself in the back seat. Fortunately, there was no traffic at all which allowed Maurice to show off all of his driving prowess… scary I must admit, however, we reached Florence's flat in no time!

We were both still fairly drunk and quite exhausted, which made us fall asleep almost immediately. I woke up late the following morning with the echoes of the bells coming from a nearby church, probably announcing the late Sunday morning mass. Florence was still fast asleep and totally naked by my side. Her stunningly beautiful contours invited me to stare at her body for about an entire hour, noticing every single palpitation of her heart, a tenuous movement that would replicate on her magnificent breasts like ripples in a serene golden reflective pond. Paris is probably the most inspiring and romantic city for lovers on earth! It is one of those things where myth corresponds to reality… or maybe reality got adapted to the myth. The city offers indeed a romance-conducive and poetic environment.

Parisians seem to be fully conscious of this so much so that flirtation is one of the favorite pastimes for all ages. Eye contact is definitely welcomed and often reciprocated which constitutes a sure sign of, if not availability, at least of a welcoming curiosity…

Florence finally woke up and we made love like in the movies. Having someone so beautiful and attractive almost requesting love from you first thing in the morning, makes you feel reassured to say the least! Florence was a bonding and extremely affectionate kind of woman, one who would make a man feel like a stallion-king when it came to love making. She knew perfectly how to turn a man into the most important person on earth probably for as long as passion would last… I was falling in love with her… yes, falling in love! It is interesting how people avoid using the term for fear of over-qualifying a given feeling or relationship to any living being. However, we 'fall' in love, don't we? It feels like being trapped by feelings beyond our free will or control, feelings that are simply uncontrollable by our minds, no matter their qualification or quantification. This is at the origin of countless dramas that permeate history through the centuries, hence creating intricate situations not only between heterosexuals but also, and especially, between homosexual relationships. Some of those have no place within certain established cultures, thus being at the origin of profound conflicts and even wars! Ah, love can indeed happen and exist in forbidden secretive gardens, in the most unexpected and conflictual situations, amongst the less likely people to fall in love, in the open or in hiding, which makes it even more exciting and mysterious, provided of course it does not constitute a deviation, in which case it falls out of the sacred and existential concept of love altogether. The fact it can originate in any circumstance is an evidence that it exists in every single aspect of our lives! It is life itself! Pure spirit indeed! We are born to love mother nature the same way we love our biological mother. She is also an intrinsic part of Nature after all! In short, love is the universal force that creates and holds everything together! We should therefore always welcome the feeling and never condemn ourselves for 'falling' in love!

The following week got underway, and Florence had to fly for a couple of days to the Middle East. I was very busy meeting with clients and visiting trade and technical associations. I had a multitude of objectives to accomplish and the prospect of being promoted, thus getting a better pay was my main motivator. Upon her return, days went by very quickly and I would spend my maximum free time available with Florence, respecting her resting hours which were critical for her to be able to face the often-gruesome schedule of a flight attendant. At the end of the day there was not a lot of time left for us to be together and more often than not we had to wait for several days before she was again entitled to take her time off. The staff at my hotel were used to her comings and goings and the male employees were delighted to see such a beautiful silhouette passing by the reception desk or the restaurant every now and then...

Despite the very short time we knew each other, our relationship was tremendously attaching to the point that I did my best to postpone my return to Brazil by several weeks and ended up staying in Paris for almost two full months as a result! It was like living in a dreamy fairy tale dreading the wake-up time and enjoying each other's company to the fullest! We were both bewitched by the entrancing passion we felt for each other. She was a very mature woman for her age, and we had a tremendously rich and free intellectual connection. On one occasion, we were having a very spirited discussion during a late Saturday lunch at one of those cozy restaurants in Montmartre (an artistic and bohemian Parisian neighborhood) and a couple of French-speaking Americans couldn't help but to invite themselves into our discussion by confessing that their imagination made them try to guess and portray our probable love story, so entertained they were by our vivid conversation and the occasional kisses we would give each other across the tiny table. After a nice introduction, we ended up having lunch together and making interesting new acquaintances.

Florence had a 'dormant' boyfriend so to speak who wanted to marry her. His name was Antoine and on one occasion we got together for a cup of coffee at Florence's insistent request for me to give her my honest opinion of him... she was a free spirit and deemed such an otherwise awkward encounter as something natural and spontaneous. He was a nice man, and I was very surprised indeed to learn that he knew pretty much everything about our relationship! He went as far as telling me, "Well, we have one thing in common and that thing is called Florence!"

When I asked Florence about it, she simply dismissed me by saying, "I don't lie to anybody, so it is up to him to accept the fact that I want to be with you, or else... he is absolutely free to go!" She was indeed a liberated soul.

As everything else in life, things evolve and sometimes simply must come to an end. This is especially true for dream like situations that come to us like a present but must for some unknown reason be returned after a while. Maybe because they are too good to last without losing their thrill. Time had come for me to return to Brazil and to my career, and Florence had found a superb opportunity to change her professional life for a much better and more exciting activity. She had been invited to form a children's support institution in Mauritius that would care for learning difficulties. This is what she had studied for, and the prospect was simply irrefutable.

We both knew that the very short yet intense time we had spent together was meant to be exactly that: an amazing discovery of a very special encounter between two beings that must be shared and enjoyed while it lasts in order to be treasured and remembered as an idyllic situation forever. As it really happened afterwards, it would help me establish some kind of ideal paradigm of love, although the concept of love does not permit any grading or conceptualization.

Each and every woman has a particularity of her own that makes us fall in love and never forget her no matter the amount of time spent together. The intensity of the relation is what really matters, not its length, and we often become captivated by details that emerge on and off subsequently only to make us feel that we have touched something of real significance in our life story. This could either be a female's fragrance, the texture of her skin, the inflexion of her voice, the usage of particular expressions, the way she expresses a climax, her maturity or the lack of it, her propensity to feel pleasure, her sensitivity, tenderness, and I could go on forever...

I must say that Florence displayed most of the above distinctive peculiarities in such an inimitable way that it made her an extraordinary woman. Each time I think of her, and I will always remember her tenderly and intensely, I can almost feel her smell or hear the intonation of her voice whispering sweet and exciting words in my ear. She will stay in my heart forever!

SÃO PAULO II

As I returned to São Paulo, I literally immersed myself into work and some months later, I finally got promoted, but as the saying goes, 'be careful what you desire because it may well come true...' I was appointed to a management position that would require me to stay in São Paulo for most of the time. Besides hating the city with my guts, it was a very boring and uneventful position unlike my previous assignment that would take me quite frequently to the Amazon and literally around the world! After six months on the job, I was mastering the technique so to speak, to the point that I would go home — I had rented a small but nice condo located in a middle-class neighborhood — fairly early and have enough time to socialize and meet new people.

One of those new acquaintances was Isabelle, a beautiful girl much younger than me, from French descent and from a very rich family residing on both sides of the Atlantic. Apparently, I was fated to remain linked to France at least for some time to come... We met at her birthday party and the attraction was mutual. She was just twenty-one but with a demeanor of a young woman who knew exactly what she wanted in life. And gosh, did she know it! In the days following her birthday she would call me almost daily and we would spend hours on the phone discussing a wide array of subjects from mundane platitudes to rich subjects like the meaning of life, religion, psychology, philosophy (she was still a student and therefore well and freshly versed in those subjects...) and of course, love. My trips and some of my life stories would enchant her as well as her female friends and I could feel that her interest in me would grow steadily and consistently. She had two brothers and one older sister and her parents were highly educated individuals albeit very snobbish always displaying some kind of irritating aristocratic look… The mother, Moyra was very fond of me, and I could sense that she was proud of the fact that her young daughter would have a friend and a potential boyfriend like me, in other words, multilingual, fairly cultivated, still young and well-travelled, and especially full of stories that would captivate her attention and curiosity. Her father, Pierre-André, hated me with his guts because in his mind I was obviously after his money… something that was never among my life priorities although I knew very well its value and of course, the possibilities at hand.

Dinners at Isabelle's were an ordeal for me, especially each time that I had to share the table with Pierre-André. I was invariably subjected to a long questionnaire about my origins, education, tastes, career, acquaintances, future projects and so on, as the man would measure both my interest in grabbing his purse but also my real money-making potential if, in the worst-case scenario I ended up married with his daughter… In this dire circumstance, he would endeavor to monetize his nightmare as he did with everything else in his life by hiring me to work in one of his numerous companies! I was very conscious of the situation and I would greatly amuse myself in sneakily manipulating the conversation. Moyra and Isabelle were also very well aware of the embarrassing situation and would do their best to pathetically help me out by trying to tally my attributes to the old man who of course would remain defiantly unconvinced… I would definitely not make things easier for him either simply by acting naturally, being myself and purposely disregarding his so called social and economic stature…

A typical question was:

"So, what are your career aims? You intend to continue involved with international trade?"

He would very ably elevate the level of my modest lumber trading position in order to encourage me to stay within the boundaries of the professional/career bullshit, his favorite topic, to which I would nonchalantly respond, "I haven't made up my mind yet, however I feel very attracted to a career change, for example, switching into something more meaningful such as art…"

His predictable reaction was "well, an art merchant can indeed become very successful as long as he develops the right connections not only within the artistic universe itself, but also to other affluent industries who can afford to pay high prices for good artists and sometimes sponsor the latter."

His sheer disappointment would cut the air like a samurai sword by me saying "no, no, sir… I want to become an actor eventually, not a trader, which is something I already am and utterly dislike!"

At this point in the conversation, he would give up on all and every attempt to sway me into his crappy business arguments only to resume the same dialogue approximately a week later when, for his downright annoyance, I would show up yet again for dinner with Isabelle.

Moyra had Mediterranean origins, so the cultural identification was easy, especially in such a culturally arid environment as Brazil. I could sense her vivid interest in marrying her daughter with someone whose only apparent flaw was being penniless, which in her view was a transitory limitation easily and promptly solved by a simple wedding ceremony, in the face of the family's fortune… This view was obviously not corroborated by Pierre-André who would rather see me being run over by a bus or any other heavy vehicle for that matter!

The butler, Roberto, had sensed the situation and was greatly amused by it! His obviously malicious glances at me, which at times I would reciprocate, would suffice to reassure him that I fully understood that he was entirely on my side!

Nevertheless, my relationship with Isabelle was getting serious and it came to a point that I had to either take the initiative to make things official, or move on with my life... besides, Isabelle was getting increasingly anxious and demanding vis a vis the issue, understandably so, I must admit, given her young age. I was quite worried, not to say terrified at the perspective of spending the rest of my life or at the very least a good part of it in that social milieu that had absolutely nothing to do with me or with my life values. But then, again, I was still quite immature, and Isabelle was like a low hanging juicy and highly appetizing fruit...

To make a long story short, I finally decided to take what would reveal itself later as an absolutely wrong and precipitous step, and we got married with all the pomp and circumstance demanded by Pierre-André, in a posh church followed by a banquet for such a huge crowd, that it gave me the impression that the entire city was there... Pierre André had obviously managed to turn my marriage into a PR affair that would yield him dividends for the months and years to come in terms of contacts, influence and prestige. Isabelle was happy as a butterfly flying amidst spring flowers in full blossom and that was what really mattered to me. We went to live in my tiny apartment in a bohemian and lively area of the city.

As expected, Pierre Andre invited me a week later to join

him for lunch at his office — he had a second butler at his service over there — and, 'noblesse oblige', would have all his luncheons in a private, cozy restaurant located on the rooftop of the building just next to his helicopter's landing pad.

"So, my dear Mr Axel, how have you been?" he asked, squeezing my hand like a boa constrictor. The man was evidently making a huge effort to appear nice to me, especially now that he had finally lost the battle... without conceding defeat for that matter, as I would soon understand!

"I am doing fine, Sir," I replied politely.

"I hope you are making my Isabelle happy," he exclaimed in a vigorous tone, very usual among executives or successful entrepreneurs who want to instill energy into a conversation or to intimidate the other person by defining at once who is in command of the situation. He finally released my hand from the uncomfortable squeeze...

"Well, sir, this is a question that you'd better ask Isabelle herself..." I replied coolly looking straight at his small and unappealing eyes. "You know women, I went on, they are never satisfied and are always inventing new necessities in order to satisfy their desires..." It was as if I had thrown a glass of cold water in his face! Suddenly his opaque smile disappeared, and his face turned solemn and almost severe...

"Well, as you know, my daughter was brought up with abundance and there is no reason whatsoever that she should live without it now... Euh... with all due respect Axel, I would be ready to complement your income if needed in order to assure that she does not lack anything..." I had gotten used to the expression "with all due respect" since I had heard it quite often only to know that every time someone would preface a statement using the terms "with all due respect", sheer disrespect for my feelings or opinions would follow!

"In the first place, I can assure you that there's no scarcity whatsoever in our lives," I scoffed back. "What you call abundance is, in my view, the vast array of superfluous and, with all my due respect as well, often stupid objects that serve no purpose but to replace what is really important in one's life…" My irritation towards the man's arrogance was growing stronger by the day, and I couldn't care less about his money especially knowing that he would extort a hefty price should I walk into the trap of ever accepting his 'generosity'.

"Mr Axel," he started off with what I thought would be a long lecture on the benefits of money accumulation, "the reason I invited you for lunch today is to offer you a position in one of my companies… a good position indeed! I think you could contribute to the development of our businesses and, who knows, build a good and profitable career in our organization."

His tactics were smart… in case I accepted the offer, I would become his employee meaning that he would be able to exercise full control of my and Isabelle's lives for as long as I stayed employed in his organization. Needless to say, my short career, despite my disinclination to pursue it for the long haul anyway, would obviously end up in Pierre-André's hands who would manipulate it at his diktat, hence maintaining me in a short leash at all times so to speak…

"Dear Pierre-André, what if I accepted your generous offer and then my relationship with your daughter went sour after some time?" I fired back sending my bullet right on target…" Would you keep my employment on my own merits or, in the event that I was the one guilty of having caused the problem with her, you would rather kick me in the ass regardless of my achievements and perceived value?"

"Mr Axel, (I hated the way he called me Mr Axel but his aim was obviously to keep the formality hence a prudent distance from me…) to be honest with you, the offer comes with some strings attached, meaning that I am making you the offer because you married my daughter, otherwise I would never present you with such a good opportunity in the face of what I would call your rebellious behavior…" He was obviously becoming increasingly irritated with the course of the conversation since I had once again managed to push him into a corner…

"In this case Pierre-André, I must gently decline the offer since it simply amounts to a disguised way for you to throw money into your daughter's life without offending me so to speak, but also without any regard whatsoever for my own professional merits… and this is something that luckily for you, I cannot accept or even admit! I apologize for the bluntness Pierre-André, however your offer in my humble opinion amounts to a well disguised bribe, nothing else."

"You are simply too proud, Mr Axel… but please explain, why do you affirm that I am lucky anyway?"

"Simply because if I were who you think I am, then your cherished money would really be imperiled! You forget that a woman in love can be manipulated in order to influence or even blackmail her own father if necessary. If your daughter was married to an ill-intentioned individual which is what you are illogically persuaded, I am, simply because I don't value money the way you do, you would be in big trouble by now! This is why I consider you a lucky man when it comes to me and to my authentic relationship with Isabelle."

"What kind of value does money have to you anyway?" he asked, defiantly trying to hide what appeared like a subtle shade of relief on his face. After all, my argument was crystal clear and carried a fair share of irrefutable logic within it.

"Well, money for me only acquires value the moment it is spent, preferably well spent. Before that, it amounts to a mere stupid accumulation to the benefit of a handful of privileged individuals in detriment of all others, since we live in a world where most people don't have enough money anyway, far from it or even worse, cannot even provide food or clean water to care for themselves and their families! Money is an energy that can be well or badly handled or, which is worse, wrongly manipulated! In the latter case, it is often the root cause of violence, wars, exterminations, rapes and so forth... this is why I despise the notion of money buildup just for building up fortunes especially when it is used as a negative energy, or simply accumulated for the sake of gathering power upon others which is frequently the case." That was precisely his case by the way...

"Mr Axel, your ideas won't take you far I'm afraid, and I remain very concerned about my daughter's future... so, please do not close the door completely to my invitation... I suggest we resume this conversation on another occasion since now I have a very important meeting to attend."

This was basically the first and the last conversation I would have with Pierre-André on the subject. Our relationship remained cordial yet with the usual and unavoidable misunderstandings that would occasionally pop up here and there in the face of our irresolvable differences.

If I was honest with myself, I had to admit that with the passing of time, my relationship with Isabelle was gradually fading. We were diametrically different in terms of temperament, character, aims, dreams, concepts regarding life values, and perception of our fellow humans. All those differences pointed inexorably towards a break-up to take place sooner or later. Sex was OK, however a far cry from Angelina's wild love-making in the currents of the Jutaí at dusk or Keiko's extreme sensitivity and tenderness which would more than compensate for her lack of eyesight and make her a true master in the art of love, or even Florence's sensuality, natural elegance and tremendous sex appeal that would make her an extremely enviable 'feline mistress' and a second to none, French lover! Women like them would greatly inspire me and awaken in me a feminine empathy that would elevate my love for them to sublime levels. Those relationships of unforgettable love filled with tremendous exhilaration would transcend any trivial and inconsequential rapports such as the one I was having with my wife. I consider myself a very wealthy man in terms of recollections I have amassed in my passion for inspirational women, meaning the majority of those that had crossed my path in life. I was capable of resuscitating smells, textures, dialogues imaginary or real, feelings and even visions of my loved ones no matter the amount of time elapsed... Indeed, it is my view that a true love never dies! It stays engraved forever in our souls and contributes to our inner growth as a human being by enhancing our sense of intimacy, tenderness and connectedness to the other.

Isabelle would definitely not fit into that category! She was hopelessly blocked by her strict education where sex equaled procreation and almost a necessary chore, just an essential part of the script of being a good spouse. My frequent attempts to make her extrapolate all those engrained beliefs and taboos inherited from her father, and abandon herself in pleasure were in vain... maybe she was not really in love with me after all, as she so often affirmed whenever we fought, which had become quite a common pattern, to be honest. Her attitude was politically correct at all times to the point of exasperation. I soon realized that I had trapped myself into a life-style and a perspective where I definitely did not belong. I grew bored by literally everything, from the sumptuous dinners at my in-laws' 'palace' that felt more like an endless abyss due to the emptiness of their mundane conversations where superficiality, materialism and sheer mediocrity would prevail, to Isabelle's growing frustration at my restive attitude towards most of the egoistic values inculcated in her brain throughout her upbringing. My relentless efforts to penetrate her persona and explore the true female behind all the veils and her well-rehearsed 'comme-il—faut' attitude, were in vain. Isabelle was not destined to stay married to me, and I not to her, period!

We divorced soon after completing two years of marriage, as expected shortly after she confessed her love to a well to do young industrialist to the utter delight of Pierre-André. Their relationship had been going on for some time and was far from being a platonic affair... I will never forget her father's disdain when I went to her parent's house for a last visit in order to politely say farewell. He probably felt vindicated from all the insolent and sometimes brazen dialogues we had had with each other, and at the same time relieved by the fact that he would never again have to face a situation where he would end up ridiculed by his own arguments...

I was obviously saddened and frustrated by the situation that initially felt like failure to me, since obviously no one takes pleasure in being betrayed or left behind, far from it. The reverse however is also true, in the sense that it is equally tough or maybe even more so to leave somebody especially without any aggravating reason that could be used as a self-justification for one's change of heart... All that being considered, a feeling of freedom and relief was starting to grow in me. Not only the freedom from the commitment to someone so diametrically different and so contrasting in terms of culture, beliefs and expectations, but mainly the relief from all that fake, miserable ego centered existence they proudly called 'normality'.

In the subsequent few months, I decided to dedicate myself to my work, albeit bureaucratic and as always quite unpleasant. It allowed me at least to distance myself from all the noise of that inhospitable city and its social castes, so attached, as is the case with every caste-based society, to the mystification of social stratification that would produce a hollow group of individuals devoid of any real interest... I definitely knew that I would not stay there for too long!

Life is made of constant change and movement, and we're all subject to it even if we prefer to persuade ourselves that we stand still in time and space! This is a risky illusion conducive to numerous mix-ups such as the sabotaging of our true self and is also one of the main paradoxes leading to the miserable status quo of most human societies. One of the measures we can use to gauge whether we are leading a satisfying existence lies, in my view, in our ability to adapt to change... So, not long after my divorce, change came knocking at my door indeed! The company needed me for a new and important management assignment that would take me first to North America, however, even before undertaking the new challenge I was requested to go to the Amazon region one last time in order to organize some remaining supplies of precious timber that my successor was not able to accomplish or, failing that, collect the amounts still due by a couple of short-tempered individuals who were persuaded they could do away with crime against the organization without being bothered. No matter my level of success in this endeavor, the timber department would be closed forever thereafter.

Apparently, my successor had not been able to perform the job and ended up resigning out of frustration or fear. The task at hand was not a simple one at all, since the suppliers were true bandits trying to make an easy buck no matter how. Dealing with those folks was complicated and dangerous as much as the treacherous waters of the Amazon River and its innumerous effluents. In fact, I was a total stranger in what had become their relatively well-known territory... To make matters even more complicated, I was supposed to close all files during a single trip, meaning that it would certainly take me several weeks if not months to complete the assignment before returning to town.

A week later I was ready to go and I confess that I was thrilled at the perspective of meeting some of my old acquaintances, especially Angelina — I had lost track of her for a very long time indeed... and some of the other intriguing personages such as the prostitutes I had spent long nights with, at times just chatting about life and about their unchecked, formidable tales over a glass of whisky... in fact many glasses of whisky! I confess I was also anxious to meet again all those unique characters I was supposed to negotiate with, since they were true legends with their almost unbelievable life stories. They were fun to be with and time would fly by listening to their sagas. I definitely needed to experience some degree of adventure after that dull period of frustration I had gone through while married to Isabelle.

AMAZON II

The flight to Manaus was as uneventful as usual and so was the subsequent connection to Tefé. Upon arrival in this little town of the upper Solimões — one of the two main effluents of the Amazon River — time would take on a completely different pace and the archetypes would change quite dramatically... Miners, lumberjacks, smugglers, assassins who would kill anyone for money and who would even have different tariffs depending on the importance of the victim-to-be and so on... I do recall meeting one individual called Rangel who would kill anybody "within the National Territorial boundaries" please (!) for what was the equivalent of US$2,000.00 at that time plus expenses, those consisting of travel, food and cheap hotels!

My arrival in Tefé was marred by an unforgettable event! Two women were fiercely fighting in the main square for the preference of someone who apparently both coveted. The fight was one of the most passionate and resolute performances I ever saw in my entire life! They were literally tearing each other apart so to speak, starting with the few clothes both were wearing under the torching Amazonian sun. The scene was one of the sexiest enactments one can think of despite the viciousness involved, since both women were very young and attractive. They had long black hair, ferocious black eyes, shining skin enhanced by the voluptuous sweat abundantly pouring along their young and athletic bodies. No one would dare intervene let alone arbitrate such a violent brawl, and all bystanders could apparently do was to hope that both would soon get tired and give up the commotion... A few minutes later both were literally naked, and sighs and groans of excitement could be heard from the small crowd, the moment those wonderful breasts now stained with blood with their nipples violently quivering and shaking in the air were displayed. I must say that a female squabble can get much more vicious than a male one maybe because women rarely settle their dispute physically so to speak as is often the case with men especially under those latitudes. On the other hand, men contrary to women tend to follow certain 'rules', influenced as they are by movies and TV shows... finally, I decided to intervene in order to avoid a potential drama unfolding, and got a couple of bruises myself before managing to finally keep them apart... I will never forget that stunning feeling of touching those extremely soft, wet, yet burning hot skins while feeling my fingers skid through the sweat and blood that covered parts of their exposed body... I will never erase from my memory the feeling, the texture, the engaging intensity of the confrontation, the extreme passion, and, last but not least, the smell of that cheap yet powerful and intoxicating perfume mixed with their sweat during those incredible moments... Later on in the day, I happened to pass by the same square and one could still see blood stains on the pavement. Maybe those stains will remain there for a long time as a symbol of how deep in hell unresolved passion can lead women or men, if left unrestrained...

The small boat that would take me up-river and then onto the Jutaí where my first supplier had his railroad tie operations, was leaving within three days, so I decided to try to locate Angelina or 'O Diabo Loiro' (the blond devil), as she was known in that remote region. Soon though my search reached a roadblock as I was informed that she had decided to head back to Chicago in order to work with her father in order to help him manage the family empire. Some people would go as far as telling me that she had been arrested in Miami and that her father had to spend a fortune with lawyers and bail payments in order to avoid her outright imprisonment for smuggling wildlife. A local woman with whom Angelina entertained a friendly rapport, told me that subsequently to her bruises with the US police authorities, Angelina had married one of her 'filthy rich' father's associates with whom she had twin boys... The news hit me like a bombshell! How come such a free and wild spirit so dedicated to nature and leading an adventurous existence by her own choice, decide to spend the rest of her life in an air-conditioned corner office in one of the Chicago towers and lead a mundane existence? But then, who was I to judge anyway, given my own rather disastrous marriage shortly followed by a divorce with Isabelle? Well, at least I had declined Pierre-André's money and figured out sooner than later that that kind of dreary life was definitely not made for me!

It is human nature to yearn for things and especially for people when suddenly those aren't available to us any longer... I had spent years without really thinking about Angelina except for some occasional reminiscences that would pop up into my mind sporadically, however upon getting that latest news, I was baffled, in a state of shock and utter disbelief! A deep melancholy took over my heart and some kind of despair invaded my whole being as I realized that we would not share those extraordinarily great moments together ever again... I would no longer hear her firm yet sweet voice questioning me about my behavior or ideas, and I would never touch her warm skin beneath the sluggishly running waters of the Jutaí while trying to penetrate her soft and welcoming vagina... We would never again kiss and lick each other languidly whilst making love and reaching one of those long and simultaneous orgasms that would propel us into a dazzling spinning motion as if trying to follow the movements of the leaves far above us hanging from those majestic trees, whose multitude of colors would then turn around in a crazy motion to the point of melding into extraordinary new tones never seen before, having the clouds and the bright moon of a clear Amazonian evening as a fabulous backdrop against that bewitching setting... She was gone as if some part of me had vanished forever to never come back.

I had never heard let alone seen Angelina again since our love affair! I wished her all the good which undoubtedly, she deserved, especially being happily married and with a not-so-boring life! I was deeply gratified to keep all those memories that I could bring back into my mind whenever I felt lonely as if I was once again close to her, holding her waist and listening to her reassuring voice! She was a wonderful woman by any account this was for sure! This is life... encounters and separations that come to us in order to yield yet another encounter... and then, the following one and so on, in a frantic dance of the chairs of existence! Genesis presupposes decay and termination of what was there before... The dawn arises further to the darkness of the night. Paulette, Sophia, Angelina, Keiko, Florence, Isabelle, and all the other magnificent women who would basically conduct, teach and enrich the truth in my life had ultimately to graciously sneak out, often independently of my own will, in order to make room to the following one. The alternative would be tantamount to creating a suffocating obstruction to what I consider to be the most important development in a man's existence — his experiences with women and their vital teachings of love, serenity and sensitivity. This however can hardly be achieved with a single woman, and the same applies evidently to a woman, due to the quasi-inherent limitations of a lifelong relationship between couples and I say this without excluding it, obviously, however they constitute very few honorable exceptions.

That same night, I went for a walk along the bank of the river and lost myself in all those good and extraordinary memories I had kept vividly in my mind from the short yet very intense period I had spent with Angelina in what amounted to a pure state of enchantment, freedom and passion.

My dreamy state came to a sudden halt however, when a swirl in the water called my attention. At first, I thought it was some kind of a fish feeding itself on mosquito's larvae or something bigger in the surface of the water, but slowly I could distinguish a silhouette emerging from the dark waters of the night heading in my direction... to my surprise, a beautiful woman reached what apparently were her clothes behind a tree and very naturally greeted me... "Good evening... quite warm tonight eh?" I approached her and to my amazement I soon realized that that remarkable silhouette was nobody else but one of the fiery fighters I had dispersed just a few hours ago at the town square! She had obviously recognized me and was gazing at me with a mixture of shame and a diabolic malicious expression. I came closer and could distinguish the recent contusions she would probably carry on her body for quite some time!

"Hi, how are you faring after what happened to you?" I asked bluntly.

"Well, before you jump to conclusions," she replied whilst dressing herself hastily, "I must tell you that the lesson I gave that stupid bitch was long due! She is very nosy and jealous, with no reason by the way, and she has been interfering heavily in my life lately! If anything, she deserved the slaps I gave her! By the way,

I must thank you for your intervention, otherwise I would have killed her... literally!"

"Slaps? Well, you are being rather modest right now, aren't you? What is your name anyway?" I asked while discovering a pair of tremendously expressive, almond-shaped black eyes in the darkness of the night.

"My real name is Isadora, but at work I am called Jade... You see, I am a dancer... or if you prefer, a prostitute! I am totally independent though, and I strictly chose the men I go to bed with... or maybe not, whenever they prefer to just share my company, or even take me to certain events as a simple escort, sometimes as far as Manaus and introduce me as their wife or girlfriend on such occasions where they don't dare introduce their wives either because they are ugly or simply too stupid to represent them... I am quite proud of my job, and I do it with professionalism and also with pleasure whenever possible believe it or not!"

"This is what I call a complete introduction," I said jokingly, and she finally smiled at me displaying a perfect range of impeccably white teeth.

Later I would realize that Isadora was a woman of character hence ready to spread her dubious credentials without shame or reservation, depending of course, on the occasion and on the person she was talking to.

"Where do you work? At the Vagão? I continued hesitantly. "That was the only well-known brothel in Tefé..."

"Oh no!" she replied, almost outraged. "As I told you before, I am fully independent, something that would be impossible in case I wanted to work there... I simply wouldn't be able to choose my partners or to practice the tariffs I want to!"

"You practice the same pricelist for every client?" I asked

trying to be polite and genuinely curious about her activity.

"Well, it depends on each circumstance... essentially it varies according to what I am expected to do and for how long. For example, if a given customer requests my services for a couple of days or more, I must charge for the time I would otherwise spend earning perhaps more money than being with him for that length of time... You see, I must survive like everybody else. The difference resides in the fact that I assume and fully realize that I depend on men to assure my sustenance whilst most women who claim to be honest and straight don't! And those who don't, end up being the most expensive, believe me... and in the end offer very little in return!"

"Well," I said jokingly, "now you just gave me the clearest definition of what opportunity cost is."

"What the hell does that mean?" she inquired not without a shade of malice emerging in her eyes.

"Forget about it, it is a silly concept utilized by silly businesspeople anyway," I replied closing the subject.

Isadora was certainly honest in her clarifications regarding her "professional" activity and I was left with the impression I was dealing with a professional of any other business branch. She was very articulate and spoke a perfect Portuguese without any of the typical accent of the Amazon region. Later she told me that she had come from Rio de Janeiro following a Greek ship captain with whom she had fallen in love and who had dropped her off in Manaus after taking her with him around the globe for nearly three years! She even spoke a broken Greek, enough to make herself understood though, which was quite an accomplishment given the complexity of the Greek language. In short, she was a very interesting, smart and captivating woman certainly far more than my ex-wife who carried all pedigrees yet was sold off to her father's milieu emulating, in the final analysis, the behavior of a prostitute in a well concealed manner of course, hidden behind the constant display of that snobbish and pathetic dramaturgy… That extremely well disguised and socially accepted lack of morals constitutes a far worse type of unethical behavior than Isadora's straightforward assumed profession no matter the integrity, honesty principles or scruples that are applied to the judgement… It was hard to admit, but Isadora showed a much higher degree of candor and openness than Isabelle, let alone her father, who would only value money and nothing else!

We stayed there for at least a couple of hours chatting as if we were a couple of old friends reminiscing about our respective lives. She came across as an inspiring woman, fairly well travelled, full of experiences some of them quite intriguing indeed. It was easy for me to understand the reasons why some men would hire her escort services and take her along to social events in lieu of their own wives. She was classy and knew how to behave according to the environment and what was expected of her.

Obviously, I do not preach prostitution as being a good thing especially for all those poor souls that are exploited by sloppy individuals or organizations dedicated to human trafficking and exploitation! Nor do I defend the attributes of the profession as such. This being said, it is my belief that society at large has stigmatized the activity either by not putting it in its right context and circumstances, or by not judging each situation with exemption and on its own merits. This lack of understanding and the proliferation of hypocritical taboos surrounding prostitution, make things even more upsetting in all of its aspects and, which is even worse, are at the origin of public health issues that arise mainly because of the discrimination suffered by the individuals who, more often than otherwise, are forced to prostitute themselves! Just to cite two definitions or concepts in order to illustrate the point, the Webster's dictionary defines prostitution as 'to use something valuable such as talent in a way that is not appropriate or respectable and specially to earn money'. I wonder how many human activities, professional or otherwise, many of them indeed despicable, exist that would perfectly fit the definition! I would even go as far as to contend that in different societies there are a myriad of activities that are neither respectable nor appropriate but still are used exclusively to earn money!

Wikipedia, in its site, affirms that 'the legal status of prostitution varies from country to country, sometimes from region to region within a given country.' In other words, its legal status is so subjective and aleatory that it varies greatly, which obviously opens the door for an infinity of injustices that root themselves probably in sheer ignorance or rather in a total lack of a more profound understanding of all the aspects involved in the activity and in its often-unfair criminalization around the world!

My final point is that one simply cannot judge and condemn an individual because she or he practices prostitution as a way of life without first knowing the individual, his true motivations, problems, life story, traumas, vicissitudes, imperatives and so on… It is exceedingly easy to categorize another human being through our own filters of fear, prejudice, anxiety, dissatisfaction or despair! What makes us think or believe that a prostitute cannot be as beautiful a person as anybody else? Or maybe a much more beautiful person than for example most 'respectable' executives who live in fear, lies, bluff, dishonesty, or criminal behavior of all kinds for that matter? Well, I've met extraordinary women in my life who were professionals of sex, and I can guarantee that they were much better human beings than the vast majority of the executives, male or female I've met. Maybe the term "prostitute" should be revisited in order to rid the terrible stigma applied to an already highly distorted issue!

To make a long story short, I couldn't avoid nurturing feelings of attraction vis a vis Isadora and a week after our first furtive encounter by the riverbank, we started a spicy affair that would transcend all my expectations towards her ability to genuinely love a man and make him feel on top of the world! She was one of the most intelligent women I had ever met, her sense of humor was second to none, and, quite obviously, she was a master in love making… We men usually think that we've learned our way in terms of satisfying a woman sexually yet after meeting Isadora I realized that I was merely a neophyte! The environment of course helped, since we were in the middle of the most astonishing nature one can imagine. She knew some incredible spots in the middle of nowhere, along the banks of the 'Igarapés' (kind of 'arms' of a given main river that can reach lengths up to hundreds of kilometers literally cutting through the impenetrable jungle). She was dark haired with masses of shiny hair descending all the way to her waist, with superbly shaped breasts with two huge nipples that would fight their way in order to trespass, like two tenacious intruders, her waves of black hair… her skin would sparkle under the sun and radiate the heat and light that her body would adsorb like a golden lizard under the scorching sun of the Amazon. We had very intense yet fairly short periods of time together and I cannot recall any other woman that would make me have sex so repeatedly during a single night! She was wild and always ready for pleasure, and she would make me have long and profound orgasms often coupled with hers…

Isadora had assured me that she was absolutely safe and disease free… I took her word for granted not without wondering how she could be so sure about it in a small, isolated town with such a precarious medical structure composed of a single, small hospital where quite often medication would have to be ordered from Manaus. Her explanation was three-fold, firstly because one of the three available doctors who would test her regularly was a specialist in the field, second because literally all of her clients were married, and finally because she would use protection whenever a doubt would arise. In any case she would favor 'well to do' men often with children hence the ones who could not afford to have a health problem of that kind. We spent all my available time together on three different occasions that I was supposed to connect through Tefé in order to reach the far-flung destinations where my suppliers were usually located. Obviously my first trip upriver was postponed by ten days or so and Isadora's clients grew very frustrated by her absence during that period… The distances I had to cover using quite varied and incredible means were staggering! Time turns into a highly relative concept as it is indeed, but it is evidenced in those remote areas, and one has to be very patient and understanding in order to accomplish whatever task is at hand, which often stands in sheer contrast with what could be almost instantly achieved in the so called 'civilized world'.

During my third, and what would probably be my last stopover in Tefé, Isadora came to fetch me at the small airport and while driving me to the hotel, confided to me in a shy manner that she had thought of a very interesting experience to be shared specifically with me, and that she could arrange the details in case I was interested. She went on enigmatically saying that she had imagined the situation with me in particular because of my acute and highly perceptive sense of the 'feminine essence".

"You are the only man with whom I can have full confidence in discussing these kinds of things," she started as if preparing my spirit for what was about to come. "Am I right to assume so?"

"Well, my dear," I replied as naturally as I could despite my growing curiosity on the subject, "I suppose so when it comes to confidence, although I don't have a clue as to what you are leading to…"

"Let us say that I enjoy sharing experiences with persons from my same sex from time to time. This doesn't mean that I am a lesbian so to speak, but merely that I can extract immense pleasure by spending some time with other women… and I do allow myself to do it sporadically! Are you shocked by this revelation?"

"Not particularly shocked, not really," I replied trying my best to sound natural. "I won't say that you do not surprise me at all, since this would be a lie, but, on the other hand, I am not shocked either. I think people are free to do whatever they wish with their body except harming it or harming someone else in the process."

"Well, all I'm trying hard to do here is to give you some hints about what I want to propose we do together… maybe by now you have already figured out what this is all about?"

"Not exactly…" I lied, since I had already a pretty good idea of where Isadora was leading to…" But I can try a couple of wild guesses, if this facilitates your task…"

"From the expression in your eyes I know that you already know what we are talking about! Come on, give me a break, will you?" She uttered laughing loudly and nervously like a little girl caught with her hand in a candy jar… "I'll put it bluntly, OK? I am suggesting a ménage à trois with me, my female friend and you!"

Now I was quite shocked indeed although very excited by the idea… Isadora obviously noticed my perplexity and tried to tame my emotion in a sweet way…

"You know, this is perhaps a crazy idea so we should maybe leave it for later, or simply forget about it altogether!"

"No, no…" I sort of recomposed myself, "why don't you let me think it over for a couple of hours and then we can discuss the issue a little deeper? You see, I am obviously attracted to the idea, but all this is absolutely new to me, so I need some time to digest it so I can give you an honest answer."

"Would you believe me if I told you that this is a totally new situation for me too?" she immediately interjected. "You probably think that because of my profession, those things are common practice, right? Well, I have never taken part in those kinds of eccentric sexual acts, simply because this for me presupposes first and foremost trust and genuine attraction towards and between all three participants, which is the case as far as I am concerned with you and Eloisa."

"And who tells you that Eloisa will be attracted to me and that I will be attracted to her for that matter?" I asked with a grain of irony…

"This is exactly why I am coming up with the idea specifically with you! Because I know you both, therefore, I can bet that there will be an instantaneous attraction between you. You will see, she is gorgeous, interesting and an extremely sensuous woman."

"I assume she is also a…"

"Oh no! Not at all!" she exclaimed cutting me off on the spot. "Not only is she not a prostitute but she is a renowned anthropologist with several articles published in the most important Brazilian and international magazines in the field, and she is married to Rogerio Batista who happens to be the richest man in the entire region!"

"Well, I hope I will not get in trouble with Mr Batista in case we proceed with your crazy, yet I must admit, very exciting idea…"

"Really don't worry about that," she exclaimed laughingly. "After all, you are dealing with professionals here!"

"I thought she was not a…"

"As I told you already, she is not! What is happening to you Axel? For you, now that you've met me, the only possibility of being a professional is being a prostitute? I am very flattered by your lofty categorization of my profession, let me tell you!"

I apologized and after some minutes of spicy jokes and a good amount of laughter, I obviously acquiesced pleasurably to Isadora's proposal!

Eloisa was, as per Isadora's description, a very surprising personage! She was petite, displaying what seemed to be a perfect body that made her look like a doll… she had lovely big, dark blue eyes and red, meaty lips that would grant her a great deal of sensuality. Her black hair was long like Isadora's, and her presence would diffuse a certain sense of finesse and sophistication. She would act as a pole of attraction as soon as she would enter any kind of setting despite her small physical stature, thanks not only to her beauty but mainly to her feline and delicate demeanor. She was one of those people who seem to know exactly their place in space in any possible environment and situation.

The three of us met in a restaurant for a light meal in order to make acquaintance with each other and also to discretely discuss the main subject that led to our meeting. I was intrigued and quite aroused by the opportunity to approach such a delicate issue with a beautiful, literate, profound and interesting woman, who was in fact even married! Our conversation ranged from anthropology, her specialty at the origin of her migration to the Amazon region, to the different circumstances that had made the three of us meet in such a remote place to more trivial aspects of our lives, tastes, anecdotal stories about our past, and so on… Eloisa was very articulate and worldly, quite an exceptional woman, rarely to be found within those latitudes! After about an hour talking as we were discussing the different aspects of Eloisa's next article, she suddenly turned to me and said,

"You are a very attractive man; you know that right? Not only because of your looks but also because of the way you stare at women as if attempting to undress them in that moment… I would definitely like to get to know you better if the opportunity presents itself!"

Her sudden interjection, so direct and down to earth, had a tremendously strong effect on me that almost made me lose control of the situation. "Well," I mumbled, almost incoherently, "I would like to know you better too…"

"Well, well, well," exclaimed Isadora laughingly, "I knew the chemistry between you both would function! What did I tell you Axel? I would love to invite both of you for dinner at home next Thursday, so you can practice your desire to get to know each other better," were Isadora's words not without a speck of malice… It was Monday and Eloisa acquiesced not before consulting her agenda probably to check whether Rogerio, her husband, was supposed to be in town or not… I obviously agreed to the date on the spot as well, with an acute sense of expectation and anticipation that wouldn't leave my mind and parts of my body for a single moment during the following three days…

I spent those remaining three days before Thursday jockeying with the office people who were wondering why my stay in Tefé was taking so long this time around! It was very easy for me to justify delays when travelling through the Amazon region and it was a piece of cake to convince them that things were as they were supposed to be, period! At the end of the day, they couldn't care less as to my whereabouts, as long as I got the job done! Not a walk in the park by any measure, let me tell you!

It is difficult to believe in the quantity of different, surprising and bizarre personages one encounters in the middle of the jungle! I had already met quite a few but I could add many more to my array for as long as I stayed in the region. Each one of them had an amazing life story to tell and one could spend hours, if not entire days listening to true or maybe not so true ones, it didn't really matter at the end of the day! Those usually spicy narratives were all highly intriguing so much so that they could easily be turned into a book by themselves! The lawlessness of the place facilitated things in the sense that most legal, social or psychological barriers would melt or simply disappear, hence every account would be told in its raw, fantastic, and sometimes unbelievable version! The fantastic reports of all those lives now coming together in such a remote place would convey a sense of comfort in one's own life story no matter how intriguing or uneventful. It was as if the life drama of one person would relativize the drama of the next one and so on subsequently late into the night, when the effect of the incredible amounts of alcohol consumed would play a moderating effect making everybody feel sorry about the next fellow but relieved about their own fate. In the end, all participants would end up having a restful sleep.

The trick or the magical empathy that enables a person to understand and identify with a different outcome to a similar situation in others, consists in the ability of the original storyteller to mimic their way of thinking and thus replicate it in imagination in order to subsequently manifest it in the context of their life story. It is maybe easier to accept feelings so clearly manifested in such a remote place, perhaps due to a sheer lack of the stresses of modern life, or the constant distractions one usually has in a big city. The fact of the matter is that we end up connecting in higher, more profound psychological levels facilitated by the perception that the so called educational or the overall social level of the other individual becomes relative and at times totally irrelevant.

After some time being immersed in that type of milieu, I could calm down and relativize many aspects of my own life especially the negative, stressful ones I used to go to bed with, night after night in São Paulo. Slowly, I started to realize the true meaning of Thoreau's wise words, in fact of one distinct word that when repeated three times acquired such a profound meaning, trivial indeed when detached in one single word — "Simplicity, simplicity, simplicity!" I was finally learning to pause in order to really enjoy being amongst people who had interesting stories to share beyond the frivolous and boring usual issues concerning money and possessions!

The prospect of having dinner at Isadora's on Thursday together with Eloisa and, most of all, having already picked a highly abrasive and exciting topic of conversation, possessed me during the three days left which seemed like an eternity! I simply couldn't concentrate on anything but the dinner, although nobody could ever make a guess about my state of mind throughout the several meetings I had with potential suppliers, who wanted to see me as soon as they knew I was in town. The meetings had at least the positive aspect of keeping me busy and forcing me to think about other things. Finally, Thursday arrived and after a torching day where temperatures reached forty-four degrees Celsius, with humidity close to one hundred per cent, I took a shower at five p.m. to come out at six thirty p.m. sweating as much as I was when entering it. After spraying lots of Azzaro, my favorite aftershave, (nope, they are not sponsoring the book!) all over my body, I dressed as casually and light as I could in order to withstand the heat of the night... my clothes however didn't differ significantly from my day's attire...

I arrived at Isadora's at eight p.m. sharp with a bouquet of almost faded roses that had travelled quite a long distance before arriving in Tefé, dangling valiantly with me on her doorstep, and rang the bell with a wobbly finger... as a matter of fact, my entire body was tremulous out of excitement and anticipation...

Isadora opened the door and after offering me a voluptuous kiss, showed me the way to an incredibly refreshed and cozy living room perfumed with a stimulating Sandalwood scent. She was bare foot, dressed in an old pair of jeans and a worn-down T-shirt that would in fact enhance her beauty in sheer disparity with the simplicity of her attire.

As I passed by the kitchen door, I could sense a delicious smell of what I guessed was some kind of a fish boil...

"I hope you like Tucunaré Bouillabaisse," Isadora asked me with a pinch of amusement in her voice. "You see, the fish has to be first and foremost very fresh... then it will all depend on the way it is cooked. This is why I prefer to prepare the Bouillabaisse with local, fresh fish from the river than to buy frozen, ocean fish that has probably lost all of its flavor and texture by the time it reaches Tefé."

"Well, I simply love Bouillabaisse! This being said, I've never tried one made with Tucunaré, but I couldn't agree more with you regarding the importance of cooking it with fresh fish," I exclaimed, as if postulating on a critical existential issue, without being able to hide the excitement in my voice.

"Now I shall have it cooked slowly by decreasing the intensity of the fire to a minimum, so that we will be able to savor it after our drinks when it shall be ready to be served… in the meantime, I shall have a quick shower and dress up for this very special occasion… Axel, the bar is just behind you, so please help yourself, will you?" and she disappeared laughingly.

I stayed alone in the living room and after pouring myself a generous dose of single malt, I started to imagine the potentially incredible night that lay ahead… Would they make good on the idea of a "ménage à trois?" Or maybe the whole thing was just an invention, a hoax, or simply a way of testing my nerves or even maybe just a deep fishing elucubration made up by Isadora in order to throw some excitement into the occasion? I would evidently prefer to imagine the former and its intricate development as the night would progress, with the alcohol playing its magic in soothing the atmosphere and in opening everybody's primordial cravings… In any event, I could safely anticipate a very interesting night with two extremely beautiful, charming, intellectually interesting and intriguing creatures, each one with her own rich life experiences. My mind would rush whilst creating a thousand hypothesis minute by minute. Maybe the whole thing was a plot engineered by Isadora in order to introduce me to Eloisa with a view to bringing us together… who knows? I was immersed in the middle of all those stimulating thoughts when a door suddenly opened and Eloisa came into the living room looking like an exotic princess, very distinguished, dressed in a long, light and totally transparent black low-necked dress that would contrast with her blue eyes, revealing a pair of imposing hard tits coming aggressively out of two generous, shapely breasts with goose bumps swelling out of a pair of sensuous dark areolas that made me feel like grabbing her and pressing her hard against my body... and this is exactly what happened when she approached me and gave me a moist kiss on my left cheek, calculatedly touching the corner confluence of my lips with hers, embracing me tight and squeezing her warm and firm breasts against my chest! I felt aroused by what was a hell of a direct inducement to my instinct of desire hence I reciprocated the embrace profusely. We probably stayed there holding each other tight for a good minute that seemed much longer given the fact that we had never been so close before. Finally, we let go of one another literally transfixed in fascination by what had just occurred,, undoubtedly willing to remain in the same position forever...

"Hello handsome, how have you been? It is really a great pleasure to see you again! I am thrilled, really!" she managed to mumble out of her apparent rapture. Those extremely warm and welcoming words would sound as an exaggeration if not preceded by our long, silent yet intense grip minutes before. I was thrilled by the prospect of a tremendously exciting evening. Eloisa came immediately across as a very intense and insightful woman as I would get the chance to corroborate over and over through the evening.

"I am fine, in fact much better now, to be honest!" I replied as a door opened and Isadora made her triumphant entrée dressed like an odalisque moving swiftly amidst an almost transparent layered pink dress displaying very subtle golden flower designs, her masses of long hair impeccably falling towards her waist and her huge dark nipples trespassing the veils each time she would make a very well-rehearsed and calculated movement. Suddenly all my doubts and conjectures faded away and I felt I was literally entering paradise!

"Here is our man!" she exclaimed with her very sexy voice. Her kiss came immediately, warm and soft on my lips and lasted enough to ensure Eloisa that we had a certain degree or rather lots of intimacy already so to speak. Then she turned around and gave Eloisa the same intense kiss grabbing her breasts and laughing loudly out of pleasure..." Oh my God, I just love these breasts!"

There was I, between two extremely attractive women, left guessing now delightfully about what was about to happen. An uncontrollable smile was involuntarily displayed on my mouth and I simply couldn't hang any other expression on my face. I felt a bit stupid but extremely happy to be there.

"Champagne everyone?" asked Isadora holding a bottle of Krug on one hand and three Champagne flutes on the other. Krug is one of the very best French Champagnes so both Eloisa and I acquiesced with no hesitation whatsoever. We sat down in what was a lovely living room and the Sandalwood scent would perfectly meld with both ladies' perfumes. The delicious Champagne would simply go down our throats with delight, waking up our bodies and spirits and guiding our eloquence towards a series of very interesting topics ranging from human relations, anthropology, politics, love and of course, sex! I was impressed with the intellectual level of both ladies let alone their up-to-date informative knowledge, given the distance between Tefé and any of the so-called civilized cities on the planet. I could easily spend the rest of my life with either, or both, without hesitation when it came to their scholarly level not to speak of course of their physical appearance!

Both were bemused at trying to find definitions that would explain their relationship, which turned out in the end to be nothing but an enjoyable love affair rather than a critical life decision to embrace homosexuality… They had met each other at the Vagão, one late evening when Eloisa's husband took her and a couple of friends visiting town for a night cap at the club. Isadora was out of duty that night and had agreed to replacing the manager, a friend of hers, who was on sick leave, and the conversation between both women flowed so flawlessly that it soon made them realize that there could be much more to their relationship than just a simple and trivial verbal exchange at a nightclub. Thereafter they would meet now and then to talk, read and after they both realized their strong mutual attraction, make love. Eloisa's husband being the typical Amazonian macho, wouldn't oppose the 'friendship' at all, on the contrary, he would favor it trusting, square minded as he was, that only an innocent and candid friendship could emerge between two women…

Finally, since it was getting late and I was very much looking forward to the 'post desert' activity, Isadora invited us to the table whilst opening a third bottle of Krug according to my still sober account" I hope you guys will also stick to Champagne. It goes very well with the Bouillabaisse and it is better not to mix it with something else that could make us sick…" Once again Eloisa and I happily agreed whilst literally attacking the Bouillabaisse which was simply delicious! The conversation revolved more and more towards sex as I felt highly privileged to be able to listen and to discuss all the enthralling aspects of the sexual involvement between those two intriguing ladies.

The tenderness with which they conveyed their emotions towards each other was so gentle yet so true and intense, that any person simply couldn't help but feel fatally attracted to both individuals.

"You understand, dear Axel, that the empathy and the unrestricted openness we both feel towards each other make us experience a unique kind of physical and emotional satisfaction that no man could ever grant in the face of his education, atavism, morals, taboos, you name it. The ideal for a woman would be to have sex with a woman in a man's body. Imagine all the delicateness of a female lover with a hard penis that would penetrate us delicately and at the same time know exactly how to caress our intimate parts the way only a woman knows…" interjected Isadora.

"What about making love with a transsexual?" I exclaimed.

"Oh, that is a totally different thing I suppose," said Eloisa. A transsexual individual usually dismisses his or her own original sexuality, his or her gender if you prefer, in favor of the opposite one and by doing so, they literally become what in fact she or he really are but, for reasons still beyond science, were born differently. What we are saying here is that in ideal terms, a woman in a man's body and, which is even more important, being able to act as both, would beat any sexual fantasy in terms of giving pleasure to a sexual partner especially if that partner was a woman."

The conversation was becoming more and more tainted by the Krug Champagne now being poured more than generously — later I understood that Isadora would get it for free by the dozens, as a gift from a rich importer in Manaus who was a good and steady client of hers…

"Why is that so?" I asked teasingly, trying hard to control my own feelings of utter excitement…

"I will try to give you what I assume to be a plausible

explanation to your question..." continued Eloisa.

"If you are as sensitive a man as Isadora has been trying to portray to me in order to convince me to be here tonight, you have probably noticed through your own relationships with women that we in fact have a very different mechanism when it comes to sexual stimulation than you men. We do not get excited by simply watching a hardened penis as most of you men suppose. Conversely, you men do get aroused simply by the sight of a naked woman and her intimate parts. Our excitement, before any preliminary physical contact or caresses, which for us are obviously utterly important, derives from a hedonistic, self-indulgent instinctive behavior. It has more to do with a reflexive feminine instinct whereby a woman, in the presence of a hardened phallus gets excited not by the sight of the phallus itself but rather by her reflexive self — awareness of her own erogenous zones that become in their turn aroused as a realization of their effect on the man's visible excitement. This is why we must feel attracted first to the man himself as a whole rather than to a couple of his isolated physical attributes. In short, our own erogenous zones awaken our sexual stimulus by themselves as if they had their own cognitive self-feeding mechanism. The man's penis if you wish is definitely not an exciting sight per se. It serves uniquely as an almost intellectual trigger to our self-feeding excitement process. To put it in simple terms, we get excited with our own selves as a consequence of our realization of the man's excitement towards us. The man is just an inspiration to our self-conscious eroticism... I can almost affirm that we get excited with our self-consciousness of our own erogenous zones rather than a mere penis... and lesbians know about that process, which I recognize, is not easy to grasp even for us women, let alone you men, isn't this right Isadora?" she concluded with loud laughter.

"Well, we will try to give you an exclusive glimpse later on into what we've been trying to convey to you in so many words," managed to articulate Isadora despite the effect of the Krug Champeane, by now quite visible in her demeanor.

"Be patient, my love" murmured Eloisa caressing my legs with her feet under the table. "There are certain things that can only be understood by experiencing them directly really…"

"Well, Axel," interjected Isadora maliciously, "What Eloisa is trying to ask you, is how in fact would you like to have this question answered… by a long explanation that will undoubtedly fall short from any resemblance to reality, or by watching it happen before your own eyes and who knows going through the experience yourself? You see, my dear, the essence of the matter lies on the individual, his interest in having real sex devoid of any constraint, as opposed to what 99.9% of all people think about sex not being even remotely aware of its real, profound meaning, which is nothing but love! It also depends on the degree and quality of the individual's sexuality and, most importantly, his or her sensitivity and the way the latter has been forged through what I would define as his deep, almost impenetrable emotional life experiences. You see, it all boils down to one's entire life learning process and the more or less rich emotional raw material that was interiorized through experience and, most of all, left inside to be further elaborated. All that put together, it has the unique power to extrapolate any gender consideration and to set free the person who will then be ready to love and to extract the utmost pleasure of each experience regardless of the person he's sharing it with, as long as there is trust and of course attraction! This being put, nothing replaces the real thing, or doing it if you prefer, right my love?" and by concluding she grabbed Eloisa by both arms and kissed her languidly right before my avid eyes!

This was the third hint as to what was about to unfold and my voice came out thick and intense, like cutting the air…" Of course, I want to experience whatever you think I should, or to very humbly offer you whatever gives you both pleasure as well!"

"Cigars everybody?" asked Isadora while leading us to her cozy living room where we took our seats amidst plush cushions that would push Eloisa and myself against each other, her left breast simply leaping out of her revealing décolleté. I could not resist and grabbed it, feeling its firmness and its hardened tip while kissing her erotically, caressing languorously her sensuous and deliciously wet lips with my tongue…

"Wow!" exclaimed Isadora. "No exclusivity whatsoever tonight folks! The idea is to share everything amongst the three of us… is this your understanding, and what you both desire as well? Let's be clear and not lose track of our original idea…"

We nodded our heads like two kids that were being asked whether they were sure they wanted ice cream after dinner…

"Should I open another bottle?" asked Isadora standing up decisively.

"Not for me please," murmured Eloisa. "Otherwise, we will fall asleep right here and all we've been telling Axel will remain a vague even though interesting theory…" And she stood up pushing and following Isadora to the room.

I stayed there by myself for a couple of minutes until both called my name in unison in between small whimpers and grunts of pleasure. I finally went into the room that was dimly illuminated yet I still could distinguish those two exuberant and vigorous young bodies intertwined in what appeared to be a strong, soaking embrace. I could smell their perfumes now mingled with the soft aroma of their bodily nectars, flowing from their intimate parts as they became more and more excited with each other…

I took off my clothes in a jiffy and lied down in bed close to them, feeling instantaneously stimulated, with my penis so rigid, that I thought it was going to somehow break in two. They turned to me pointing at every direction with those majestic breasts and their hardened nipples and protuberant areolas, glowing and reflecting the light of the candle that was placed on top of a little table enhancing even more the sensual atmosphere of the room.

Then, they slowly started to lick my entire body stopping at the most excitable parts, licking and sucking them sluggishly, taking their time to drive me crazy with their superbly resourceful mouths and tongues…

From time to time, they would meet in the middle, somewhere on top of my body, and kiss and lick each other so languorously and gracefully in a very delicate and warm way, exuding levels of pleasure that only two females could mutually attain with such tenderness. Eloisa was now performing marvels on my penis with her mouth, letting her breasts caress my belly whilst Isadora would infiltrate from behind and suck her clitoris and pussy with a delicate intensity right in front of my eyes which would allow me to watch the entire scene whilst receiving Eloisa's extremely electrifying caresses. I was immersed in a total and reckless tumult of my awakened senses leading me inexorably to an uncontrollable paroxysm of bliss. Then, presumably minutes later that seemed an eternity of pure frenzy and delight, she would delicately push Eloisa aside coming over me and guiding my cock towards her clitoris, performing small circles around it and massaging it almost frantically around her excited vulva, finally having it penetrate very slowly into her welcoming, warm and extremely lubricated vagina.

I then performed several 'pussy eating' sessions, sucking and licking the clitoris and vulvas of one, whilst penetrating the other until they both finally reached a long orgasm almost in a perfect unison...

I do not know how many times the two would reach a passionate orgasm simultaneously or otherwise but all I know is that I had more than one intense orgasm myself either through intercourse or during superbly performed oral sex, before falling fast asleep, very late at night, literally consumed and totally out of energy. I slept between both, feeling their soft skin and their sensual perfumes and listening to their deep and fulfilled breaths... I would awaken several times during that short night enjoying the intense delight of feeling those two warm, wet bodies against mine. I was amazed not only by the experience itself but also by the fact that I had gone through it quite naturally, which had allowed me to observe, feel and most of all actively participate in the love making of two women in love having wild sex. I must say that I learned a lot that night mostly about tender sex, about how to really give pleasure to a woman, about altruistic pleasure, about learning how to please myself by pleasing the other, by taking my time to enjoy the intercourse or other forms of sex without seeking frantically to reach an orgasm like most of us men instinctively do, as if we were racing to reach the climax... and then what? We tend to fall asleep ignoring completely whether our female partner, laying at our side, has had a good time or not... generally not!

I owe a lot to Isadora and Eloisa. They helped me demystify and better accept the gay phenomena and to discover the probable reason why gays seem to have much more fun when having sex than heterosexuals... it is probably because somehow all barriers tend to fall apart in order to eradicate the most difficult and obnoxious one which is called discrimination! Once that despicable barrier is set aside, all the others pale in comparison hence are fairly easily surmounted. I must also admit that, in the case of Isadora and Eloisa, sex was much more intense, sensual, and profound than most heterosexual sex I had ever practiced before. Reality was that I had fallen in love with both women, their openness, their natural way of accepting and loving each other, and all I really desired that night was to eternalize those fantastic hours we had spent together sharing an incredible amount of pleasure and passion! Obviously, those were very intimate feelings which faced tremendous, not to say unsurmountable barriers since any possible or even imaginable sustainable kind of relationship with both was simply unfeasible! In the end, I had to sadly realize that I'd better leave them to their own destinies whether together or not, whilst keeping them forever inside my heart as a fond memory of a highly relished and unique experience and an impossible sweet dream. This didn't mean however that we didn't repeat the experience in the following days!

I will always be intrigued by the natural propensity that we all have to fall in love as opposed to the often lofty and unrealistic standards or at times even barriers we self-impose on ourselves in order to accept such a simple and instinctive fact of life! We are simply incapable of accepting the fact of falling in love unless it musters all of our acquired filters of social convenience and acceptance… Some of us are more predisposed than others thus more inclined to admit it, at least to ourselves but still not without going through some worthless feelings of self-criticism or guilt! This being said, I am convinced that all of us fall in love more often than otherwise during our lifetime, censuring ourselves outright maybe out of fear to the point that we hurry to erase the impulse and with it the extraordinary feelings that derive from the latter. It is like throwing away the baby's bath together with the baby so to speak! By either accepting it and enjoying it, as we always should, or going through it surreptitiously because of our marital situation, taboos, inhibitions or even sheer fear or plain timidity, I can guarantee that we all fall in love several times during our lifetime, often in the most unexpected situations. We simply cannot control it, which certainly adds to its magic, to the passionate emotions it awakens in us, bringing us back to life often after long periods of sedation, re opening the doors to what is perhaps one of the most powerful feelings a human being can ever experience… simply love…

No one can deny the thrilling feelings of elation we experience whenever we catch the eye of a beautiful, highly attractive individual sitting in front of us in a café or in a restaurant, no matter what the prevailing life circumstances of both. All of a sudden, the entire world comes to a standstill, and we get the feeling that only the two of us matter. If the glare and the stare continue thereafter, a tacit complicity is immediately established, and a vast array of possibilities arise! Naturally, during the extent of that subtle flirtation, a series of amusing or sensual scenarios pass through our minds and we feel like standing up, grabbing the individual and flying far away to any destination, preferably an exotic one which enables us to stay isolated from the rest of the world, possibly for eternity! Love at first sight as the one I just described is commonly dismissed as being just a passing feeling, a fancy caprice of the mind bearing no importance whatsoever. In my view, however, this is a wrong attitude to have since one can, even for a short amount of time, feel true passion for another being, and live through the situation be it of short or longer duration, literally as a serendipitous encounter of one's sister soul. Love cannot be categorized or weighed as we often do with everything else in our lives. As such, we simply cannot predict when it will 'hit' us hence we are unable to choose between different preconceived, socially acquired parameters such as race, color, culture, archetypes, circumstances, timing, and so on. On the other hand, there is intensity, but even this can be influenced by timing and circumstances. In other words, we can fall in love with someone who ultimately does not become a long-term match for us simply because of the overall context of our lives or even the particular situation of a given moment, such as the environment, commitments that can or cannot be postponed, other people surrounding us, and so on. This however does not invalidate our feelings of love and attraction since those are indeed uncontrollable. They are there simply manifesting themselves like a wildflower waiting to be picked and smelled by an individual in love before offering it to his or her beloved person. Love is always perpetrating its magic of creation since it is at its very core, its very womb, whenever it occurs, enlightening our existence! If we could only reset the civilizational clock and create a culture whose consciousness would be just love and its manifestations, we would certainly be a completely different and much happier bunch!

Instead, and quite unfortunately, we live in a terrible world of fear, full of crazy menaces often created by ourselves, ranging from extremism, absurd fanatic theories, all out wars, hatred, despicable events involving children, all that worsened by illogical, self-centered, corrupt and incompetent governments. Those so-called leaders represent enormous political and social threats due to their greed as well as their total lack of real, validated knowledge of the populations they supposedly serve, let alone a reasonable amount of necessary wisdom to govern in this complex world! Had they at least some of these values or some understanding of the utterly absurd situation we're currently immersed in on a global scale, it would enable them to establish decisive democratic values with a view to create a better society!

Amidst the complete mess we live in today's world, one of our main concerns is about sex and its social, political and economic implications! In the end, sex is manipulated, mystified, distorted, commercialized in the sense of using it for publicity purposes, leading to all sorts of felonies and wrongdoings that are committed under its banner. Different cultures and religions use sex to define or influence any given social order with a view to serve the interests of a few who compose its structures of power. Evidently that goes far beyond considerations of simple procreation which also by the way merit strong governance...

We have created an absurd and socially unsurmountable distinction between sex and love that is at the origin of a huge confusion leading to its wrongful manipulation to all sorts of purposes ranging from money all the way to unspeakable crimes!

My involvement with Isadora and Eloisa albeit shocking to many, has been one of the purest love experiences of my entire life in the sense that the three of us trusted each other to the point of abandoning ourselves totally in the experience. And it ended up being a fantastic voyage into our deepest feelings and instincts which was achieved under the auspices of pure pleasure, another highly distorted notion! My question therefore remains perhaps unanswered in the breezes of the Solimões... What is more meaningfully enriching and significant, the planetary mess we're all immersed in, or the possibility to express love in its most touching and intense form no matter the set-up, the arrangement or the sex of the adult individuals involved in the experience, as long as it is consensual and natural? I guess deep in ourselves, we all know the answer!

Perhaps my life story is permeated with love stories by the simple fact that I am always open to experience love… and love is literally everywhere! Quite often I surprise myself talking to a flower who generously lent me its perfume, or to a tree, majestic or small, even insignificant, it doesn't matter. What matters are the feelings that emanate from my chest in recognition of the flowers or the tree's detached, disinterested generosity and the subsequent feeling of well-being and belonging that I experience towards them, or maybe with them! A perfect parallel can easily be traced here with my amazing adventure with Isadora and Eloisa. They were two flowers in full bloom offering their most intimate feelings to me and expressing them through their erotic perfumes and their tremendously attractive bodies…

Following that fantastic night, I left Isadora's home filled with sentiments of love, bursting with feelings of tenderness and with the sole certainty that I wanted to repeat the experience over and over again! I was feeling ecstatic like a boy that had been told an exciting secret but knew that as long as he kept it a secret, he would be entitled to get more of it!

And so it happened. I was happy to learn from both my 'partners' that my feelings were reciprocated, so we spent the following week literally in bed except for short intermissions to take care of some daily chores mostly designed to ensure our privacy and to get us some food. I called some of our main suppliers and the office a couple of times to fill them in with some uneventful news and to get further instructions from my also uneventful boss. Isadora called some of her customers to tell them that regretfully she was ill in bed, and Eloisa called her husband to say that she had to stay with Isadora to help her heal from a most horrifying flu... it was like three kids building a thick wall on a pebble beach, stone by stone, in order to assure their right to full privacy ultimately allowing the three of us to enjoy the presence of one another, our full and unrestricted nudity — the hot weather allowed us to stay naked 24/7, enjoying the continuous vision of our bodies and especially our uncovered sexes, and to perform sexual intercourse as many times and as long as we felt like it... Pure bliss and delight! I had never learned so much about feminine sexual stimulation simply by watching both performing it on each other... Only a woman knows exactly how to do it properly and I had the immense privilege of not only watching it but discussing it, asking any question I wanted to, and finally practicing it myself on those tremendously sexual females! As an example, clitoris stimulation is obviously better performed with one's mouth and tongue, and it can be tremendously exciting for a man to do it to his companion, slowly, as sweetly as possible, and in repeated movements. The texture, the hardening of it, the gradual wetting and the crescendo towards the climax, are in my view second to none elements that serve to arouse a man and make him reach a profound orgasm thereafter...

I was feeling very excited with that colorful relationship and with all the new sexual and personal experiences it entailed, but I was also conscious that all that passion was eventually designed to come to a close sooner rather than later. It was like an impossible dream momentarily come true for the three of us, as if the universe had generously come to a halt in order to allow three inhabitants of planet Earth to experience joy through a highly innovative and open relationship allowing the discovery of unimaginable sensual prowess and the unconditional surrender to their most hidden desires.

A week flies indeed, especially when you become immersed in such a sui generis experience. All three of us knew deep in our hearts however, that since we would not be able to eternalize the experience whilst upholding the same intensity and meaning that made it so unique, we'd better say goodbye keeping forever in our souls those fond and unscathed memories of something very difficult to reveal to anyone without raising perplexity… We thus decided to part ways without any plans for an encore whatsoever. And so, we did… I never met or heard about Isadora or Eloisa again. And that was OK… it simply was the way it should be.

A few days later I travelled back to São Paulo in order to update my top management on the 'situation'. Obviously, my mission was far from over since I simply hadn't been able to close all the files, I was supposed to close in order to move on with my career as an international trader. I was well received and was happy to learn that my promotion was ready, solely waiting for me to conclude my job in the Tropical Trading department and close the latter for good. My new assignment involved more sophisticated products such as metals and minerals which would make me travel worldwide, a pleasant perspective that could ultimately take me back to Keiko's and perhaps Florence's arms?

At that particular juncture I was like a navigator without any defined course… as the saying goes, "there're no favorable winds for the directionless navigator!" I was a bit lost in terms of what I wanted in my life. I was lucky however to have a highly rewarding and understanding boss who had noticed my hesitations towards my life objectives, so one day he came to me with a very enticing proposal consisting of my spending some time at their Toronto offices designed to acquaint myself with the metals and minerals business so that I would gather real elements and an 'on the field' experience about that trade even before starting my new assignment. The so-called training period would consist of about three to four months which would subsequently still allow me to conclude my job at the Tropical Department despite that short intermission.

NORTH AMERICA

I obviously accepted the offer since I had nothing to lose in the first place, and a month later I was taking off for Toronto. I was settled in a small, fully furnished apartment located in the posh Yorkville neighborhood and became immediately delighted with that city. Toronto is an extremely livable and pleasant city, with almost all the advantages of New York yet lacking the disadvantages of the latter. It is a clean, beautiful, civilized, safe and very welcoming city. Its size is still tenable notwithstanding its cosmopolitan allure. One can find everything in Toronto, from a second to none education, excellent infrastructure, superlative quality of life, to being the third theatre city in the world coming just behind London and New York. Food is excellent and restaurants boast an extremely varied and high-quality cuisine for literally all tastes. My office hours were reasonable and since the team was aware that I was there only temporarily, no one was afraid of my potential competition which could represent a threat to their jobs. I was entitled to a small company car and to some long weekends and took great pleasure in travelling to nearby picturesque towns such as Niagara on the Lake amongst others. I was not particularly interested in female company since the very intense period I spent with Isadora and Eloisa had seemingly fulfilled my sexual appetite at least for some time… but life knows better.

On the eve of what had been announced as supposedly being a beautiful long holiday weekend I received a surprising phone call from a woman, that went more or less like this,

"May I speak to Mr Axel Mavromatis please?"

"May I ask who wants to speak to Mr Mavromatis?"

"Well, this is an old acquaintance of Mr Mavromatis…" the voice came softly. "This is someone that he knows pretty well and who misses him dearly, and eugh… thinks of him quite often…" At that point of the conversation, I had figured out who was at the other end of the line and couldn't hold my surprise…

"Angelina??" I guessed without any particular effort and most of all without trying to disguise my excitement.

"Yes, you bastard! How come you disappear the way you did without communicating with me for ages?!"

"Thank you! I return the compliment," I mumbled, my voice literally quaking without being able to hide my emotion. It is interesting the way we feel stirred as soon as we get in touch with someone who represented something important in our lives. "You are calling me from Chicago, I presume?"

"Yes, handsome, and I want to see you right away!" She hadn't changed a bit judging from the bossy tone of her voice…

"Well, I'm afraid this won't be possible. However, I can try to catch the first Air Canada flight and meet you in Chicago by tomorrow! We have a four-day long weekend in Canada. Does this sound early enough to you?"

"Don't be so old fashioned, you silly boy! I can pick you up say in a couple of hours, and we could spend the weekend in New York with some good friends of ours who live in a great place right in the heart of Manhattan!"

"Ours? You mean that you plan to come with your husband? What's his name if I may ask?"

"Gerry… he will be joining us tomorrow since he's caught in a board meeting until later tonight and he is dying to get to know you after everything I told him! You know, I told him literally everything about us and our crazy love affair in the jungle! Axel, please get your passport right away and do meet me at the private terminal of the Toronto Pearson's airport in precisely three hours, will you? and remember to bring your stuff for the long weekend!" She hung up abruptly as if she didn't want to run any risk of getting a 'no' for an answer. That was no doubt Angelina at her best.

I confess I was left very excited by the short conversation, especially with the prospect of seeing Angelina again after all those years despite the references to Gerry, the husband! I hastily prepared a small suitcase with the essentials for a long weekend and headed to the street looking for a taxi, a rarity on the eve of a long weekend, to take me down 401 to Pearson airport. After some forty minutes or so I was lucky to find a cab driven by a big-bearded man wearing a turban, someone who is known as being a religious Sikh and who is quite commonly found driving taxis or limousines in Canada. The man was extremely gentle and drove me silently all the way to the opposite side of the commercial flight terminals to an elegant private hall where a beautiful hostess welcomed me not before checking my name and passport against a prearranged short list of expected guests. The lounge was very well outfitted with elegant furniture and also well supplied with all sorts of drinks and appetizers designed to satisfy even the most demanding of tastes. I grabbed a couple of magazines and entertained myself for just a little more than one hour, when the attractive hostess came to me and announced the arrival of what was supposed to be Angelina's plane. Custom clearance was granted before boarding further to which we headed to the tarmac.

I was expecting to see a small airplane piloted by Angelina herself, as the image of her old hydroplane back in the good old days of tropical fish smuggling in the upper Jutaí river came back to me… instead, as I came out of the terminal building, I was utterly impressed to see a huge, shiny Gulfstream jet that looked brand new as if just popped out of the assembly line! As I boarded the impressive airplane, I was immediately transfixed by its superb and very spacious interior which had been luxuriously appointed displaying what was probably Angelina's extremely good taste, and elegantly equipped with a series of amenities beyond imagination. There was even a standing bar beyond which and to my surprise, I could perceive Angelina in person sipping a glass of Champagne. To say that she was looking gorgeous, would be a gross under- statement! She was simply splendidly dressed in what I could only guess were very expensive clothes enhancing even more her striking good looks. In contrast to all that opulence, I was wearing one of my very old jeans and a worn-down tee-shirt, not even wearing socks as I usually did during summertime, and negligently displaying what I would call a 'historical' pair of old and rundown sneakers stained beyond hope!

I grabbed Angelina and hugged her tightly, taking all my time to feel the familiarity of that body and its alluring smell after all those years that seemed now more like a flicker long lost in space and time!

"How have you been, my love?" She whispered in my ear. "I have missed you greatly!"

"Really? I replied dreamily, resolutely hunting for her familiar lips and for one of her intimate and languorous kisses…

"No, no, my dear!" She exclaimed pushing me gently away from her with a smile, "things have changed, and, in as much as I love you and know that I always will, I now belong to Gerry so to speak… I mean I'm in love with him," she mumbled trying her best to reshape the outdated notion of 'belonging'. "Please understand that I want to be your best friend, however my life is now so different and so satisfying, that I simply want to keep it that way! I don't want to ruin it although I can assure you that if I could stop the earth and jump out of it with you for a couple of hours, we would definitely fall into each other's arms and repeat all those fantastic experiences we had the privilege of sharing in the Alto Solimões!"

It felt like a cold shower suddenly pouring over me and flooding all and everything I had imagined from the moment I had received her call! We men often live our fantasies in all their grandeur and end up creating castles out of the blue only to see them collapse before our eyes, plummeting our egos in the depths of the deepest, miserable, and hopeless hole! And this was exactly how I suddenly felt, wishing I could roll back time and find myself safe in my tiny and familiar living room in Toronto with no plans whatsoever for the long weekend! I simply could not portray myself having long and mundane conversations with Gerry in New York — suddenly I hated his name — To top it all he knew everything about us and about our sexual prowess in the Rio Negro or the Jutaí according to Angelina!! Maybe he was some sort of a pervert who would get excited by meeting someone who had had incredible sex with his wife in the past? or even maybe to experience some sort of distorted excitement by having the spicier passages described to him for the tenth time or so by the performer himself?

Angelina broke the silence with a laughter, evidently grasping my state of confusion, "Come on, Axel! Aren't you the one who wisely taught me that life is an ever-changing dynamic, a constant movement, and that we either should roll with the punches or cunningly withdraw from the battle all together and stay safely behind? I feel that you are surprised at the news of my life, and I understand it, however if I really, really meant something to you, you would have contacted me a long time ago before it was too late, wouldn't you?"

She had a point. Angelina, like all the other marvelous women I had gotten involved with had had their importance in shaping my life for sure, however the truth was that I had never felt compelled to share my entire life exclusively with only one of them except for my honest try with Isabelle but that had proven to be a mistake probably due to my very young age. In this sense, it had never crossed my mind to go back to any one of them with a serious intent of founding a family in the traditional sense, especially considering the precepts and the burdens imposed on such undertaking from our western, so called civilized society.

"I guess you have a valid point here," I replied coming out of my torpor trying hard to uphold my statement with the right attitude. "OK, so let us try to be great friends! I promise you that I shall do my very best for this to become a reality, how about that?"

"This is my guy!" she exclaimed whilst giving me a very civilized kiss that felt diametrically distinct from the ardent kisses, she used to amaze me with in the past, while taking me by the hand and showing me my seat that looked more like the comfortable TV couch I had in my tiny living room, than an airplane seat. "We must get seated and fasten our seat belts for take-off... they will only take off when we're ready, so let's do it before I get a call from Vivian asking me whether we are on time for dinner at her home in Manhattan tonight!"

The flight was as smooth as silk and a highly trained flight attendant served non-stop hot appetizers, caviar blinis and delicious finger sandwiches all washed down with Dom Perignon vintage Champagne. By the time we landed at La Guardia airport, I was feeling sort of legless however still in control of my reflexes. It occurred to me that Angelina was certainly one of those very wealthy individuals to the extent of having a special license to land her private jet on a non-private commercial runway just for convenience purposes…

A stately brand-new black Rolls Royce was waiting for us on the tarmac with an impeccably dressed driver holding the back door open for us whilst a couple of airport personnel loaded our bags in the trunk which closed automatically with an elegant "click" ensuring it was well locked. The imposing car then silently slithered through the tarmac guarded gates and headed towards Manhattan making me feel like a grand Pasha on a flying carpet!

The car took us straight to mid-town Manhattan somewhere between Madison and Fifth Avenue and entered a big, underground private parking under what could be perceived as being a very posh neoclassic building.

A stylish elevator took us to the penthouse, not before a code had been carefully typed by the driver on a discreet console by the side of the story keyboard indicator. The elevator door opened directly into the apartment entry hall which was as big and aristocratic as many living rooms I had seen in my short marriage to Isabelle…

Angelina took me by the hand reassuringly, sensing my unease especially in the face of my poor attire amidst such grandiose surroundings and steered me into the most spectacular living room I've ever seen in my life. We took quite some time to cross it in order to reach four or five big, elegant French doors leading to a fantastic terrace with an unencumbered view of the New York Central Park and parts of the Manhattan impressive skyline right across. The Big Apple in all its splendor was appearing before us offering all of its grandeur to the delight of our senses... I could not take my eyes from the majestic scenery and stood there with Angelina, motionless and speechless until a sweet voice broke the enchantment reaching out towards our direction...

"Well, well, so here he is, I presume, our very famous Indiana Jones straight from the Amazon jungle!" exclaimed Vivian, a voluptuous looking woman, one of a kind who seemed to look through you as if you were totally translucent, making you feel vulnerable to her invasive charm, unable to hide anything from her shrewd and penetrating glance! Obviously, she had been very well briefed on all the details of our past exploits from Angelina herself, and certainly had a pretty accurate description of who I was. She stared at me persistently with an enigmatic smile, giving me the impression that she wanted to dissect my psyche in order to make sure that I matched the description given to her by Angelina, presumably over innumerous glasses of wine or cups of Jasmin tea during confidences made on sunny or rainy afternoons on that incredibly stunning terrace. Suddenly I felt that being rich was not such a bad thing after all!

The fallacious drawback still existing in my mind was that the very rich people I had wasted a portion of my life with, in Brazil, had left me with feelings of disdain at the idea of having lots of money, due to the fact that they were totally ignorant individuals. They were indeed the image itself of mediocrity, completely transfixed by money, without the necessary cultural, traditional or spiritual attributes one needs in order to be able to enjoy it and share it with others out of love and compassion! Money is a powerful energy that can be used for making good thus generating happiness, or for gathering power in order to subjugate others into moral or material slavery ultimately leading to decadence and demise!

Vivian embraced me tight and gave me a generous kiss, evidently welcoming me warmly into her home. A minute later, a tall, dark haired, handsome and well-dressed middle-aged man came to the terrace and introduced himself as Patrick, Vivian's husband and the father of their three children.

"It is a great pleasure to meet you Axel! You can't imagine how much I look forward to your telling us more about your adventurous stories, apart from the very thrilling and spicy ones we have already heard from Angelina, as well as to confirm some rather unbelievable accounts that our dear friend has been telling us over the recent years and that sound rather eugh... how should I put it? Quite incredible I must say! Should I trust your friend, what do you think?" And he laughed out loud as if trying to be heard through the dark alleys of the park.

Patrick had a British accent, and I was soon told that he had come from London while still fairly young in order to establish and expand his family's business having to do with private equity investments in the US. Apparently, he had been quite successful, at least judging from his car and his home, two of the main hallmarks that attest to the reaching of the paramount heights of the so-called American Dream. Later Angelina confided to me that he had multiplied his family fortune many times over...

Our conversation was very fluid ranging from platitudes to a variety of more important existential topics and we immediately felt empathy for each other. I was told that we were still waiting for another guest whose name was Amanda, a neighbor living in the same building, just two floors beneath theirs... I couldn't avoid noticing a very subtle yet evocative expression in Patrick's eyes when the name Amanda was pronounced.

We were very comfortably installed on the living room's plush cushions and divans, sipping yet another glass of vintage Champagne when I could faintly hear the doorbell ring from afar, followed by very fast steps which increased in intensity until a gorgeous creature displaying a catlike, svelte and graceful figure literally broke into the living room distributing kisses to everybody, fortuitously including me as well!

"Let me introduce you Amanda, Axel" said Vivian not without a very subtle teasing tone in her voice. At that very moment, I sort of understood that there was certainly something cooking in the minds of our hosts with regards to a possible flirtation between Amanda and myself...

I was simply paralyzed staring at that new dazzling personage standing before me watching me and measuring me in detail from head to toe, probably wondering where the hell I was coming from dressed like a street beggar although she was not so differently dressed either! She was wearing a pair of jeans, very fashionable for sure, and bearing the name of one of those filthy expensive couturiers from Madison Avenue, a pair of old looking sneakers and a décolleté black T shirt that would put in evidence a pair of fabulous, very firm breasts whose strong and protuberant nipples would give me the impression of trying to break free and jump towards the ceiling. She was extremely beautiful with a feline demeanor, shortly cut black hair à la Chanel, that would enhance her slinky looks and give her a light, yet very elegant appearance! Her voice was firm and sexy showing determination in sheer contrast with such a delicate figure... She came across as one of those spirited individuals who can solve any problem in the spur of the moment... It was as if nothing could get in her way that wasn't readily solvable or surmountable no matter how intricate or convoluted. Her presence and charisma captured every single available space of that huge living room, and her insouciance gave us all a feeling of well-being and curiosity vis a vis her intriguing and gracious young self.

"So, you are the fellow I have been hearing so many intriguing stories about, that I have decided to call you 'the expected one', did they tell you that? Finally, I can put a face to the legend, and I hope you will be staying long enough so that we can show you some of the good things that we have in this incredible city. Have you been to New York before?"

"No, this is truly my first time ever and I very much look forward to getting to know at least some of the wonderful museums, music halls, theatres, that are world famous and that make this city such a great place to visit let alone live in it like you do. But to answer to your question, I am staying for the long weekend."

"Wow, this is far too short a visit! New York is a city where you need several weeks if not months in order to get a real sense of it, its people's vibrant spirit, all the intriguing underground spots where you can enjoy the best artists performing just for their own fun, not to mention theaters, museums, music halls where you have different shows and at times fabulous, second to none events going on! New York offers absolutely everything for all tastes, endlessly! Perhaps the only good news about your short stay is that you will be enticed to come back for more, and this is something that I can guarantee in advance! In any case we shall do our best to show you as much stuff as possible in these meagre four days, right Angelina?" I could glance a malicious expression in Angelina's face…

Amanda's reaction after knowing me for just a few minutes sounded like a tacit approval of what she had imagined from Angelina's descriptions as well as an open invitation for me to come back. I could feel from the inflection of her voice that much had been said about me by Angelina from the time we split in the upper Solimões until that evening… I felt proud and secure, obviously helped by the Champagne that was so freely flowing down my throat…

"Well, judging from my first impressions I am pretty sure that I shall probably be coming back! To be honest however, I must say that Angelina knows me well and she knows of my preferences which unfortunately exclude crowded cities and favor instead places like small villages in the middle of nowhere which is where we met by the way! This being said, New York is New York and I heard and read enough about it and all its wonders to feel attracted to it even without having ever been here! So, Amanda, I look forward to your chaperoning, of course if your timing permits!'

"Don't forget to take this guy for a walk in the Central Park between one museum and a theatre! This will allow poor Axel to breath some fresh air and acknowledge that at least some trees have survived civilization and are still there, standing tall in the midst of this concrete jungle!" interjected Patrick with his British sense of humor.

I confess that I felt welcomed and at the same time extremely attracted to Amanda. Angelina obviously had sensed it all and threw invocative glances at me from time to time. She had obviously planned the encounter not only with a view to allowing me to have fun and enjoy Amanda's company, but also in order to help clear the situation in anticipation of Gerry's arrival scheduled for the following morning. I felt comforted as well as

222

reassured by her wise strategy especially now that I had met Amanda.

The dinner was simply as fabulous as can be. We were served Iranian caviar with blinis together with a series of other exquisite appetizers, followed by what the chef (yes, there was a private chef in the house working exclusively for Vivian and Patrick) called 'crispy pheasant with foie gras', with a highly delicate sauce that turned out to be a perfect combination. All sorts of side dishes were also served, all perfectly matched by two bottles of a 'Premier Grand Cru de Pomerol', a superlative Bordeaux wine. For dessert, a grandiose soufflé au Grand Marnier made us all want to scratch and lick the bowls where it had been served so that absolutely nothing would be left over! Homemade delicious petits fours followed, together with a variety of choices of vintage cognacs, portos and 'eaux de vie'. By the end of the dinner, it was already past midnight and further to some pleasant platitudes we all decided that it was time to get some rest...

The following morning greeted us with a radiant sun hitting Central Park and creating a colorful display of the gorgeous summer leaves. The sky was blue like no other as so often happens in New York that time of the year and, by the time we were all up and ready for breakfast, the penthouse was strikingly clean and tidy as if nobody had been having dinner there the night before, a result of the early work of an army of employees who served and cleaned the house even on weekends and holidays!

By the time I reached the sunny dining room contiguous to the kitchen, one of the three existing in the apartment besides the tabled terraces, it was as if I had practiced my morning jogging in the face of a true labyrinth of corridors, private offices, bedrooms and living rooms that composed Vivian's and Patrick's magnificent Manhattan home. Angelina and Vivian were already there sipping their coffee and chatting like good old friends do. As I arrived, I was immediately followed by a tall and handsome young man in his mid-thirties, impeccably dressed for the occasion. He went straight to Angelina and gave her an impassioned albeit quick kiss on her lips that made me feel awkward to put it mildly…

"Let me introduce you to Gerry, Axel," said Angelina standing up quite abruptly, genuinely surprised by his impromptu arrival straight from Chicago.

"Uau," he exclaimed smiling and displaying a friendly, self-assuring attitude, "this is indeed a special occasion! Axel, I must confess that until fairly recently I had to put up with Angelina murmuring your name in her dreams in the middle of the night, presumably amidst fabulous jungle and exotic river settings, not to mention the exploits of the dream, since she would invariably tell me that she could not remember a thing when waking up! Ha ha… Now I can finally put a face to the legend and stop being jealous of a ghost for heaven's sake!" I was flattered and at the same time humbled by such an open and spontaneous posture coming from a man who certainly had to put up with, for sure more than once, the not so pleasant recounts of our Amazonian passion.

Gerry had a commanding tone in his voice, even when making fun of the rather embarrassing situations he apparently went through with Angelina regarding our past relationship. I was frankly very proud to hear that she would dream of me, and I surely knew all the potential contents of her dreams… He would come across as one of those determined kind of individuals whose way of life was intrinsically connected with convincing and influencing people as well as solving intricate business problems. He displayed balance, quick thinking and a good sense of humor, besides good judgement certainly commensurate with his life story and childhood which, as I learned later, was one of love, stability and understanding. As I got to know him better, I could not help but involuntarily and quietly, of course, compare his upbringing to mine, one of total chaos and disarray that would make me look like a miracle in the making for people who would get to know even a tiny fraction of my terrifying and mindless childhood...

There is nowadays scientific evidence available whereby violence in any shape or form inflicted on children may cause damage in their genomes by affecting specific genes which, as a consequence, are passed on as a damaged formation through at least three generations... Three generations to heal wounds that we thought would disappear during a lifetime or even before! Imagine the Syrian war with all of its unqualified violence perpetrated against children, and its dreadful consequences ensuing for at the very least three generations and this if one assumes that the perpetration of violence would somehow and miraculously cease in the first year after a durable ceasefire! Whenever I happen to watch those horrifying war scenes on television with children being violated, wounded or killed in front of the cameras, I simply cannot fathom how we, as a species, will survive our own deranged selves and consequently our inherited violent genetic behavior towards our own race not to speak of the other species that consequently suffer from our presence on this planet.

Gerry in fact represented quite the opposite of all those crazy yet realistic thoughts that had surreptitiously crept into my mind. He reflected the hope that still outlasts the prevailing negativity that pervades our planet. By observing him present his ideas and defend his points of view with such assertiveness, things would fall back into place and the world made sense all over again... I could easily understand the reasons why Angelina had fallen in love with him and had subsequently chosen him to become her husband among a crowd of potential candidates she most certainly had at hand.

Amidst all those conflicting thoughts crossing my mind, the now recognizable quick and light steps approached the dining room in a crescendo and I could visualize Amanda rushing in to join us for breakfast. She erupted into the room spreading around a fresh, spring like perfume and kissing everybody affectionately. Oh God, how sexy she was, so elegantly yet simply dressed in a tight, carelessly unbuttoned blouse with no bra underneath which would leave us all guessing her superb breasts, perfectly matching a pair of pants that would put her terrific body in full evidence. Her Chanel hair style meticulously cut would harmonize with her discreet but sensual make-up and would provide her with that highly provocative slinky look... to top it all, when kissing me, she murmured "how are you today, handsome?" in my ear, a clear sign that she wanted to give me some kind of a telegraphic exclusive message... I felt good and extremely delighted by such attribute, especially in the presence of Gerry who, in my view, would definitely deserve the accolade and even more...! fortunately, he didn't get any!

Finally, Patrick arrived with a sleepy face, and we could all enjoy each other's company not to speak of the delicious breads and French croissants that were of course freshly home baked together with outstanding homemade jams, delicious omelets with all possible ingredients, exquisite cheeses and so on.

At one point, Amanda interrupted everybody to announce in a quasi-official tone that she would take care of me for the rest of the day by taking me to places such as museums and art galleries that everybody else knew just too well hence not needing to bother to come with us. Was she smart, oh boy, yes, she was! Needless to say, all the others immediately understood the message, so much so that no further questions were asked except for Angelina who quite undiplomatically said, "He is all yours, as long as you deliver him back here no later than Tuesday evening for me to fly him back to Toronto…"

To make a long story short, later in the morning following that sumptuous breakfast, we left Vivian's and Patrick's home, went directly to the Guggenheim Museum, spent around two hours there and the following three days in bed in her gorgeous apartment making love like two wild animals in full mating season!

Amanda was an accomplished lover and to be honest, after three days in her home, or rather in her bed, all I could possibly describe were her sleeping quarters and how busy and entertained she kept me for the entire three days and two nights! We made love in all possible and conceivable situations and positions, like two very thirsty kids who discover the juice dispenser with no restrictions from the adults! Our smells fused and our tastes intermingled to such an extent, that in the end we felt a complete bond as if the entire situation was part of a predetermined script planned by an expert in matching couples through love making… which made me eventually think of Angelina and her probable planning of the whole thing!

My suspicion was finally proven right by Amanda, who at one point confessed the plot by exclaiming "|Oh boy, Angelina was right, you are a hell of a lover! She was right to advise me that the best strategy was to take you straight to bed!" I had mixed feelings about the compliment, on the one hand feeling like an object of desire manipulated by the two, and on the other proud that my sexual prowess had been so prized and recognized by two very special women… In the end I decided not to give any importance to Amanda's comments following Angelina's complicity in the story and fully enjoy it instead.

Amanda was sweet… literally! Her soft yet firm skin had a sweetened taste that would perfectly match her perfume of choice. The mixture of both would result in a highly sensual fragrance and a very distinctive appealing taste that would make me constantly come back for more! Even though we stayed tightly together, cuddled to each other, making love and laughing like two teenagers during almost seventy-two hours, she was still smelling as if she had just walked out of her morning shower. The woman was incredibly sexy and attractive to the point that I declined any invitation to break for meals in the kitchen, asking her to bring them to the bed instead. By Tuesday evening I was really distressed at the prospect of leaving her to fly back to Toronto with Angelina and Gerry…

I left Amanda's apartment to join Vivian and Patrick's lavish loft not without first promising her that I would come back at the first opportunity! As I reached their fabulous home, Angelina practically pushed me out the door, telling me that Gerry had to be in Chicago early enough to join some kind of business dinner. I apologized for my possible delay, greeted Vivian and Patrick in a hurry and jumped into the Rolls Royce elegantly parked on the building's private parking space facing Central Park. The majestic car roared its potent, yet extremely silent engine and we arrived at La Guardia in a jiffy.

"So, my dear Axel, am I right to presume that you both got along quite well judging from the amount of time you both spent together visiting the New York museums?" asked Angelina not without a mischievous tone in her voice and a sarcastic smile on her lips.

"Well indeed," I replied without hesitation, returning the irony. "You can ask me anything you want about the Guggenheim, the Metropolitan and especially about the Natural History Museum and I will not disappoint you! Now on a more serious note, Amanda is an extraordinary lady! I thank you for introducing her to me, and by the way, I thank you both for the marvelous weekend." I completed the reply in a respectful tone.

"Well, we are happy to know that both of you matched! I was sure about it! And by the way Axel, needless to say the Gulfstream will be at your disposal whenever you wish to fly back to New York again, respecting Gerry's business priorities of course."

That phrase sounded like music to my ears especially considering the fact that I had just left Amanda's still hot sheets after such an extraordinary and amazing weekend! At that point here I was falling hopelessly in love with Amanda and with her intense ways of expressing her love and appreciation towards me in such a short period of our acquaintance. Gerry had an evocative grimace on his face, giving me the impression that his mind was divided between the conversation which he was only vaguely following, and the details of his business affair slated to take place later on that same evening in Chicago…

"Thank you, Angelina! I truly appreciate your offer which I will make good with enormous pleasure, and rest assured that I shall be forever grateful for your initiative to introduce me to Amanda, and most of all yours and Gerry's generous attitude towards me after all these years!"

"I never forget my good friends, my dear Axel, and you must know that you have been and still are one of them with the particularity of having dedicated yourself to me during a very special and sensitive period of my life giving me exactly what I needed the most at that time… love, tenderness, understanding and trust" Gerry's grimace changed completely upon hearing that last phrase which prompted Angelina to look at him straight in the face and proclaim with a very serious expression." Nothing new to you, right my love? You know from the very beginning that this guy here occupies and, most importantly, will always occupy, a very, very special place in my life!"

"Did I say anything?" was Gerry's short and assertive reply, before adjusting his sitting position and resuming his ruminations probably about the deal he was about to button up later on with his business associates…

In no time we landed in Toronto, and I disembarked after kissing Angelina and hugging Gerry good buy and thanking them profusely once again for the incredibly good time I had had in New York.

A taxi-limo driven by an imposing bearded man wearing a turban drove me back home to Yorkville and I spent the rest of the evening on the phone romanticizing with Amanda… spending a fortune indeed but it was worth its while!

The following week was extremely busy, mostly spent in dealing with awkward technical terms like 'Contango', 'Backwardation' amongst others, all of them part of my intensive training in the metal trading business… boring really! Every evening of that week I would spend hours with Amanda on the phone carelessly vis a vis my modest telecommunications budget, and by Wednesday she would surprise me by happily announcing that she had it all figured out by arranging for Angelina's jet to pick me up once again at Pearson airport on Friday evening to fly me to New York where she intended to spend an entire week with me before flying back with me to Toronto on the following Friday for yet another week with me... Her suggestion was then for me to try to take a week's holiday in order to spend it with her at her second home at the Hamptons... she had a country house in Southampton more specifically in a place called Sagaponack. She then would fly back with me on Sunday evening and happily "cook for me" in Toronto during the subsequent week... I immediately accepted her proposed schedule as well as the invitation without a blink, instantly trying to find a good excuse that would allow me to take a week off so early in my training period, whilst feeling extreme pride and excitement at the prospect of spending so much time with my newly found love!

My feelings towards Amanda besides attraction and falling in love, were a mixture of pride, extreme joy and blissful anticipation towards all the fantastic situations including the exploration of a new way of life that was suddenly opening itself before my senses regardless of how long it would last! And deep in my heart I knew that it would certainly not last forever. The best of all was that I felt so welcomed and admired for my eclecticism that I was invaded and fulfilled by sentiments of peace and complete detachment from the usual and anxious internal dialogue which normally takes place at the early stages of a romance. Obviously, money, lots of it by the way, facilitated things and I must say that this time around I had decided to let go of my philosophical principles and enjoy myself delving in a whole new set of impressions and amenities that only money in such incredible amounts can provide.

Notwithstanding, I was still the same wild and indomitable soul that would view money only as a means to enjoy life by spending it more or less openhandedly according to the circumstances that would come my way, obviously without relinquishing acts of charity commensurate with one's affluence… I had to admit however that Amanda's rapport to the apparent vast amounts of money she could dispose of was a far cry from Isabelle's, my former wife, and Pierre-André's, her materialistic obsessed father. For them, money was an end in itself whereas for Amanda money equaled good life and helping others! In this regard, we were equals so to speak, with the difference that she had loads of it and I had almost none! Besides originating from an affluent milieu, she had inherited a fortune from her former husband, a highly successful businessman associated with Patrick in a number of common ventures.

Time simply flew at a staggering speed in the following two weeks, which seemed like a dream to me. I went back to New York for the first weekend, and I must confess that my exposure to art and museums remained dismal, not to say non-existent since we basically couldn't separate from each other except for a couple of superlative meals in posh restaurants in Manhattan. One of them, La Côte Basque, introduced me to the best possible roasted duck one can have, even surpassing what is considered to be the best of the best prepared by the famous restaurant in Beijing where Peking Duck was invented! The secret, I guess, is that they roast the duck and then remove the skin with all its fat (ducks tend to have a very fatty skin), throw away the fat, recompose the duck, and serve it as crunchy and tasty as can be… all that accompanied by excellent Bordeaux wines, inspired us to… go straight back to bed!

The rest of the time was spent in Amanda's home and the staff were given two days off which ensured our total privacy. In my humble opinion, nothing matches an entire weekend of flirtation, passion, and full intimacy without having any obligation, requirement, commitment of any sort, you name it! Even words become superfluous, just a way to have a good laugh with one another before plunging back into the sweet lethargy of exploring each other's bodies just to discover new concealed pleasures that only an extended time in full intimacy without any mental hesitation, shyness or acquired reservations are able to provide! This assumes a total complicity from both partners which happens naturally within the mutual pursuit of perfected pleasure. Amanda was a true prodigy in mastering the art!

I had managed to get the following week off as suggested by Amanda, not before being forced to fly back to Toronto on Sunday evening in order to attend a stupid meeting to which I had been summoned by the hierarchy who were probably jealous of my recounts. I then flew once again to La Guardia on Angelina's Gulfstream on Monday p.m. The pilots and the flight attendant this time around treated me like someone belonging to the family and did all they possibly could to keep me happy and entertained! Oh, that V.I.P. life flying from one private terminal to the other was becoming almost a routine for me — I was feeling like an important and very interesting guy after all!

Finally, on Monday evening Amanda's driver took us to Sagaponack aboard her 'top of its class' Bentley.

I simply cannot find words to describe the magnificent, gorgeous surroundings of what Amanda referred to over the phone as 'my country house'. It consisted of a stately manor home, comprising an Olympic size, heated swimming pool, two impeccably maintained tennis courts, a private pathway to a secluded beach, workout state-of-the-art facilities, a private SPA with a Burmese masseuse on demand, horse stables for ten horses with its training grounds, and all possible amenities such as a barbecue lounge that would make many restaurant owners feel diminished and jealous, and I could go on forever. The mansion itself had ten suites differently and finely decorated for every possible demanding taste, two splendid living rooms with majestic fireplaces leading to a patio followed by lawns that would stretch for maybe half a mile or so, a superbly welcoming and very well-appointed dining room and so on…

"My guess is that I'd better enjoy all this as quickly as possible before we spend the entire week in bed!" I said to Amanda teasingly whilst kissing her lips in a soft embrace…

"Well, we'll be busy with other things too this time around my love… I have invited a group of friends for dinner tomorrow, and I am sure they will insist in reciprocating, so, my dear savage cave man, prepare yourself to socialize a little bit although I happen to know that this is definitely not your favorite pastime… you see, I want to show you around so that my friends don't think you are a mere mirage or an invention I made up just to impress them!"

"If you say so, "I replied nonchalantly. "Why the hell people like to meet other people even though they don't have a clue as to what they will find? It sounds to me like the collector's syndrome… I know him, her, them… On top of that, in a year's time you will all probably be making fun of my stories and guessing what the hell became of me…"

Amanda looked at me straight in the eyes with a dismayed expression and exclaimed,

"Well first of all, thank you for the hint! I didn't know that your intention is to disappear to the point that nobody will know your whereabouts! You did it with Angelina, but we all thought that Mr Mystery would remain afloat this time around! Not a problem for me, my dear! I can occupy my time differently without you, that's for sure!"

I started to realize that Angelina had tried to nail me down to Amanda maybe to keep me close to her in a certain way… My reply came in a rather trenchant way.

"Wow, wow, wow, let us slow down here. In the first place I am not a pastime to anyone, no matter how convenient you may find me in order to occupy your time! All the money in this world cannot buy me as a pastime or as an exotic entertainment to anyone! To put things in a clear perspective, I am not here for you to merely occupy yourself! This being said, I am a free soul, thank God, and I realized some time ago that my life is nothing but an ever-changing chain of events that take me randomly wherever fate wants me to be! Why? I honestly don't know, but this is how I have chosen to spend my life making the very most out of every single moment! This is all that exists anyway, the present moment! I therefore can sincerely say that I love you now! Tomorrow is anybody's guess! This feeling is pure, devoid of any second thoughts, interest, calculation and so on… but it can only be valid for the present moment, for now, since in any case this is all there is! Therefore, my proposal to you is, let's make the very best out of this marvelous week that fate presented to us. Now we're together! Afterwards is a word that I usually throw to the universe to act upon without expecting any specific answer! Simply because there is no answer, Amanda! Everything is possible and the present moment is all there is even if destiny has conspired for us to stay together forever! But this will only be known in hindsight!"

We just had our first disagreement in the short period of time we were together. I had touched her paradoxical feminine feelings of possess/dispossess, a feature that after all is part of a woman's essence. In other words, a woman is made to protect, to embrace, and to hold the male obviously up to a certain point or up to her own convenience... then if things get rough, comes a feeling of liberation, especially if the male ends up getting codependent vis a vis the woman, which is something the latter will immediately detect through feminine sensors that are well developed in the female psyche. There is here a distinction to be made between codependence and interdependence. Interdependence is a condition of being mutually reliant on each other and this denotes balance, whereas codependence is a dysfunctional behavior that can yield compulsive, unhealthy relationships where mutual reliance becomes totally asymmetric, hence unbalanced. I expressed this to Amanda in order to make the point that a possessive relationship invariably ends up in tatters therefore she'd better not even go there. She understood my point not without putting herself on the defensive by assuring me that this was definitely never the case when it came to her loving relationships! I acquiesced without further arguments.

She later explained that, in her opinion, my chief feature in terms of attracting women was my sense of independence coupled with my highly developed feminine instincts. That combination according to Amanda would radiate a subtle type of energy that only women could detect but that would generate an immediate attraction towards me as a male, as paradoxical as it might seem. That, according to Amanda would be at the core of my highly developed sentiments of tenderness, my almost feminine intuition, however when combined with my masculinity, would become explosive. What I called the possess/dispossess syndrome present in women, would be totally neutralized by that feature of mine which would create a challenge to women... followed by feelings of tender attraction as an attempt to harness that subtle coexistence of feminine/masculine attributes...

I confess that I was very flattered by her remarks, which showed that she had been analyzing me, maybe in order to understand and decipher what Angelina had probably confided about me or at least her vision of me.

Amanda had what one could define as a slinky and extremely graceful feature when it came to her sensuality. I simply could not take my eyes off of her, and I would stay fixated on every detail such as the gracious back of her neck, her delicate ears, her perfectly proportionate nose, her tender and always warm cheeks, her low neck that would reveal the start of her splendid breasts, and her velvet like skin that would transmit a sense of purity yielding tenacious attraction. Her demeanor was alluring and glamorous in every movement of her extremely well proportionate body, and this would add to her enigmatic stance. That woman wouldn't stop a single male or female head from turning upon her passing by!

We went straight to a perfumed and sumptuous bed after a light dinner prepared by her maid who would not hide her joy and curiosity of having me around, maybe an evidence that Amanda would not take anyone to the Hamptons except on some rare and very special occasions, as she would herself later confirm.

Our love making that evening was the most tender experience I had ever had, maybe a result of our previous vivacious conversation. We needed to release all that contained energy that had stayed somehow blocked despite all our frank and direct exchanges or that stayed in the realm of the thoughts we both wanted to express to each other but finally didn't. It was as if we were in a transcending experience where our bodies knew exactly what to do to extract the maximum pleasure from the other as if blindly guided by a universal entity brought upon us to make us love each other to the utmost with no restrictions whatsoever! We then spent the entire night intertwined with each other, so tightly knotted as if to intimidate and scare away any potential interference in our deeply loving emotions... I realized once again that love can only be positive, be good, that love is the purest, the most beneficial feeling that our bodies and souls can and must experience! There is no place for taboos, moral limits or any other restrictions to the most sublime act resulting from feelings that have been so generously bestowed upon our species by higher, universal forces! The real spiritual crime concerning love in any of its forms, is to not pursue this sublime sentiment and the pleasures it generates in us, instead of the false moral constraints that have been developed through the ages in order to enslave us, often favoring the greed of sick, ill-intentioned individuals, governments, entire societies or religious groups, that have usurped the truth and created deviant ideas of this lofty feeling to serve their own, hidden and often terrifying interests...

By finally unwinding from all that energy, whilst hearing Amanda's regular breathing and feeling her heartbeat, I sensed an invasion of joy and fulfillment. I could hardly sleep, often awakened by disturbing thoughts only to fall back into sleep reassured by her presence!

Once again, I had been gifted... I was in love! Life had a meaning, it smelled good, I felt excited at every perspective even the most trivial one like having breakfast, as long as I knew that Amanda would be by my side! We had an entire week ahead of us, certainly better than just one day, however still too short a period, but we also had eternity if we so desired! We were free! Love is freedom! True love is the most liberating feeling a human being can have!

We sat for breakfast at a cozy dining room leading to an internal patio full of flowers. We could not take our eyes off each other and here and there we would express small laughs at our bewilderment towards all those beautiful feelings that had possessed us so unexpectedly. From time to time our skins would touch and a spark of electricity would penetrate our beings filling us with contentment!

The morning was gorgeous and sooner than I would have honestly expected, almost that entire magical day had passed not before allowing us to enjoy the company of each other in a long brisk walk by the property and by the sea followed by a late light lunch.

Rigorously on schedule, in the late afternoon, the same smiling lady of the night before came in to announce that Amanda's friends were already waiting in the east side living room...

"How many are there, my love?" I asked Amanda, eager to figure out up to what extent our magical moments would be gone...

"Well, they are four couples, four lovely couples, you will see, who can't wait to meet you... you see my love, ever since I divorced, I have never introduced anyone to them, and I have consistently rejected every attempt of theirs to make me date some of their friends..."

"So?" I asked rather cynically...

"So, you should consider yourself a privileged soul my love! This being said, beware of my friends... they like to protect me, and you can bet they will scrutinize you from head to toe before emitting any opinion, and in case they disapprove of you, they will not mince words in order to protect me!"

"I didn't know you had put together a jury to have me

inspected so thoroughly. If they don't approve of me, I probably know the outcome, but what if they do approve of me? What comes next?" I asked with a naughty expression.

Amanda was obviously embarrassed by my question like a chess player facing a risky move by her opponent. "Well, that is a secret," was her reply to me, denying my expected boyish gratification... I let the issue go, not without making a mental note to return to the subject at the first opportunity...

The happy bunch waiting for us in the living room located in the east side of the mansion were exactly that... a happy bunch! As we came in, they stopped laughing and gazed at me from top to bottom eager to draw the first conclusions of the encounter before I could even open my mouth to say hi! It is very interesting to be observed by people who want to get a precise definition of yourself fairly quickly, instead of giving time to time in order to get to know you better, at your own tempo, allowing themselves the possibility of even making mistakes in their first judgements and correcting them as the relationship evolves. On the other hand, you remain in fact the only one in command of the encounter and its ensuing account, having the ability to adapt it or even change it altogether as you see fit. The fun of the situation is that you can gauge other people's misconceptions about yourself and still wait for a better approximation or guesstimate without having to move a finger. All you have to do is to observe and play with their body language! Communication encompasses a lot beyond the verbal ability which quite often is at the origin of significant misunderstandings.

Amanda grasped the momentum immediately and took the initiative to introduce me...

"Hi everybody! Let me finally introduce you to my savage

friend who came straight from the Amazon jungle to meet with us! Axel, please meet my very good friends with whom I share incredible moments with here in the Hamptons!"

I greeted everybody politely, still in command of the intense exchange of energy between us yet quite bored with the reiteration of the introductory allusions about myself as the indomitable being from the confines of the jungle! I tried not to lose control of the communication that had been established and the feverish, intense and palpable thirst for more of me! I was greatly amused of course!

Finally, a beautiful and elegantly dressed woman broke the silence and with it the enchantment of the furtive communication that had been going on.

"I guess you know by now that we are all extremely curious to hear your stories from the horse's mouth, Amanda has been telling us incredible things about you ever since she met you a couple of weeks ago, and we are all eager to hear additional details from the one who was there, in person, — all those exciting stories!"

A series of "yeah, yeah, right" arose from the small crowd obviously giving me very little chance to stay silent.

"Well, first of all you should consider that everything is in the eye of the beholder my dear friends. Reality is that my stories are not so fantastic or even exceptional by any shape or form! What happened is that some peculiar facts came to me in a very special set of circumstances of my life which made me process the events in such a way as to extract very unusual, almost intriguing aspects of the latter. It was like watching a movie and cherry picking the scenes that count the most for the script… with the difference that it was not a movie. It was hard core reality indeed!"

"Well, guys, do not expect Axel to sit down and recount his life for endless hours because, amongst other reasons, this is his first visit here and I have put together a weeklong program to entertain him... so maybe he never leaves!" she finished with a laughter.

Finally, it was agreed that I would tell them parts of my story by dinner time, since we already had four invitations confirmed for the days to follow.

We then spent the rest of the day together touring the place and having a lovely lunch in a nice seafood restaurant in the neighborhood. The late afternoon tea took place at the McCormick's, yet another gorgeous property by the sea.

I was pampered by everybody, and I confess that I enjoyed it greatly! Those people, despite their sophistication and savoir faire (they were all highly skilled professionals with university degrees and doctorates from the very best American universities such as Harvard, Yale, Stamford, MIT and so on) treated me like one of their own from the very beginning, respecting and even valuing my humble beginnings and my life struggles to merely survive, a stark contrast to the vast majority of the so called Brazilian elite who, far from being even remotely educated, had completely lost their sense of dignity, ranked close to zero if not below from an erudite or cultural standpoint, and, with the exclusion of some rare and honorable exceptions, treated people as a monetary value where mere wealth would constitute the entire substance of an individual. Quite sad and despicable indeed...

We had highly inspirational and moving intellectual exchanges through the ensuing week and in the end, I had made eight new and exciting friends from different walks of life, all with very interesting stories and, most of all, wide and open-minded interpretations of their own lives which contributed to making them highly interesting and intellectually rich!

I will always praise Americans for their capacity of self-evaluation, of bravely recognizing their shortcomings despite the huge dominance of the American influence in the world and starting all over again whenever necessary! Their resilience is indeed second to none. This is why they have built such a great country, which, despite its multiple problems, remains the number one country on earth in terms of opportunity.

Amanda and I had to literally steal time for ourselves by inventing all sorts of excuses in order to avoid being caught into an endless series of social requests with her lovely friends. They wanted to be with us and somehow my life stories and my experiences in the Amazon jungle and elsewhere in the world acted like a magnet to their imagination. I treated them all with due respect but also conveyed a sense of freedom, of detachment from the pretentiously stylish aspects of their lives and a certain intimacy to the wild and the unknown, something they were not used to in their sophisticated and contained milieu. Like everybody else in their entourage, their lives, albeit intellectually rich, lacked a little bit of spice, of madness so to speak, of daring and an out-of-the-beaten-path creativity, all of which were an inherent part of my life circumstances. For them, I was a free spirit, which is something they simply could not afford to be in the face of their business and social commitments. In fact, they had to nurture an image of modern, open minded entrepreneurs which meant that their dreams of freedom had to be found in the many books they read, most of them self-help or philosophical works or even esoteric studies in the form of exploratory essays. Listening not only to my stories but mainly to the interpretations I had made of the different personages that participated in my random and erratic life trajectory, exerted a fascination on them especially considering the authenticity of the narrative and the sagacity of its multiple details.

The week went by faster than we would like it to, and in literally no time we found ourselves on the following Saturday ready to drive back to New York for me to fly back to Toronto the following day. We arrived in Manhattan on Saturday early afternoon and went straight to bed in order to enjoy each other's intimacy throughout every single moment left before my departure.

We made love intensely with an unrevealed yet unsettling intuition that this would perhaps be our last encounter. We both had no physical restrictions whatsoever towards each other and the anxiety of the separation gave our sex a special flavor and an impulse to devour each other's being in an egotistic impulse to carry the essence of the other away forever. Our bodies fused and our sweat gave us both a salty, familiar taste, that we would certainly miss in the future.

Deep in her soul Amanda was certainly not looking for someone like me to be part of her life for the long stretch. She needed a companion from her milieu with a more stable background than mine, someone who would be able to sit down for hours on lazy Sunday afternoons and play bridge whilst making spirited jokes about common acquaintances and their softhearted adventures not without a well contained amount of socially accepted folly. I, in sheer contrast, represented an indomitable, quite non-accommodative soul, too far from her familiar and comfy life-style, distant from the well-established limits of what she was able to tolerate from a companion in the long haul. Her orderly and secure upbringing hence her way of reasoning as well as her accepted social values were too deeply engrained in her mind, carefully crafted from generation to generation of her ancestors despite her high cultural level which allowed a certain openness to novelty. I was conversely, along with my crazy stories and set of rebellious convictions, just fine and acceptable for a couple of sunny days at the Hamptons. Amanda and her friends in fact enjoyed my company, and my out of the box ideas as long as they were not too far from a well-chosen bottle of Sonoma or French expensive wine that would facilitate their own introspection. This being said, at the end of the day as the effects of the Bordeaux wine would recede, they would definitely feel reassured by their possessions and cozy way of life. A glass of exquisite "XO" cognac would finally reinforce their conviction about their "well and smartly chosen" existence. The elegant settings of their multi-million-dollar posh domiciles represented in fact an unbridgeable fortification of their own beliefs by somehow materially re-affirming, through the ramparts of their manor homes, their certitude about their predictable paths through life…

There is no way I would fit in for the long haul, no matter how Amanda would welcome it, and she probably would, extending our exciting and lively love affair not without the expectation that I would somehow change and ultimately adapt myself to their modus vivendi. But I knew that even if I had the means and the willingness to hang around for a while, the whole thing would sooner or later collapse like a house of cards! Not that I was better or worse than them… I was simply not part of that entourage and was very dissimilar indeed, to put it mildly.

I therefore boarded Angelina's as always impressive G5 on that Sunday afternoon knowing, deep in my heart, that I would probably not see Amanda again at least in the foreseeable future! Nor the now almost familiar and spectacular Gulfstream jet for that matter. She had probably reached the same conclusion without daring to articulate it to me or even to herself… It was too early for that and after all there was no harm in keeping the dream alive for a while.

During the following weeks we had several conversations over the phone and together reached the conclusion that the best course of action was to give ourselves time to ponder what we really expected from each other.

Two months later, I was summoned to go back to São Paulo in order to finally pass the torch… I was polite enough and politically correct to call my new friends in New York to say goodbye and to thank them profusely notwithstanding that strange feeling whereby I was closing that chapter for good. Amanda and I had had a couple of final talks and both of us had decided that our short relationship, albeit great, could not be extended for all the good reasons we both had extensively debated, therefore we lovingly decided that we should part ways, at least temporarily…

Angelina was determined to foster my situation with Amanda and as such had even offered me a good job position in one of her enterprises which would enable me to move to New York and even get a Green Card in order to become a US resident. Needless to say, and although that gesture of hers was very enticing to me, I politely declined not without second thoughts though, but in the end, I was deeply convinced that I simply did not belong to that reality. I was finally maturing and my growing critical need for the essential was becoming an intrinsic part of my soul, which, by the way, seemed to be in a hurry now! I would obviously only be able to de-code those signals at a later stage in my life as is usually the case.

Angelina knew that my farewell was likely a final goodbye

so much so that she didn't harness the courage to fly to Toronto to have a goodbye dinner as she had promised to do. She called me and all she could say was, "You should know that you represent a lot to me, and that I shall always love you!"

"I know... I love you too!" was all I could say in return before hanging up and crying like an abandoned child.

Once back in São Paulo, and after being introduced to my new metals trading team, I was unexpectedly requested by management to go to the Amazon, more precisely back to the Jutaí river region one last time for a final attempt to recover over three million US dollars still unaccounted for and that had been paid in advance to a ruthless French/Algerian individual by the name of Youssef, with the expectation that the latter would supply a substantial tonnage of rare minerals in return. This was my new specialty so to speak yet Youssef was still part of the old guard, with whom I had had many tough exchanges in the past in order to make him deliver what he was supposed to in terms of sawn timber. My new boss thought that although the assignment at hand was not strictly part of my new responsibilities, it was an excellent opportunity to improve the company's cash position whilst presenting me with the last of those unpleasant challenges which consisted in recovering money that had been unprofessionally advanced to dishonest individuals by stupid or worse, corrupt executives...

AMAZON III

I took off on a Saturday afternoon from São Paulo to Manaus and I confess that I was not sad at all with the perspective of spending what were supposed to be my last couple of weeks in the jungle. I looked forward to the peace and quietness of some of those familiar places that were extremely far away from the so-called civilized world yet recognizable enough to me to the point that I could almost call them my second home. I also looked forward to the fantastic and delicious Tucunaré (river fish) that I had learned to enjoy eating during my now countless expeditions to the region… and, last but not least, I had kept vivid in my mind those fabulous remembrances of the pinnacle of erotic pleasure represented by Eloisa and Isadora!

I decided to have a short connection and flew directly West from Manaus to Tefé in order to spend the night there before joining Youssef on his river boat that would take us upriver in the Solimões and from there into the Jutaí river region in what was supposed to later become the 'Cujubim' reserve — the largest sustainable development reserve in the world encompassing six million acres. Once there, we would spend a good week touring the region and meeting Youssef's mining teams who supposedly would show us the rare minerals ready to be delivered to Tefé by small boats and from there flown over to São Paulo…

My night in Tefé was calm as I shared a couple of beers with my old friends at my favorite restaurant where Tucunaré, the outstandingly delicious fish, was served fried next to the bank of the river, literally being transferred directly from the water to a piece of solid hardwood where it was cleaned still alive, and from there into the frying pan… a cruel, yet delicious. tradition.

I learned with surprise and admittedly much to my regret that Isadora and Eloisa had recently moved to Paris, France, in a bid to strike it big in some sort of a new cabaret that had just been inaugurated in the 'city of lights'. Eloisa had obviously left her influential husband . I could hardly contain my frustration in the face of what would have definitively been a night of reencounter between the three of us! Simply fantastic for sure! But reality is what it is, and my recurrent fantasy regarding those outstanding lovers had no other option but to come to a close!

The following day started at five am sharp with myself punctually positioned with my backpack next to Youssef's characteristic Amazonian boat, painted in bright yellow with dark blue stripes which would give it the allure of one of those elegant and pleasant boats usually anchored in one of those very charming little harbors of the Côte d'Azur in southern France. Probably wishful thinking on the part of Youssef who, as I learned later, was a wanted felon by the Europol police organization in Europe, for a series of financial as well as other, hidden crimes. He happened to simply hate the Amazon region yet had no choice but to live there at least temporarily since there existed very few better hiding places on earth as far as he was concerned.

"Ho, ho, ho, this is what I call a punctual man!" a hoarse and guttural voice made itself present preceding a big, bearded and badly dressed individual who, despite his coarse appearance, did not lack a certain degree of charm, I must confess…" How are you Axel? It has been a long time since we met when I was still dealing with the timber business, eh? I learned that you went to

Toronto and became an expert in the minerals business, so I look forward to a long and profitable business relationship between us! Now, you probably have a lot to teach me…" was his ironic exclamation followed by a vulgar laughter that would expose a mouthful of gold fillings which would undoubtedly put him in harm's way in the face of the value of the gold in his mouth. There was no doubt that gold was worth well above the value of human life in the ruthless milieu he used to hang around.

"Well, it will all depend on the speed you intend to supply what has already been contracted and paid for, or repay the three million dollars you owe my organization!" was my blunt reply without mincing a single word!

Youssef threw me an icy glimpse whilst mumbling something that sounded like an "of course" which made me immediately feel that my task amounted in reality to mission impossible! Our first exchange had been indeed indicative of the difficulties I was about to face with the man…

The old engine started with a lazy purr that would thereafter persist for the rest of the trip however as we distanced ourselves from the bank of the river, a splendid tropical sun made its grandiose appearance through the top of the huge tree canopies as a promise that destiny had good things in store after all, despite Youssef's now evident antipathy towards me. Our speed was definitely not impressive at all and according to Youssef, who knew the place like the palm of his hand, we had to navigate for at least a good week before reaching the mining region I was supposed to inspect. Two old and dirty looking hammocks would serve as our beds throughout the entire voyage, and we were supposed to sleep in alternate shifts most of the time lest we wanted to make sure the voyage wouldn't last forever!

Youssef was a born storyteller and he had loads of attention-grabbing stories, some of which were very exciting indeed, others rather boring really! This would make things easier to bear since I was a good listener and my instincts made me feel that I didn't want to disclose my own life stories to this kind of an individual anyway... so I thought better he do the talking anyway!

He defined himself as a Berber who was accidentally born in France, a country he disdained for obvious colonial reasons. He had a reasonable historical knowledge about his country of origin and hailed Algeria, rightly so, as being at the origin of the invention and manufacturing of different human tools especially war tools like blades and swords dating back to the Middle Paleolithic period, in other words, around the year of 30,000 BC. Youssef claimed that his family's heritage came from a direct lineage from the Berber King Masinissa (circa 150 BC) which would of course attach a certain degree of nobleness to his ancestry. He was without a shadow of a doubt a remarkable storyteller whose accounts were rich in details and descriptive intensity. I listened to most of his stories silently for endless hours, watching the waves created by the propulsion of the boat, half-hypnotized by the continuous resonance of the engine and the swinging of the hull, gently swaying through the ripples created by the treacherous currents of the river.

His unmissable stories, some of which were of course hard to believe, would frequently take place in the desert, on the occasions when Youssef would go back to Algeria on holiday which would allow him to return to his hailed origins. There, in a not-so-distant past, Youssef and his black Arabian stallion would often rescue defenseless, eroticized and gorgeous "odalisques" who were hopelessly lost, laying on the desert sand, alone and desperate just waiting to be found by Youssef under a moonless starry night. Of course he was young and extremely handsome in those days, and most of all didn't have that protuberant, colossal belly that would follow him around, permanently and everywhere, obliging him to carry it at all times as an undesirable bastard child! Needless to say, he had been extremely athletic in his youth, which would grant him the strength and more importantly the imagination to grab those poor, desperately lost, yet exquisite creatures by the arm, catapult them on to the back of the horse with a single, uninterrupted movement, and charge ahead in a most impressive gallop in the middle of the mysterious yet inviting darkness!

Other accounts had to do with fierce fights against individuals emerging from enemy nomad tribes, generally with a view to defend an honorable cause or, once again, the honor of a dame belonging to his own dynasty... The stories were long and plenty of details aimed at giving the listener a full sense of the context of any given situation of the narrative imaginary or otherwise. Listening to him had the advantage of accelerating the passage of time which would somehow mitigate the boredom of our long and monotonous journey...

In reality I knew that Youssef had grown up in the outskirts of Paris in a poor neighborhood built by the French state in order to accommodate poor immigrants who didn't have enough means to afford adequate housing. His upbringing had therefore been harsh with a father who would not take no for an answer. Life was taxing from all angles which gave young Youssef a spirited character often resulting in aggressive attitudes towards what would have otherwise been customary, everyday life circumstances. Every single occurrence described by Youssef regarding his past, would therefore be presented and tainted with strong, dramatic colors that would portray him as the hero of every single episode composing his existence!

The hard fact remained however that as a kid, he had to defend himself quite often from gangs of older boys who would terrorize the streets of his neighborhood and bully the young ones in order to rob them of their meagre savings. That dreadful environment had taught Youssef to become a first-class street fighter which served him well in terms of allowing him to survive in that urban jungle. Interestingly enough though, Youssef kept his dignity intact and never joined any of those thug groups. He grew up to become one of those fearless, cunning individuals who regretfully carved his way up, economically speaking, by associating himself with the underground business world, ultimately becoming involved in a series of outlawed financial activities obliging him to escape prison by finding refuge deep in the Amazon jungle. But before ending up in the Jutaí riverbanks, Youssef had gone through the most unbelievable set of circumstances escaping from police through several cities in the six continents ahead of deciding to finally go incommunicado deep in the Amazon region... quite a saga!

Well, that was the character of the individual I had to deal with inside a tiny boat for a period of more than 15 days if all went well, which of course I doubted. To his merit, he knew the region and the habits of some of the tribes we would come across in our journey quite well, so there were no worries from that standpoint... my real concern was Youssef himself and his confrontational attitude towards me. In fact, I had the feeling that he was afraid of me especially due to the fact that he knew that I was aware of the quasi-unsurmountable debt he had contracted with the company I worked for and was there to collect. That, plus his constant defiant attitude made me seriously doubt the existence of the minerals he had agreed to deliver. This made him feel extremely nervous and it was quite obvious that he had decided to play the game as it went, rolling with the punches so to speak, and improvising most of the time in order to come across as a serious and reliable supplier of minerals. I must say that Youssef was basically a serious individual, with a rightful demeanor but I would never be able to tell whether he had been corrupted by my predecessor and ended up seduced by the amount of money at stake — quite a lot of money for Youssef's standards!

So, amidst a series of epic and at times unmissable episodes about Youssef's thrilling life, six days went by and in the end, I was getting quite anxious to get to the place where the minerals were supposedly stockpiled and ready to be loaded aboard the first available boat capable of carrying such a heavy cargo. To celebrate what was supposed to be the last day aboard before reaching our final destination, Youssef practically exhumed a whole bottle of Jack Daniels carefully hidden like a treasure in the tiny basement of the boat exuding a heavy smell of fuel due to the proximity to the engine, and served us two huge doses before raising his glass and, to my utter bewilderment, stating literally,

"Axel, I must tell you that I shall never deliver those minerals since they simply do not exist and never existed! So let us finally celebrate the truth!"

That memorable statement was followed by sarcastic and extremely strident laughter that I shall never forget! We both stood there staring at each other, with me taken aback, saying nothing, as if that highly surprising and unanticipated revelation had taken away all of my ability to utter a single word!

After some time that seemed an eternity, I mumbled, "Nothing, really nothing at all, Youssef?"

"Zero!" was his short and trenchant reply followed by yet more scornful and golden laughter.

I didn't know what to say except for aggressively questioning him about the utility of the trip... and the huge amount of time and money spent for absolutely nothing!

"What am I supposed to do, Youssef?" was my question as if asking for a solution from the very man that had the firm intention of stealing from the company the full three million dollars!

"Well, Axel, go back to São Paulo and tell your stupid bosses to go fuck themselves! This is the price people pay for being stupid! I am not referring to you of course, since I know you're pretty much a smart fellow at the end of the day," was his ironic answer while pouring another very generous dose of Jack Daniels in my glass.

"You must be wondering why I decided to disclose this to you instead of endlessly continuing that comedy of hide and seek. Well, it is simply because I have a very enticing proposal for you... why don't you come and work with me... as a partner of course! With all the contacts you have in the US, especially with that billionaire bitch you fucked with all over the Amazon, we could land a couple of very profitable deals that would allow us to make a piss-pot full of money and retire somewhere in the Côte d'Azur! You see, interesting news spreads very fast in this fucking place and I happen to know all about your recent trip to the US and the fact that you stayed with Angelina in her husband's mansion fucking like two rabbits in his own bed!"

At that point, I simply lost my temper and my rage was such that I could no longer control the situation, and all at once, I jumped like a leopard punching Youssef hard on the chin so strongly that I had the impression of displacing his jaw, besides perhaps breaking my hand in the process! He lost his balance for a while and fell back on one of the poles of the boat on his back. In the meantime, and amidst all that upheaval, the boat had totally lost its course and I instinctively turned around to grab the wheel in order to restore its direction, when I suddenly felt that massive hit in the back of my head that catapulted me half unconscious into the darkness of the night and headfirst in the tumultuous and dark waters of the Jutaí!

All I remember was Youssef's cries fading away in the dark whilst desperately screaming my name and frantically yelling in all directions downstream in order to locate me in the darkness of the moonless night amidst the turbulent and agitated whirlpools created by the rapid currents of the river. I was voiceless and could hardly keep myself afloat after the violent blow to the back of my head and I could hear Youssef's voice becoming more and more inaudible as I felt my body being carried speedily by the rapids of the river towards what seemed to be a distant riverbank… I knew that I had to struggle in order to stay afloat and especially stay conscious after the ferocious jolt I had received from Youssef whose voice had now simply gone totally silent in the darkness of the night.

After drifting for around an hour or so and struggling desperately to stay conscious, I could feel my feet touching the muddy riverbed which subsequently became full of pebbles which made me believe that I had finally reached the riverbank. I tried to stand up on my feet still feeling a great pain in the back of my head, let alone my probably half-broken right hand, but could hardly find my balance. I then decided to crawl out of the water to no avail due to the very high density of the vegetation in that particular spot. I crawled a considerable distance downstream, with almost no visibility whatsoever, trying my very best not to be pulled back to the middle of the river by the strong currents. I finally reached a point where I could vaguely perceive some kind of a clearing in the riverbank, so I started to crawl towards that direction when, as I reached the shallows of the river, I suddenly felt an acute pain as if something had bit me in my lower leg… immediately after, I could scarcely distinguish the sleek form of a multi-colored snake swimming away speedily towards the riverbank and swiftly crawling inside the vegetation where it instantly disappeared…

I finally reached the clearing spot and endeavored to climb out of the water with all my remaining strength when I suddenly started to feel my muscles gradually going dormant and becoming practically inactive despite my desperate efforts to continue ahead. I finally reached a fairly dry spot and at that point in time I could no longer feel the outer or peripheral muscles of my body! It was a horrendous feeling of almost total paralysis and I finally realized that I had most certainly been bitten by what was probably an Aquatic Coral Snake, one of the most poisonous if not the most poisonous snake of the Americas! The gradual feeling of paralysis of my muscles was certainly due to the powerful neurotoxins released by the snake's bite! Before any further consideration, and while I was still conscious, I reached for a sharp stone and used all my remaining strength to create a deep cut encompassing the two almost invisible marks of the snake fangs in my leg until an abundant amount of blood started flowing from the cut. Then I took off my shirt and created what resembled a rope and used it as a tourniquet firmly attaching the upper part of my leg with it as tightly as I could. In the ensuing moments I felt a surprisingly comfortable sensation of latency in practically my entire body despite some difficulty in breathing, before gradually losing my senses and every notion of orientation. Then, I gently passed out amidst the timeless immensity of the Amazon basin…

I am not sure how many hours, that seemed like entire days, I spent immersed in a complete state of delirium punctuated by hallucinations that were in their turn alternated here and there by episodes of full clarity and, lastly, enlightening ecstasy… I must confess though that during those hallucinations I had a clear intuition that my mind/body situation was just the same, only performing and reacting in what felt like a different dimension. In other words, the hallucinogen state I was immersed in seemed to be clearly a reflection of a totally new dimensional environment, instead of any deregulation of my state of mind per se as a result of the poison running in my veins… I therefore felt as an explorer of a brand-new world, a distinctive reality that was unravelling just there, before my eyes, whilst triggering the awakening of what seemed to be a brand-new set of unfamiliar senses! All that revolutionary perception was unraveling like a totally new awareness which in a way was shielding me from panicking in the face of the most awkward and terrifying situation I found myself somewhere along the banks of the Jutaí river! My own familiar senses would be challenged by unfamiliar emotions and feelings that in their turn would create juxtaposed, multi-dimensional realities. Colors would change completely as would the entire setting, making me transcend into diverse existential scenarios that were quite intriguing and stimulating! For example, not only could I fly, but I could also transpose myself to any given situation of my past and rearrange entire scenes by reordering a given condition to my own liking! Amongst those highly lucid yet inexplicable perceptions there was a particular one that made me feel as if my body would shift through some kind of conveyance towards that unforgettable night with Angelina and that incredibly hospitable tribe, where I was given that mysterious concoction made out of snake blood mixed with other kinds of wild roots and herbs that gave me an extraordinary energy at that time... the most intriguing aspect of that vivid, albeit hectic and feverish voyage all the way back to that specific episode, was that I could now make a clear connection between the snake bite and the brew I was offered on that occasion. It suddenly occurred to me that maybe, or rather probably, that drink mixture provided me with some sort of partial immunization against the extremely toxic venom of the Water Coral snake scientifically known as the 'Micrurus Surinamensis'! Hadn't I been provided with some sort of inoculation, I should have probably been dead within a few hours from the bite at best!

The human body has a huge capacity of storing memories especially if those include physical distinctive events, and to revive them in case of extreme necessity, which was definitely the case vis a vis what was happening to me by resuscitating that distant drinking ceremony! This was certainly the reason why I was still alive albeit in a highly perilous situation... I was getting hungry but had absolutely no strength or enough lucidity to look for food... water was not a problem given the frequent tropical showers which would allow me to drink by simply opening my mouth and swallowing, albeit with great difficulty in the face of the inflammatory process triggered by the poison that would generate a slowly suffocating effect. The fact of the matter was that I would alternate between a complete hallucinogenic, totally oblivious, yet highly intuitive state, to a highly clear and lucid state of mind, and then dive back into a comatose condition. The periods of lucidity were scarce and very short in time, but I could realize that they would gradually increase as time went by. The periods of hallucination were bizarre and eccentric since they would for example make me travel back to significant periods, people or events in my life or even to events, persons or places; I simply could not connect to anything at all… entire theories would come and go in a flash and I often desperately wished to have access to a pen and a piece of paper in order to note them down!

Strange yet mind-blowing, stunningly beautiful women I had met in the past and complete strangers would come and sit by my side and offer me caresses that would placate my despair and pacify my often-excruciating muscle pain. My perceptions of them were extraordinarily clear, and I could distinctly grasp what went on deep inside their beings. I was able to sense an unbelievable multiplicity of profound and very authentic feminine instincts as if being my own, and even feelings and perceptions that resembled rare and exotic flowers waiting for someone to smell their exquisite aromas… and to meld into their spiritual beauty. It occurred to me that all those women parading in my imagination, or otherwise in different dimensions, were possibly nothing but a metamorphose of myself into different beings exhaling pure and unrestricted love! It is a fact that each and every woman hides, deep inside, her own and unique mystical footprint composed of all the nonphysical elements that are part of her inner self and ultimately differentiate the feminine from the masculine. My hallucinogenic state in a way offered me the prerogative to read into some of those different feminine mystical footprints, go in and out of them, and to desperately fall in love with them since there were no more filters or social veils whatsoever. It was as if those dancing creatures, imaginary or otherwise, belonging to separate dimensions pertaining or not to my past were there, just waiting to be uncovered and passionately loved! Then there was also the purely physical component brought about by that ecstatic state I was immersed in. I could literally feel the soft touch of women's skins coming into contact with different parts of my body and giving me an incredibly pleasurable feeling of warmth and comfort somehow quelling my excruciating pain! It was as if a second, separate reality, completely detached from my agonizing quasi moribund condition would come to my rescue in order to keep me alive…

I would also traverse long mental stretches of what appeared to be sustained, totally lucid periods of perfect reasoning, bearing absolutely no connection with anything I had ever thought or imagined before. As such, love would come to my mind as a perfect all-encompassing entity that would express itself through the entire spectrum of reality be it spiritual, physical, known or unknown. Love is love, period, no matter the conduit of its expression. Physical love, or to put it plainly, sex, is obviously one of the most crucial and encompassing expressions of love and it is the one thing that allows two individuals to fulfill their cosmic destiny of pleasure, ecstasy and procreation! Nobody should be afraid or ashamed of surrendering completely to love, in any of its shapes or forms. We fear love because we fear our potential failure to perform although it is never a matter of performance, as well as our extraordinary power to surrender to pleasure! Pleasure is often viewed as something prohibited, a sinful expression of the self, made illicit by society. The truth is that pleasure, sexual pleasure to be more specific, is the utmost spiritual expression borne by our universal bodies without any restrictions or boundaries! Entire societies and their deceptive man-made beliefs have turned that wonderful cosmic energy into something shameful, restricted and reprehensible. That vision of truth suddenly manifested itself in an extremely vivid image inside my mind as repeatedly and desperately as the feelings of my utter sufferance as the poison made its way through my veins…

I was not afraid at all though. Anyone who had the opportunity to spend the night in the Amazon jungle knows that most animals are nocturnal and as such come out to hunt in the middle of the night creating a deafening, continuous racket, a tumultuous pandemonium intertwined with the furor of life and death occurring just there, everywhere, repeatedly, a sheer expression of the eternal drama between hunter and prey… My perception was one of full awareness of all those expressions of life and death surrounding my body, which had the effect of soothing my spirit and somehow appeasing my pain. I was in fact taking an active part in that dance in a crazy alternation that would in fact place my entire being on a thin razor's edge where fear simply could not subsist! I would also alternate between what I thought were long periods of sleep probably necessary to compensate for my exhaustion thus helping me recover at least some of my energy, and endless hiatus of what seemed to be a half-awakened state… As time went by, I started feeling increasingly hungry to the point of grabbing whatever was in my reach such as rotten roots and fallen leaves in order to placate my insatiable appetite…

As I started experiencing increased periods of lucidity all those hallucinations which at least served to mentally propel me away from that miserable condition, gradually faded away and I started to feel increasingly anxious with the deplorable situation I was incontestably in… at one given point, my desperation grew to such an unbearable extent that I convinced myself that death would be the only plausible outcome left for me in the face of my dire circumstances. The dark, moonless night had fallen and even darker clouds were auguring a stormy night. I had already noticed that the level of the river had swollen consistently presaging not only the start of the rainy season, but also the thaw of the snow that had accumulated in the Andes' Mountain peaks during the winter season of the southern hemisphere. That phenomenon is the main factor behind the yearly flooding of the entire region which allows its splendid flora as well as its unbelievably rich fauna to regenerate from the ravages of the dry season.

The rain started falling quite heavily, and the riverbank started to gradually disappear under the increasingly strong currents of muddy water that would wash everything away no matter its size or weight...

Suddenly I could faintly discern a moving heavy tree trunk some one hundred meters from where I was, floating towards me at a frightening pace whilst I had the neat impression of hearing voices... I thought that I was once again hallucinating since I was still barely conscious, nevertheless all of a sudden, I felt the shock of the tree trunk hitting my body in its passage and making me almost lose consciousness. The last thing I could think of for the last fraction of a second before passing out for good, was that I was most certainly facing my own death. Strangely enough though, immediately thereafter, a feeling of well-being invaded my body and my mind, followed by another one of great relief... then all became dark, and I finally fell into deep unconsciousness...

BORN AGAIN

My unexpected awakening was the weirdest thing that had ever happened to me, so much so that it took me some good minutes to realize that I was not dead nor dreaming! In reality, I was being hastily transported on some kind of a makeshift stretcher, and all I could see was the tree branches and farther away their drenched canopies passing by, very fast, over my head... It took me quite some time to realize that I was being carried by supposedly two individuals who were holding the stretcher above their heads maybe out of precaution so that I wouldn't fall off and eventually get so scared to the point of running away... as if I had any energy left for such an epic move! I decided instinctively to stay motionless perhaps as a protective measure, thus avoiding any possible reaction originating from those who were beneath me. The rain was not abating at all, quite the contrary, and despite being totally exposed to it, I was invaded by certain instinctive feelings of protection despite the almost unbearable pain let alone the fact that I was soaked and in the twilight zone of what remained of my consciousness. I was also impressed by what seemed to me like being a very well-organized rescue operation.

I couldn't possibly tell the distance that had been covered between my rescue at the river-bank and our arrival in what appeared to be an Indian hamlet in the middle of nowhere! By then I was in a really bad shape and could hardly distinguish one shadow from the other, let alone make sense of what was going on in my surroundings. All I could discern were voices, however, I couldn't grasp a single word of what they were saying to one another… Finally, a hand introduced delicately some sort of pipe in my mouth, and I instinctively inhaled the smoke, just to lose what still remained of my distressed consciousness instantaneously.

I had several dreams during my long sleep — subsequently I was led to understand that I had slept for three days as a result of my exhaustion, combined with the smoke I had inhaled… some sort of sleeping, relaxing drug. One of those dreams took me back to Tokyo and to Keiko. She was holding me tight in her arms while caressing my chest the way she used to do, so tenderly, that I would infallibly fall asleep in her arms. She would then hold me there for a long time, no matter how long it took for me to wake up. She would then sing one of those Japanese lullabies, so soothingly that at times I would fall asleep all over again… seemingly my present drowsy condition was fusing with the oneiric state of my mind and would carry me all over to the other side of the globe and into Keiko's welcoming and familiar embrace…

Suddenly I felt a warm touch right in the region of my leg where the snake had bit me. Without knowing whether I was still in Keiko's dream, I looked down and to my surprise there was that sublime creature posing her lips onto my horrifying and repulsive wound, and then sucking it in order to extract what seemed to be a mixture of blood and a yellowish substance that appeared to me as a disgusting cocktail made of the poison of the Coral snake together with some kind of an infectious substance, probably the product resulting from the reaction between the venom and my blood and tissues… The young woman would then pull as much liquid as she could from the open abscess and spit it out in some kind of a big clay bowl placed by her side. I immediately understood that she was trying to empty the wound of all the poison and impurities as well as to provide the necessary asepsis in order to stop and prevent further infections from occurring.

After a long period of time, perhaps a good couple of hours, or even more, she finished her nauseating job and disappeared only to come back a couple of minutes later with a fumigated piece of strongly scented wood and, after delicately turning my head to the opposite side, she applied vigorously the glowing ember right onto the wound! I heard my scream for a fraction of a second before passing out yet again!

I woke up without any pain, which was an extraordinary feeling of relief! Moments later the same young woman re-entered the place where I was laying down, allowing me for the first time since she had started taking care of me, and thanks to my newly gained lucidity, to be able to discern the flawless beauty and exquisite elegance of that breathtaking young woman! She was entirely naked which allowed me to admire her voluptuous body whose forms, in close competition with sheer perfection, reminded me of the Venus de Milo statue sitting at the Louvre Museum in Paris. She moved around effortlessly, practically gliding between objects making no noise whatsoever, which would add a sense of softness to her extremely graceful presence. She would avoid staring into my eyes although I could intuit through her discreet and tactful demeanor that she was totally aware, not only of my obvious presence but also of my circumspect attitude and of my still partial and highly distorted perception of that entirely new and unpredictable situation. All of a sudden, she turned towards me and started gesticulating, twisting her arms and fingers in all directions, emitting discreet sounds, trying desperately to tell me something but it was too early for me to be able to follow her attempted reasoning and what she was trying to articulate! All I could grasp was that she was probably trying to describe the situation where they had found me in the middle of the jungle, and subsequently decided to run a considerable risk in transporting me, in all comfort I must say, back to their hamlet. The impression she gave me was of a professional healer judging from her totally unaffected attitude towards me and my nudity, since they had undressed me probably to examine if I had more wounds to other parts of my body. Given the intense heat and humidity that was probably also done in order to make me feel more comfortable. Her shyness and ensuing formality towards me made me think that I was probably the first white man they had entered into contact with. As such, I could hardly imagine her contradictory feelings by having to take care of what in appearance amounted probably to an extraterrestrial being...

They kept me incommunicado for a good couple of days except for Yana's constant presence and dedicated care! She would feed me by bringing small portions of food that I would rate as being different yet tasty. It was generally cooked fish or some kind of barbecued meat from some small animal... monkey meat? Subsequently my bet would prove to be the right one!

She had mentioned her name several times and made sure I would mention mine in return so that she would avoid any possible ambiguity. As soon as she felt secure enough, she started mumbling my name each time she wanted to call my attention. I felt gratified to hear it come out of those flower-like, magnificently shaped red lips! It made me feel greatly honored to be recognized by someone as pure and authentic as Yana! She would sense my satisfaction and would usually smile and caress my hands in return, in a clear demonstration of trust and affection. Her nudity was simply so naturally perfect, that my persistent staring at her glorious forms was unavoidable yet she would go about her business in a reassuring display of normalcy, as if my codes of conduct were totally alien to hers. Once again, I was instantly swayed by what I like to call a totally unsullied insight, one of those genuine feelings that penetrates one's mind without leaving a single gist of doubt behind. In one word, I was bewildered with the feeling of literally falling in love at first sight with that fantastic and unique creature whom I had barely seen let alone communicate with! I had that very intense hunch each time Yana would pronounce my name or each time I would pronounce hers, that there was a full sentiment of trust and assurance as if love was flowing from our mouths! It is incredible indeed that endless accounts, countless literary volumes, tomes after tomes have been written through history in an attempt to describe and define love only for it to be unveiled and blossom in its entirety within a wild and unique impulse, promptly, from a single word pronounced in the right circumstance! Love is an energy that flows out of the womb of creation to indefinitely multiply itself in a multitude of forms, colors, textures and dreams... love is creation itself but we consistently fail to recognize it as such, and stubbornly keep looking at the opposite direction in our interminable quest for forged satisfactions that lead to entire lives wasted in what I would appropriately define as counterfeit existences. All socially accepted definitions of the term love are nothing but mere man- made 'fake legitimacies' of what cannot be legitimized simply because one cannot legitimize what is! Those definitely fall short of any real understanding of the true meaning of love!

It was really astonishing that Yana and I had managed to create such a vibrant emotional bond in just three days of silent body language communication! There was I in the middle of nowhere, thousands of miles away from any so-called civilized spot, having barely survived what was usually a fatal snake bite, desperately falling in love with a woman I barely heard the voice of let alone establish any familiar emotional link. Maybe the explanation was just that! Maybe the very fact that our connection had immediately yielded such significant, strong and likely mutual feelings of affinity and attraction to each other was precisely because we had absolutely no past ethnic or cultural bonds whatsoever yet had been intensely communicating for three days in such pure, natural and spontaneous circumstances...

Finally on the third morning, a very imposing man came in and silently sat by my side with a purposeful expression. My impression was that I was being examined by a specialist doctor who was supposed to give me a clean bill of health or prescribe further treatment. He stared at the bite wound for quite some time touching the surrounding area delicately. Then he took both my hands with his own big, strong ones and stretched my arms behind my head so strongly that I couldn't avoid screaming out in pain. He then immediately released them with an expression of approval on his handsome face. I understood that he was looking for any signs of paralysis left by the potent venom that was certainly still running through my body albeit at a far less critical concentration. That was followed by a vigorous body massage that made me feel relaxed and tonified. Then, he stood up laughing loudly in a clear sign of satisfaction which gave me comfort and made me feel like a schoolboy passing a medical examination... He finally pointed to his powerful chest and introduced himself simply as "Guinaré".

I was definitely thankful to those strange and completely unfamiliar individuals who had gone out of their way to first rescue me and save my life and then heal my wound and patiently resuscitating me from the near-death condition they had found me in. I later understood that they were watching me slowly die for hours at the bank of the river, hesitating before intervening since I looked very strange and scary to them. Most probably, and thinking about their generous yet risky attitude, if I had suddenly died from the poison, it would have arranged their affair in a far better fashion! Instead, the violence of the trunk suddenly hitting me while still alive, awakened their survival instincts and propelled them to my rescue!

On that same day in the early afternoon Yana came in with a radiant smile on her face and gestured repeatedly towards the entrance of the shack, signaling that it was time for me to try to stand on my feet and walk out! I first sort of panicked, not only because of my still frail physical condition, but mainly due to the potential unexpected situation I was about to experience by meeting other members of Yana's tribe…

Albeit hesitantly, I walked out of the shack only to find myself surrounded by a crowd of about 1,000 individuals; men, women and children, all trying to get a good sight angle of what appeared to them as a highly awkward creature. The vast majority were smiling at me as if saluting my coming back to life! They kept on staring at me silently in sheer expectation of my next move or gesture. I slowly raised my right hand and waived it in an innocent salute to all, to which the small crowd responded with friendly gestures and lots of laughter! I later understood that laughing for that tribe was a sign of friendship and approval…

Guinaré, the same big man who earlier in the day had performed the medical examination and the very relieving massage, came forward and took my hand reassuringly, showing me the way to a big shack next door to where I had spent the last three days being treated. We entered it, and as soon as my eyes got used to the almost total darkness of the place, a slow burning rudimentary candle yielded some frail lighting through which I could distinguish a small elderly man sitting on a solidly built, single trunk wooden bench smoking a pipe, exhaling a perfumed smoke that reminded me of sandalwood.

Guinaré pointed his big finger towards the sitting man and mumbled some incomprehensible words while simultaneously crossing his arms as if holding a baby within them. I quickly understood the allegory and that I was in front of someone who had fathered at least someone else, probably more than one individual in the tribe, and if by any chance one of those individuals was Yana, it meant that I was in front of the man whose wonderful daughter had spent three days taking care of me. The only gesture that came to my mind was bending forward in a tentative sign of respect and gratitude. The man on the bench laughed in return which made me feel that he had probably understood the meaning of my gesture. Then, we spent around fifteen minutes in complete silence, and finally the old man broke it up by what seemed to me like a quick question addressed to Guinaré who replied also in very few words, abruptly ending the dialogue. He then once again took me delicately by the hand and guided me out of the shack. Once outside, under a torching equatorial sun, I was quite surprised to observe that most female members of the tribe were very beautiful and surprisingly well-kept women, especially if one considered the rough environment they lived in.

Inversely to most snapshots that portray native, bush populations in the wild whose female members, despite being very young women are generally portrayed as being precociously haggard, these had nothing to hide, quite the contrary! Their voluptuous forms and radiant smiley faces would transmit youth besides joy and pleasure, two highly important components of a life worth living!

My first impressions in observing that remote and certainly still unheard of, indigenous population, were therefore remarkably positive, agreeable and relaxing... Instead of feeling threatened in any way, I felt welcomed and, I dare to say, my presence almost appreciated by most individuals I came in contact with.

Taking a day at a time can produce true miracles... After around forty days (I was noting every passing day by carving a small mark in a beautiful flat stone that I had found near the river) my understanding of the tribe and its habits had significantly evolved and I could now decipher some of the ideas they expressed through their guttural language coupled with gestures and at times hilarious facial expressions... I must say that the fact that there was no formal linguistic understanding between me, and the members of the tribe would provide a direct, unfiltered de-codification of significant aspects of their social and cultural life, something that would have been otherwise lost in translation so to speak...

For example, I finally came to understand that the old man I had met in my first foray out of my 'recovery ward' was some kind of a great and venerable chief of the entire tribe, someone who would be revered as a father by all. This being said, the legitimacy of his standing was solely due to his extensive knowledge and wisdom in the guidance of his people rather than any heroic combat exploits or the like as it is often the case not only in primitive societies but also in some of the so-called developed ones... He had also genetically fathered some of the members of the tribe who, as I understood later, didn't inherit any social privilege for that matter! Subsequently I also understood that physical love was completely free and devoid of any sense of possessing one another despite a monogamist precept whereby loyalty was strictly observed and respected for the entire duration of a given love relationship between a man and a woman. In other words, a man and a woman could fall in love and make love without any pre-condition or entitlement of any nature upon each other and this, for as long as the relationship brought satisfaction to both partners! Love was viewed solely and purely as an act of... love... period! Not as a means to declare a possession on another human being thus preventing the latter of being entirely free to choose and, what was more important, to change partners when things got difficult, or the relationship turned sour... The maternity issue had also been creatively solved by the fact that all women were considered to be the common mothers of all newborns! That commonality would persist forever meaning that any given member of the tribe could address any older woman as his/her own mother, and moreover exercise a choice over his/her own preferred motherhood! The chief of course knew the genealogic ramifications of the tribe and kept a thorough record of the latter hence avoiding any undesirable incident that could result in an incestuous relationship.

This was a totally innovative, ethnic concept, extremely difficult for me to grasp let alone comprehend from a purely cultural or philosophical standpoint. It was indeed very hard to accept that innovative social structure especially on every occasion that I imagined a possible relationship with Yana, with whom I was falling deeper and deeper in love with the passing of time... Needless to say, my attraction to Yana, deep in my western societal indoctrination, obviously presupposed monogamy and fidelity for life since I simply could not envision ever losing her to someone else at least at that stage of events!

Much later I evolved into a more intellectual understanding of their social organization from what was initially a purely instinctive one.

One interesting aspect concerning the effects of the passing of time in those latitudes, was that my body was getting gradually exposed and adapted to a radically different diet, intensive physical involuntary exercise, a torching heat together with a merciless sun that had turned my skin color into a dark golden tan obviously helped by the daily use of a mixture composed of crushed red seeds from 'Urucum' (an Amazonian plant) together with essential oils extracted from different plants and local kinds of exotic nuts. My hair was growing longer and acquired golden reflections too, whilst my feet had developed such thick soles that I definitely stopped using my old sneakers for good and started to walk and even run on the narrow and winding paths in the middle of the jungle following my fellow hunters with total ease. I felt healthier and stronger, and my night sleep was uninterrupted and relaxing like never before. The main metamorphosis however had to do with the fact that my thinking was becoming much clearer by the day, besides being much more focused on the present moment and on my immediate surroundings rather than lost somewhere in the dead past or galloping towards a non-existent future as was often the case with me in the past. I felt pleasure in noticing that my concentration and lucidity were much more acute and perceptive. Finally, I could observe that I was more alive than ever, teeming with a renewed energy that I had never so consciously enjoyed by being present and centered without the constant fears that had permeated my past life.

I could hardly imagine the origins of that tribe, totally isolated in the middle of the Amazon basin, probably for centuries if not millennia, having migrated from Africa to the Americas, maybe some 80,000 years ago, withstanding a huge number of unspeakable and at times unsurmountable challenges, being almost decimated in the process before reaching the jungles of South America. Their culture had survived and evolved by developing an acute instinct of survival, definitely needed in order to face the enormous amounts of adversity in crossing the globe, confronting freezing cold temperatures contrary to the ones of their original habitat, all this and more, probably causing a lasting rupture from their inherited values. This, in turn, had eventually yielded a tremendous number of instinctive tenets and ingrained precepts obtained through centuries of very risky trial-and-error endeavors. The accumulation of all those threats and challenges through the centuries had resulted in what appeared to be substantially defined cultural genetic markers in sheer contrast to our contemporary Western culture. Our so called 'civilized' cultural values, judging from the deplorable state of our societies, have been lost in time probably due to an overdependence of the individual in technology which produced a human being totally devoid of its original instincts, physically weak and highly vulnerable when compared to our fellow animals or to indigenous peoples like the ones I had the extreme privilege to come into contact with.

Both indigenous peoples as well as animals are born with a full set of instinctive and survival genetic markers which allow, for instance, a filly or a colt to walk away from their mom sometimes within a few minutes after being born! Likewise, a baby "Indian" as they are commonly called, develops his or her physical independence from the parents much sooner than a baby born in a big city, surrounded by the latest state of the art obstetric technology amongst others... As I spent more time in the jungle with those intriguing individuals, I could witness that their risk avoidance, albeit existent in order to guarantee their survival as a species, was much slighter than ours which resulted indeed in a much more exciting existence enriched by the lack of fear from their own unavoidable failures, which ultimately served just as a lesson learned in order to increase the chances of success in the next trial. They had instinctively developed the notion that errors, and the ensuing potential consequential failure of a given undertaking were nothing but a necessary aspect in their learning process that was centered in developing a harmonious society rather than creating sophisticated instruments or techniques designed to mitigate the probability of failure itself! The result of this highly developed cultural atavism was evident in their joyful and smiley way of life, practically devoid of unjustified fears, sadness, resentment, hatred or negativism. Just imagine if our children could be taught that failure is a good thing, an intrinsic aspect of any learning process...

The result of their instinctive acceptance of a trial-and-error survival practice, had created a society based on the precept of respectful polygamy where, whilst meticulously excepting all potential incestuous or consanguineous sexual relationships, there were no 'legally' established couples except where both individuals wanted and decided to stay together, whether granting procreation in the process or not. This social organization evidently had a tremendous positive effect on the development of authentic physical characteristics and moral values that permeated the everyday lives of those creatures. For example, the majority of them were good looking, which is rather rare in autochthonous groups around the world! I couldn't avoid establishing a mental and purely imaginary correlational link between the fact that they could freely choose their mating companions with the extraordinary beauty of the majority of the individuals composing the tribe! One would contend that we too can freely elect our wives and husbands with whom we shall subsequently found a family... This is probably the case in some instances. However, I would also contend that when this happens, it does happen in concealment of all the highly complex social rules and precepts we must follow and blindly obey in order to, amongst other things, mitigate our risk of failure! I probably don't have to cite any statistics pertaining to the ever-increasing divorce rates in our modern societies! I could also observe with great interest and delight that there were no visible signs of feelings of jealousy, possession, or any predatory competition amongst the members of the group. The elderly man I had met with Guinaré earlier on upon my arrival was considered the Chief of the entire tribe as well as the father of all of its members which would bestow enormous respect from all when in his all-encompassing presence. This would instill confidence in one another and avoid all animosity or feelings of bitterness among the members of the tribe.

I was slowly fathoming that I had potentially met the idealized society so ably described by the German philosopher Nietzsche — 'A society in which will reign not the Judge but the Creator'. Then, another thought, amongst many, crossed my mind as a result of my acute observation of their social organization — there was no ugliness per se, either physical or spiritual so to speak. A beautiful and moving innocence prevailed in literally all members of the tribe! As I would come across an increasing number of individuals, I realized that the vast majority were amazingly kind, welcoming, generous and accepting. Ethnocentrism was indeed a non-existent idea in the face of the single ethnic group composing the tribe, however I had a very clear feeling that it was also a totally unfamiliar psychological perception when it came to their connection to me, a completely different and unknown kind of being! It became more and more evident to me that their kind and peaceful conduct, achieved through several generations had become engrained in their DNA. The fact is that new scientific research is now finding evidence that certain persistent detrimental behaviors, such as alcoholism, as well as some difficult to treat traumatic conducts (as, for example, those resulting from a certain number of war scars, be it physical, psychological or both, suffered by veterans) end up getting ingrained into the DNA of the bearer of such conducts and are, subsequently, genetically passed on to the next generations! My impression however is that the recently developed research in this domain has understandably focused on the negative aspects of the equation since, after all, the end objective is to find potential cures to the terrible consequences of such findings in society and its individuals. The positive consequences stand on their own merits though and would probably constitute the first embryonic results of the research for potential cures. This is precisely what I was witnessing, a society that had managed to carve good deeds into their genetic markings, generating wonderful individuals with astonishing results in their physical, psychological and sociological attributes.

Conversely, I must sadly admit that our societies are marred in discrimination and fear let alone ethnocentrism, which most certainly generate all the ugliness, evil and dreadfulness we have to bear in our often, self-defeating quest, for a better world. I would go as far as affirming that most of the so-called civilized individuals are genetically modified in the most negative sense of the word, carrying terrible and too often difficult to eradicate signs of heinousness. We are therefore hopelessly lost in the societal quagmire we have created through several generations practicing deceits designed to accommodate ourselves ultimately in order to force us to bear the imperfections of our social surroundings to the benefit of a few malevolent individuals, instead of challenging and fighting back through a natural process of trial and error like the people I was starting to realize I had the extreme luck of being in contact with...

We have very little indeed to be proud of in the so-called developed world, be it Western or Eastern it doesn't matter now that globalization tends to eliminate all useful, hence necessary, differences! Yes, necessary in order to give us at least the chance of a more objective judgement! Instead, we find ourselves immersed into a vicious circle of misconceptions, fear, aggression, and lies upon lies disseminated by social media platforms designed to conceal the terrible truth which becomes more and more evident as we head relentlessly towards the destruction of our own habitat!

This amazing culture that destiny put me in contact with was a living proof that it is perfectly possible to lead a highly suitable and fulfilling life based on the amalgamation of the two main universal forces of Love and Nature, both concepts that are probably inherently associated! The results were so obvious that my impulse was to tour the world with the sole aim to preach what was being revealed to me as a critical combination essential for a balanced, harmonious life = Love + Nature!

For an outsider like myself, one of the obvious, natural and apparently conflicting life preserving solutions they had mastered through the centuries was birth control! That goal was achieved through a two-prong approach. Firstly, the determination of whether a woman could bear a child from a given mate was done by a council of sages composed of seven women and three men and presided by the old Chief himself. I was led to understand that several parameters were taken into account such as physical and mental fitness, intelligence, potential genetic connections, age, willingness of the mother-to-be to bear and co-educate a child, loving relationships, and, most of all, the tribe's material capacity to add yet another member to its ranks without sacrificing the common wellbeing... The second important element to ensure birth control, was a combination of several roots found in the surrounding jungle which were cooked together for days in order to produce a powerful spermicide water soluble powder. All adult men who would reach the age for sexual intercourse as determined by the tribal traditions, and who met the established preconditions for such, were supposed to drink it once a week until such time that they were allowed to procreate. The onus of contraception thus fell on the men not the women of the tribe.

I soon understood that those 'primitive' individuals had naturally developed and successfully applied the concept of sustainable development into their small society. Conversely, our unsustainably overcrowded 'civilization' is mired in conflict, unspeakable violence, fear, ignorance, hunger and misery, just to cite a few, in an era of superlative technology yielding useless and hopeless longevity that should otherwise give us all the benefits of organizing our societies so that abundance could benefit all! The paradox is indeed as obvious as it is unbearable!

The plain truth is that we have lost our sense of commonality, of human cohesion, and we are faced with a total lack of true, honest and legitimate leadership in the entire world! This has resulted, amongst other detrimental realities in a chaotic and senseless multiplication of our species, spurred by what I would call 'visionless technology' that in the end works against us instead of favoring the improvement of our own quality of life on this earth. We end up over consuming literally everything in a disorganized and unplanned manner, mercilessly destroying our own habitat including the ones of our fellow animal and vegetable species, in total disrespect of ours and theirs very existence on this planet!

Notwithstanding the huge laundry list of the so-called global leader's shortcomings that should bring shame and dishonor to all of them with absolutely no exception whatsoever, some of the most catastrophic ones are the total disregard to the environment, widespread corruption practices, definitional distortions of all kinds and I could go on. More than likely, the worst one is the total lack of any kind of organized birth control policies. I must stress that when it comes to leaders, I include here not only political but also religious, business and macroeconomic institutions, world thinkers and planners, Think Tanks, and so on. When it comes to birth control, it is maybe preferable and more politically correct to call it 'Demography planning' but whichever the chosen term, its absence no doubt constitutes a real drama unfolding before our eyes with no real and empowered advocates seriously studying the issue with a view to providing solutions thus sustainability to our battered world. It is unthinkable and even unimaginable to conceive that the world population can maintain its growth at the current rates without depleting the planet of all its vital resources in the not-so-distant future, the very resources which are themselves critical to mankind's survival!

And still, not a single world leader is capable of coming up with proposals or at the very least with fresh ideas designed to harness this quagmire or at least to launch a global pragmatic debate, preferring instead to bestow potential solutions to the so-called technological advances that will emerge from thin air! Well, there's simply no time for such! We must act now if we want to save mankind from a complete collapse of vital resources that, whether we like it or not, do not belong to mankind alone but must be shared with all the other species on this relatively tiny planet...

And, quite paradoxically to say the least, here was I bewildered by some one thousand five hundred individuals who seemingly had harnessed the mystery by having quite naturally developed the common understanding that any given ecosystem, or habitat, no matter how extensive it appears to be, can be quickly destroyed. Our competitive and voracious nature favors the systematic creation of imbalances as a function of our insatiability which unfortunately represents by and large our western way of life.

Those humble yet wise people had conversely created a social structure with clearly defined and accepted canons, designed to preserve the quality of life of the group and of its surrounding environment which are co-dependent. How come we, the so-called civilized society, with such sophisticated means and resources are literally incapable of conceiving simple and logical solutions meant to improve our life on this planet whilst preserving the latter? Our solutions are often sophisticated to the extreme and they end up generating problems which more often than otherwise supersede the pursued potential solution yielding a diabolic virtuous circle of problem-solution-problem, always benefiting the lucky few fortunate ones who are devoted to finding technological solutions to literally everything without measuring any consequences since they know that anything that can potentially do wrong will ultimately represent yet another opportunity to seek corrective action through even more sophisticated technology!

Artificial Intelligence is definitely a case in point! Without extending myself in an infinity of examples, we could just consider the new fad called the driverless car which could potentially create many problems such as terrorists breaking into the system of a given car and sending the driver into an abyss or a crowd, or kidnapping the latter, or even programming a series of vehicles such as buses, trucks etc. and command them from afar for criminal purposes. Another emblematic consequence of the so-called AI — Artificial Intelligence — indeed a huge alienating factor in vogue — is the potential of becoming a chronic unemployment generator! Nobody can really affirm today at least with a certain degree of certitude where resides the boundary between the multifunction robotic executing machine and the monster with the potential of dominating us all! I hope this existential conundrum rather than a technological one will be solved in due course before we mercilessly destroy what will be the remains of our species!

Yana and I were hopelessly falling in love with each other, and it became exceedingly difficult for us to hide our feelings from anyone who would come our way. We would not even touch each other except for the casual touching of our arms or hands, however we would spend hours 'talking' to each other through a mixture of sounds and gestures which had the benefit of teaching me the first sounds, words and very short sentences used in their communication. With the passing of time however the situation started to become quite unbearable to the point that one day, after having spent maybe a full year amongst those fantastic people I decided that it was time for me to arm myself with courage and go talk to the chief himself. My skin was very tanned as a result of the daily application of the protective mixture containing 'Urucum' and my equally heavily sun-tanned hair had turned almost blond and had grown as long as everybody else's together with my beard, some sort of a privilege of mine since no one else could display it and that exerted quite an irrefutable attraction amongst females…

I had the clear impression that I had evolved to become very appealing to most women who would invariably give me generous smiles without controlling their impulse to touch me each time our paths would cross… I was walking barefoot all the time without any problem as well as totally naked like everybody else, and my muscles had hardened and had acquired the features of a true athlete. I often realized by watching my reflection in the river or ponds surrounding the hamlet that I had gotten quite a compelling allure that I definitely didn't have in my past life. Most members of the tribe were slowly becoming used to seeing me around and I realized with pleasure that in a certain way I was slowly but surely becoming accepted by them as being yet another member of the group despite my strange and different looks…

My self-esteem had reached its pinnacle. However, I must admit that this was mainly due to all the wonderful women who had shared my adventurous life, even those whose participation had been modest in terms of the amount of time they had spent with me. For someone who had come a long way in terms of self-esteem, I must confess that my transformation into a fulfilled, thoughtful and contemplative man had everything to do with my fantastic, loving relationships with women. I owe them practically every positive achievement I had in life in particular my clear discernment that was about to propel me towards the most critical and important choice I had ever made in my life.

So, under a sunny sky, on a beautiful day, I decided to approach Guinaré to ask him what his opinion was about my idea to consult with the chief about a possible intimate relationship between me and Yana. To my surprise and as soon as he understood what I was alluding to, he gave me a reassuring laugh and immediately took me by the hand and guided me towards the chief's now familiar shack. Admittedly there was absolutely no bureaucracy regarding the tribe's decision-making process! As soon as we entered the place, a familiar smell guided me through a smoke trail all the way to the same bench where the Chief was sitting and smoking his pipe in a meditative mood as if he hadn't moved from there, ever since the first time I saw him...

As I tried to utter some words to thank him for receiving me and to introduce the subject, the Big Chief ordered me to shut up with an easy—to-decipher abrupt gesture performed with his right hand... after some minutes that seemed like an eternity he raised his eyes and stared at me with a sharp, piercing resolve and kept his eyes focused on mine for a very long time before saying very slowly in a clear intent of trying to make me understand... "You love, Yana?"

Guinaré started gesticulating frantic signs designed to make me understand more clearly... he was a first-class mimic translator, no doubt about it!

"Oh yes, very much Chief," I muttered using a couple of words I had learned from Yana, shaking my head without a single clue as to what was to follow... Guinaré of course sort of translated my words, and I truly hoped that he was being precise...

After a concise monologue pronounced by the Chief, Guinaré made a big effort so that I would understand as clearly as possible the Chief's reply that went more or less like this,

"Because you are a good and sacred soul, and despite your impure blood, I bless you and permit that she becomes your wife... your blood is impure and we will bear the consequences, whichever those will be... But you can only father one single child during your lifetime, and you will never, ever leave our tribe! In case you try to escape we will have no choice but to kill you!"

The conversation was over, and the Big Chief went patiently back to his pipe...

As I walked out, there was a small crowd surrounding Yana and seemingly waiting for me as if everybody had guessed my intent in seeing the chief. Word of mouth was the communication of choice indeed! Guinaré raised my arm in a victorious and welcoming gesture, shouted three words and the whole crowd cheered in jubilation as three very strong and familiar individuals grabbed me and raised me high off the ground throwing me into the air three consecutive times! Then, they put me back on the ground and everybody rapidly disappeared leaving me alone with Yana.

After a very long silence and keeping herself strangely away from me as if preparing for the worst, she finally spoke,

"So, I think the Big Chief was nice to us," — she said with an uncertain voice — "Now you are the only one to decide if you want to stay here forever, or leave! What is your decision?" These people were very direct and our Western habit of taking time to think about something before deciding, no matter how serious the issue, was simply incomprehensible to them.

So, there I was, just after a short year further to my rescue having to make a crucial, life sweeping decision that would simply turn upside down literally all aspects of my existence forever! In a matter of minutes my entire life unfolded in my now suddenly highly agitated mind and my brain instinctively started to process and measure a myriad of viewpoints and circumstances that had contributed to who I was in the present moment. The conclusion was simple and straightforward, I liked for the better the person I had become in the jungle than any recollection of myself during my entire past existence! Besides, by now everybody certainly thought that I was dead somewhere in the Amazon… so why bother anyhow.

I grabbed Yana by the waist and finally kissed her lips without any restrain or fear that someone could catch us.

"I love you, Yana," I said in their language, while placing her right hand on my heart as I had seen other members of the tribe perform several times, "and my decision is to stay here forever close to you!"

She had an outburst with a mixture of tears and laughter, and for a furtive moment I could perceive the Chief observing us very discretely from a small opening of his shack, before quickly disappearing back into the darkness of his home…

We were finally allowed to live together under the same roof and both of us spent the rest of the day literally quivering in anticipation of our first romantic night in those fantastic surroundings…

As the last rays of sun disappeared behind the canopy of the majestic forest, and a faraway thunder announced an approaching storm Yana and I took shelter in her shack preciously pre-arranged and incensed with an exotic perfume by some very caring women who had obviously anticipated my decision to become part of the tribe even though my 'impure blood' would always make me look awkward vis a vis my tribal peers.

Ever since that unforgettable night, a decisive life experience filled with love that changed my existence forever after, Yana would follow me like a shadow no matter where I went and would offer me her undivided attention and care whenever I expressed a need or desire. I later understood that this behavior was expected from any woman who wanted to bear a child of any given man obviously with the previous blessing of the Chief, of the ten sages of the council, and ultimately of the entire tribe! We had gone through the three levels of scrutiny, and I was extremely honored and delighted to be somehow considered a member of that fantastic group of global voyagers notwithstanding my different ethnicity!

I must say that the permission given to a member of the tribe to have a child generated not only with a stranger but, and this was indeed extraordinary, with a white man with no knowledge, history or any past tradition whatsoever was unheard of in the entire annals of those formidable individuals! By that time, I had barely started to grasp some of the fabulous secrets of what living in and from the jungle meant… and those marvelous and generous creatures were ready to disclose much more to me, a perfect stranger!

All taken into consideration, and since the ruling roots of that society were, at the end of the day, of a matriarchal nature, Yana's desire had indeed a bearing in the decision-making process of the tribe… and it was now obvious that she prevailed!

Yana and I had decided to bear a child however we both agreed that we should wait some time in order for me to get fully engrained in their culture so that our child would have a father completely acquainted to the way of life and the vicissitudes of that intriguingly beautiful yet often hostile habitat. I made real efforts to absorb as much as I could from their culture, always being very careful not to interfere in any way thus avoiding any potential disruption of their highly well-adjusted existence. It was definitely me who had to learn from them, as my knowledge was definitely useless for their fantastic way of life! I instinctively knew that it was up to me to get adapted to their modus vivendi that went back millennia in terms of adaptive survival experiences rather than try to interfere in any shape or form no matter what my logical reasoning was. My critical views regarding our western society were so trenchant that I had simply lost all interest in teaching them anything emanating from a culture that was heading decisively towards its own demise! The problem remained however that the failure of our societies would drag too many innocent hostages down the same drain! Hence, for all those reasons amongst many others, I had definitely decided to stay there for the rest of my life! I wanted to be one of them, period! I had no anguish vis a vis my decision or any regrets for that matter. On the contrary, I felt a deep sense of peace and relief to disconnect from the entire paraphernalia created by our civilization and to feel absolutely free from all connotations of the word 'possession' be it material or personal and from the unavoidable fear of losing those same possessions for whatever reasons. We all lose them anyway sooner or later!

Another year went by, and, in a beautiful full moon night, my love took me by the hand and led me slowly to the bank of the river, the same river that had so inadvertently united our destinies… she then took me in her arms, kissed me languidly and made passionate love to me.

She then sat by my side, stared at me with her gorgeous almond-shaped eyes, swept a couple of stubborn tears that were rolling down her face and said, "I am expecting our baby, Axel."

We stayed there for a long time embracing and kissing each other with caring tenderness.

We were happy.

MON RÊVE FAMILIER

Je fais souvent ce rêve étrange et pénétrant
D'une femme inconnue, et que j'aime, et qui m'aime
Et qui n'est, chaque fois, ni tout à fait la même
Ni tout à fait une autre, et m'aime et me comprend.

Car elle me comprend, et mon cœur, transparent
Pour elle seule, hélas! cesse d'être un problème
Pour elle seule, et les moiteurs de mon front blême,
Elle seule les sait rafraîchir, en pleurant.

Est-elle brune, blonde ou rousse ? – Je l'ignore.
Son nom ? Je me souviens qu'il est doux et sonore
Comme ceux des aimés que la Vie exila.

Son regard est pareil au regard des statues,
Et, pour sa voix, lointaine, et calme, et grave, elle a
L'inflexion des voix chères qui se sont tues.

Paul Verlaine (1844 – 1896)